THE
SECRET
IN THE
BIBLE

TONY BUSHBY

Best–selling author of 'The Bible Fraud'
and 'The Crucifixion of Truth'

Joshua Books

joshuabooks.com

Joshua Books

All correspondence to the publishers
PO Box 5149
Maroochydore BC 4558
Queensland Australia

First printed and published in 2003 by Joshua Books

Second printing 2005

Without Prejudice

Category: Author: Religious & Theology: History: Ancient Mysteries

ISBN 0 9581891 4 5

Master Distribution through Joshua Books
www.joshuabooks.com

TONY BUSHBY

Tony Bushby was born in Australia in 1948. He is the author of a number of journalistic reports on the subject of Near Death Experiences and publisher of specialist material on esoteric subjects.

In 1985 he began an investigation into the origins of Christianity and revealed new evidence about the cover-up of Jesus' twin brother in his groundbreaking book, *The Bible Fraud*. That topic is now the subject of an upcoming British TV documentary and *The Secret in the Bible* is a natural follow-on from the earlier work.

Tony Bushby now spends much of his time in Cairo, Egypt and researches regularly in the Rare Archives Division of the Alexandrian Library at Alexandria.

ALSO BY TONY BUSHBY

'THE BIBLE FRAUD'

To order, see the website: www.thebiblefraud.com

**'How well we know what a profitable superstition
this fable of Christ has been for us'
Pope Leo X (1513-1521)**

What others have said...

*I thoroughly enjoyed Tony Bushby's The Bible Fraud. Its tale ended my own
research into the origins and source material of the Bible (not for a book! Just
my own curious hunger to know!). This author has done in a careful and
extremely well researched book, far better than most in this genre, because of the
attention to detail, which, I have confirmed myself over the past twenty years
from various sources, is validated and more accurate than many academic papers
found in our universities. It is undoubtedly the most important book on
Christianity and the Roman legacy ever written, and most likely will have the
least impact because it explodes the mythology and power basis for a religion
which will be impossible for most to swallow. A truth that will choke rather than
enlighten. I look forward to his next book and I do hope that it opens eyes to
the true wonders and we finally put away the destructive toy of over simplified
pacification tripe that exists in 'political commercial establishment religions.*
MAE, Isle of Sanday, Orkney, Scotland

Why weren't we told about this earlier?
Juliana O'Brien, University Theological graduate

The ramifications of this evidence are impossible to calculate.
Rev. Herbert O'Brien, Ordained Minister of the Reformed Baptist
Church, Melbourne, Australia

*The Bible Fraud is a real eye opener. It is well documented and easy to
understand. Everyone should read this book to understand how we have been
deceived. Especially all Christians who think they know the truth. You will
never think the same once you have read this book.*
JS, Jacksonville, Florida, USA

I wish to thank you for exposing the fraud of the Catholic Church. I have spent most of my life researching the Bible and the history of this world. (I have written a book on the subject.) What I would not write about, except on the periphery, was of Jesus, for I found much about his life that was strange.
NS, New Westminster, B.C., Canada

I just received the book The Bible Fraud and I'm very pleased with the truths coming out in this publication. Many of the truths that Tony has spelled out in this book has been known by myself and others for a long time but never the whole story as set up in this book! Thank you Tony for putting it all together!!! I'm looking forward to the new book Tony is writing …
REE, Minot, Nevada, USA

This is the first time in my entire life that I have read anything of this nature concerning the person of Jesus Christ. I have long loved the reading of scripture since a child and committed much to memory. To think… that the loved and respected writings may be a fraud is difficult to receive. I will continue on the journey.
RL, Kent, Washington, USA

If the general public were to read this book, it would cause much angst and awe. Can it change history? Yes, I think it could.
JF, Niagara Falls, Ontario, Canada

I think that this book is one that has been awaited for a very long time by so many people, and it gives everyone something to think about.
DG, USA

I can only say that all heretofore thoughts concerning the NT have been laid to rest since reading The Bible Fraud. It brings a perspective to light of "religion" that should be compulsory reading for all honest people. It demonstrates how "religion" was shrewdly used by the ancient rulers much as it is today. The old thought about "the more things change, the more they stay the same" is markedly demonstrated in this publication. Kudos to the author. Can't wait to read the sequel.
WB, Independence, MO, USA

I was ordained as a Baptist minister in 1963 and began pulpiteering in New Jersey. There were doubts since my high school days about the "conversion" I was led to by the preacher in the small church near our Pennsylvania farm. Questions like, Is there a heaven and hell? Why does praying seem to be just a talking session with myself and the environment? Why hasn't the world changed for the better over the 2000 years since this Jesus we talk about was allegedly here? Why doesn't this resurrected Jesus talk with us as he allegedly did to other people on earth? Why aren't prayers answered? Why do professing Christians seem little different from "unsaved" people in their daily living and speaking? Why so many contradictions and confusing statements of lawyerese in the Bible? etc. etc.

It took about four years for me to realise that my doubts had a very real basis, because churchianity isn't what it's cracked up to be when you actually begin pastoring, getting to know the people and the politics and personalities that make them click. So I left that world and began working with my hands to earn a living and doing some things closer to my talents and likings, like performing and teaching music, home improvement contracting, etc.

I kept searching for truth, but never could make sense of the thousands of religious groups and ideas making the rounds. In 1993 I married an equally "religious" Georgia girl. We discussed these dilemmas together and realised we had the same misgivings and questions regarding life and its many puzzles. In our searches we came upon the site with information regarding Tony Bushby's The Bible Fraud. We ordered the book and our questions were finally answered!

Looking back at the seminary I attended in Philadelphia, Pennsylvania, I remember their quoting the "church fathers" and all the various propoganda that keeps their graduates mired down in the lies of history. Mr Bushby's research revealed all the answers which had eluded us through the years, because we didn't know where to look, or we were afraid to search too deeply for fear of losing the "faith" which might "save" us from an unknown future of "suffering for our sins."

In conclusion, my life has changed drastically after reading The Bible Fraud, because I now know why I had doubts about my faith through the years. I now have the courage to try to help people see a better way than the fearful lives they live under the lies of the suffering in hell and living under the list of don'ts that deprives them of a life of joy and happiness. Why would a loving God want his children to live such guilt-ridden and sad lives as punishment for sins? Reading this book is truly a path to the truth which make us free! Thank you, Mr Bushby, for your fearless, meticulous research into a field full of superstition, fear and untruths.

BB, MDiv, DC, Shiloh, GA

The Bible Fraud was ABSOLUTELY FABULOUS. Tony Bushby has confirmed for me what I have thought to be true for quite a while.
JAM, Goulburn, NSW, Australia

On the other hand, a real truth seeker will realise that a guy who brings his bedroll to a library so he can research night and day would be an infinitely more reliable source than a writer whose main focus is fame and ego enhancement.
Claudia, USA

I read Tony's first book, The Bible Fraud in March 2002. I had been a believer in the Christian faith for 58 years. I no longer believe the Christian myth in the New Testament gospel accounts.
TD, Dunlap, Illinois, USA

Please send my congratualtions to Tony - whoever he is, wherever he is - for The Bible Fraud. How simple and straightforward the truth is, when unearthed in such a practical way. The results of his unstinting investigation will surge across the world. I hope he keeps his head well down.
FB, Llandudno, North Wales, UK

I was truly impressed with the amount of information and references supplied. He deserves a lot of credit for his work.
EP, Toronto, Ontario, Canada

The Jewish side of my family has always taught us to question, which I have passed to my children. Without questioning issues, you may never find the real answers. This book answered many questions that I have sought answers to.
NT, USA

How sad that we have suffered the long years of history so dreadfully deceived.
M & MD, Hastings, New Zealand

A job well done Tony. Someone had the "guts" to put it in print.
ES, Swan Hills, Alberta, Canada

THE
SECRET
IN THE
BIBLE

II

MATTERS OF CONFIDENTIALITY

To provide the new information presented in this book, the author was obliged to comply with two separate secrecy agreements specifically established to contain the release of 'sensitive information'. Therefore, some insights were not directly divulged, the main one being the 'seven things' said to have existed before the creation of the world. The Rosicrucians called them the *Seven Unspeakable Secrets* and the 'Legends of the Craft' of Freemasonry originally referred to them as *Seven Steps of the Winding Stairs*. However, ancient rabbinic tradition openly maintained that the Torah was one of those 'seven things' and the extraordinary Secret it holds made it greater than the combination of the other six secrets. The other delicate issue was the true extent of subterranean chambers below the sands of the Pyramid Plateau at Giza. Nevertheless, previously undisclosed information about the Bible, Solomon's Temple, the Great Pyramid and the Sphinx is publishable outside secrecy agreement commitments and that wisdom is revealed in this book.

II

THE SOUL'S SECRET

In each of the sixteen chapters of this book, one special word is written with something different about its presentation. Those words are NoT misprints or typing errors, but are intentionally altered or 'coded' to spell out a special message. Those persons who search and record them in the order presented will find revealed a deep ancient secret that rests below the pages of the Bible; a deeper secret than what is openly revealed in this book.

That sixteen-worded sentence was extracted from the ancient *Book of God*, a mysterious old document written on a fabric of an unknown nature, and highly regarded by the Ancients thousands of years ago.

The 'coded' clues are called *Words of Truth* and there is no glamorous earthly prize for their discovery, excepting hidden treasure to nourish the Soul. A special page is provided towards the end of this book to record each particular word upon its discovery.

CONTENTS

ACKNOWLEDGEMENTS

In the long gestation period of this book, friends and associates freely provided help and support and without their assistance, the new information now presented would never have eventuated. Therefore, sincere expressions of appreciation are extended to the following souls who, with kindness and understanding, played a direct and unrecognized part in enlightening mankind: Christopher Ebbett, for providing the peace and tranquillity of the farm cottage to finalise the manuscript; Tristan Rankine (Tri-Star), for making the link between ancient Egyptian and Australian Aboriginal culture; John Telfer, for research assistance, insight, and dedication; Tony Skerrett, for the loan of his personal computer at a critical time; 'Little Light Feather', Michelle Brooks, for her friendship, loyalty, hospitality and inspirational conversations; Julie Allan, for research and recommendations on manuscript development; John Bannister, for his business acumen and the vital role played in final publication; Virginia Cass, for her superb cooking that kept me alive; and Nigel Cass, for his untiring assistance with complex computer matters.

Sincere thanks also go to my brother Phil, and my nephew Damian; to Lara-May for the use of her home, and Jan McClusky for her endless and fascinating inspired advice; to Peter Ritchie, for his learned recommendations on cover design, and to Annette Ebbett, who provided the light in the darkness, and opened the final door.

CHAPTER ONE

THE KNOWN EXISTENCE OF A 'SECRET'

In a cavern in the Spanish region of Sacro Monte, carefully sealed with great blocks of hewn stone and guarded by two vertical stone pillars, a bizarre discovery was made. A dozen skeletons, dating to 2000 BC, were found sitting in a perfect circle around the central corpse of a woman wearing the remains of a leather tunic upon which was inscribed '22 strange geometric patterns'. Archaeologists also discovered a curious assortment of artifacts associated with ritual performance: a human skull, seven rainbow-coloured clay discs of the type usually identified with solar worship, an unusual lantern, and seeds of the narcotic opium poppy. Anthony Roberts, in his book *Giants in the Earth,* hypothesized that the central woman was an adept and spiritual guide who led her initiates into an astral state of contemplation. 'The people who made this magic trip', he said, 'had never returned from its mystical revelations and this is quite possibly by choice'. It is clear from the cave discoveries that those people knew the Secret in the Bible and willingly experienced it right into physical death itself.

A clue to the motive behind their ritual suicide is preserved in secret manuals that provide the key to unravel a great riddle that Pythagoras (c. 580-500 BC) called, 'the Mystery of the gods which has been hidden for ages of generations'. In the ancient world there was widespread belief in the existence of exalted knowledge that was accessible only to initiated people, knowledge that, by definition, conveyed a sense of awe. The fundamental nature of their illuminated teaching enters into an esoteric domain that dwells between history and legend and connects directly with a transcendent realm. Evidence that special insight was concealed from the masses is mentioned in the oldest religious texts available to mankind: the Dead Sea Scrolls, the books of Enoch, Esdras and Jasher, the Holy Koran, the Talmud, the Mahabharata, the Old Testament, Gospels and Epistles of the New Testament and the personal records of some early church presbyters.

The concealed message that the Bible holds underscores the mystery teachings of the Secret Societies of Freemasons, Rosicrucians, Knights Templar, the Eastern Star and others that many people in the outer world have never heard of. It was everyday knowledge that great secret systems flourished in the East, in Chaldea, Egypt, Assyria, Greece and Italy, and among the Hebrews in Babylonia and Phoenicia, the Druids of Britain, uncivilized African races, and later, among Muslims. 'I received from the messenger of God two kinds of knowledge', said Prophet Mohammed (570-632). 'One of these I taught...but if I had taught them the other it would have broken their throats'. Gautama Siddhartha (c. 568 BC), Buddha, also referred to undisclosed knowledge, saying; 'O disciples, the things which I have discovered and have not told you are more numerous than those which I have told you'.

© Alexandrina Archeological Museum, Egypt

This ancient terracotta plaque records the presentation of two scrolls of different kinds of knowledge, and published here for the first time. The figures are wearing the typical conical headdress of ancient Babylonian gods.

A Masonic initiate into the Mysteries, Dr Lawrence Buck, explained in his book *Mystic Masonry* (1922), that in ancient Secret School ceremonies, and in all great religions:

> ...there was always an exoteric portion given out to the world, to the uninitiated, and an esoteric portion reserved for the initiates, and revealed only in degrees, accordingly as the candidate demonstrated his fitness to receive, conceal and rightly use the knowledge so imparted. Few professed Christians are, perhaps, aware that such was the case with Christianity during the early centuries.

That a certain 'Secret' predated and became part of Christianity is clear by the esoteric narratives in canonical Christian texts. Paul (Saul) described his knowledge of a man who had personally 'experienced' the Secret, one who had, in his lifetime, received the highest initiation. Paul said of him:

> and I know that this man was caught up into Paradise: whether in the body or out of the body I do not know, God knows: and he heard things that cannot be retold, which is not lawful to repeat.[1]

Paul's words are almost identical with those recorded of other initiates as they referred in awe to the extraordinary substance of the ancient Secret. Another New Testament statement also attributed to Paul declared that, 'the wisdom is spoke only among them who are perfect', the plain translation of that sentence being, 'they speak of the Secret only amongst the initiated'.

Presbyter Hippolytus (170-236) wrote that a 'great, marvelous, and most perfect mystery' was revealed to him in the second grade of initiation. The illuminated teachers of humanity...Socrates, Pythagoras, Aristotle, Virgil, Homer and Apollonius of Tyana were all initiates in the ancient Sacred Mysteries...they knew the Secret knowledge. Other recorded initiates include Plato (427-347 BC), Plutarch (46-120), Celsus (c. 178), Clement of Alexandria (160-215), Plotinus (205-270) and Porphyry (233-304). Both Plato and Plotinus subtly described the 'divine visions of the Mysteries' as a secret science sought by many but known only to a few. Ancient Egyptian priests referred often to a 'Secret Science' known to them and so awesome was its power they taught it to no one who had not been firstly prepared, tested and accepted.

The Mystery Schools arose from the highest aspirations of the human mind, the desire for knowledge of eternal verities. Celsus, a second century historian and author, wrote a work called *True Discourse* that was subsequently destroyed by St. Aurorius Augustine (354-430) in the fifth century.[2] Celsus was an acknowledged expert on religious institutions and an important intellectual opponent of the early presbyterian movement. He wrote about pre-requisites for admission into the Mysteries and advised those wishing to learn the Secret; 'Let him approach whose hands are pure and whose words are wise'. Clement of Alexandria, wrote that teachings of the Mystery Schools concerned mainly Nature and the Universe. 'Here ends all instruction…Nature and all things are seen and known', he expounded. The Mysteries were closer to science and philosophy and more holy than the religion that was preached to the less mature in intelligence and morality. A few early presbyters were initiates into the Lesser Mysteries and their writings showed they fully appreciated the delineation between the esoteric (inner or hidden) and the exoteric (open or apparent).

However, not all presbyters were admitted into the Mystery Schools. In his book, *The Apology of Tertullian*, the 'barbarous, uncouth' Quintus Tertullian,[3] today called the Bishop of Carthage, expressed anger at his refusal of entry because he objected to the penalty of the promissory oath. Oaths were accompanied by peculiar rites intended to increase the solemnity and reverence of the act and often required some form of personal sacrifice. Tertullian (160-220) would not swear to 'the invocation of Deity to witness and avenge as a consequence of violating the oath' and refused to be bound.

In the fourth century, leading advocates of the Christian church developed a secret worship from which a major portion of the public was excluded, and the custom of communicating only to a portion of the community became known as the 'Disciplina Arcani', or 'The Discipline of the Secret'. The privacy of the sacred rites performed was guarded with utmost care from the obtrusive eyes of all who were not qualified to be present. The words, 'Let none who are simply hearers, and let no infidels be present' were proclaimed in a loud voice at the commencement of every ritual performance, and those not acknowledged were dismissed before the door was locked and guarded. The formula for expelling the unwanted at that point was loud recitation of the words, 'Holy things for the holy, let the Dogs depart'. St. Augustine said that candidates involved in the ceremonies went veiled in public, and after baptism, the veils were removed as an emblem of the liberty of the spiritual life that was obtained by knowledge gained from the secret ceremonies. When fully initiated they were called the *illuminati* or Illuminated because they had been enlightened to secrets that were concealed from the general populace. So complete was the understanding of some early churchmen of hidden mysteries, and initiation into them, that St Ambrose (333-397), Bishop of Milan, wrote a book called, *Concerning those who are initiated into the Mysteries*. So ancient were the Egyptian revelations, the great ecclesiastical historian Johann Mosheim (1694-1755) admitted that 'the origin of the sacred, mystic and celebrated Discipline of the Secret used by the fathers in the early church was to be found in the Mysteries of pre-Christian Paganism'.[4]

Another Christian Saint, Gregory (540-604), Bishop of Constantinople, recorded his knowledge of concealed doctrines:

> You have heard as much of the Mystery as we are allowed to speak openly in the ears of all: the rest will be communicated to you in private; and that you must retain within yourself…our Mysteries are not to be made known to strangers.

In the 1950s, classical scholar Professor Morton Smith of Columbia University, USA, discovered a rare Gospel when researching old manuscripts in the Mar Saba monastery in the Judean Wilderness. That Gospel proved to be an earlier version of the canonical Gospel of Mark, and attached to it were a series of writings purporting to be from the pen of Clement of Alexandria. In his book, *The Secret Gospel* (1974), Professor Smith recorded information from a previously unknown letter written by Clement that revealed that the newly-discovered Gospel, today called 'The Secret Gospel of Mark' was 'hidden, and even now carefully guarded, being read only to those who are being initiated in the Mystery'.

Further evidence of concealed information in Christian writings is found in the records of St Jerome, (d. 420) who confessed of it in an unguarded moment. Jerome said he found a Gospel written in Hebrew at the library collected at Caesarea by a person called Pamphilius. He said that he 'received permission from the Nazarenes, who at Beraea of Syria used this Gospel, to translate it...and which is called by most persons the genuine Gospel of Matthew'.[5]

Writing later to bishops Chromatius and Heliodorus, Jerome complained that the translation of that Gospel was 'a difficult work' because the original author 'did not wish it to be openly written':

> For if this (Gospel) had not been secret, he (the original author) would have added to the evangel that what he gave forth was his; but he made up this book sealed up in curious Hebrew characters, which he put forth in such a way that the book, written in Hebrew letters, and by the hand of himself, might only be possessed by the men most religious; who also, in the course of time, received it from those who preceded them. But this book they never gave to any one to be transcribed, and its text they related some way or other in secret.

St Jerome admitted, not withstanding that he tried to translate it twice, that the 'secret' and 'genuine' Gospel of Matthew was almost unintelligible to him. Jerome did not know the Secret being revealed in this book, for had he done so, he would not have had difficulty in translating the work. He was an uninitiated man and, as the Secret unfolds, it shall become clear why he had translation problems with that particular Gospel. Consequently, ancient church records revealed that two early Christian Gospels, Matthew and Mark, were known to have contained some mysterious sort of 'secret'.

Textual evidence of a hidden belief was further supported with the 1945–46 discovery of a particular document in a sealed funerary urn near Nag Hammadi in Syria. It was one of 52 manuscripts bound in 13 books and now called the Nag Hammadi Scrolls. The cache of writings were found literally 'buried in the desert' after a storm had blown away sand and exposed the sealed clay container. The writing of interest is the Gospel of Thomas, but it would have been more aptly called the 'Gospel of Hidden Knowledge', for that is precisely what it is.

© Archives de Histore.   Photo by Jean Doresse

The Syrian Desert site where the Gospel of Thomas was discovered. Note the holes where searches were unsuccessfully conducted for additional scrolls.

The Gospel of Thomas received its great publicity because of its sometimes-close links with the canonical Gospels and modern synopses of those Gospels often compare the parallels to Thomas. Unlike the canonical Gospels, however, it is almost void of both narration and any discernable outline, and suggests a more mysterious route to enlightenment. It is composed of 114 sayings (or logia) and the possibility that the Gospel Rabbi Jesus knew some of the sayings it preserved is generally conceded. The origin of that Gospel is not known, but the church claimed the collection of mystical sayings was assembled sometime around the mid-second century under the pseudonym of Didymus Judas Thomas. He was Judas Khrestus in the Gospels, the twin-brother of Rabbi Jesus, and the untold story of their lives was the nucleus of this author's earlier book *The Bible Fraud*. Some material in the Gospel of Thomas is thought to be much older than canonical writings and internal evidence suggests that it may have originally been an Essene composition. However, one thing is for sure: whoever wrote it was an Initiate, and knew the Secret in the Bible.

It appears that the original collection was theologically neutral but went through an evolutionary process until it received its name, and the sayings recorded in it were applied to Rabbi Jesus. However, the important point is the fact that the Gospel of Thomas opens with a short statement advising readers that it was composed of 'secret words' and persons 'who find the interpretation of these sayings will not taste death'.[6] That profound statement immediately suggested that the document 'held some form of sacred intention and its clues to the existence of an immortal status were supported with this additional passage: 'The Pharisees and the scribes have received the keys of knowledge and they have hidden them'.[7]

That passage confirmed that scribes concealed something special in ancient times and that information was subtly encoded into not only the Gospel of Thomas, but also into major sections of the *Old Testament* when it was written centuries earlier. Special secret knowledge was known and possessed by certain members of the priesthood but withheld from the public for thousands of years. But why…? Maybe a clue rests in this statement:

> And he (Jesus) took him (Judas Thomas the twin) and withdrew and told him three things. When Judas Thomas returned to his companions, they asked him, 'What did Rabbi Jesus say to you?' 'If I tell you just one of those things which he told me, you will pick up stones and throw them at me'.[8]

The curious assertion by Judas Thomas inferred that what he had learnt from Rabbi Jesus was unbelievable to the ears of common people. That, and other statements in ancient writings, served to highlight the fact that a unique Secret was in circulation in some quarters and was known to, and used by, various sects, orthodox and heretical, Jewish, Islamic, Gnostic, Essenic and Christian. Its existence was a matter of common knowledge to certain people and this book systematically reveals what it was.

The secret books of the Essenes

The Essene movement, one of three religious sects that flourished in the Roman provinces around the commencement of the Christian era, was specifically established to preserve the Secret. In Philo's first century book, *About the Contemplative Life*, he spoke of the Essenes as 'the ones who recognize the truth' and whose sect was inspired into existence to preserve the secret knowledge in the Bible. Their organisation was a full and special branch of the Mysteries and knowledge of their doctrines was revolutionized by the Qumran Scroll discovery (The Dead Sea Scrolls). Some of the books found in that cache were purposely written to conceal ancient high wisdom and clandestinely pass on to initiates a certain esoteric knowledge.

Two primary secrets or mysteries played significant roles in the thought of the Dead Sea Scrolls. The first was the 'mystery of Sin' followed by the 'mystery of what we will Become' (The Secret of Becoming) and the Scrolls urge continued investigation into those mysteries because that led to paths of truths and thus revealed the roots of evil. Sin was the name of the Babylonian Moon-god, 'Lord of the city of Ur', and was believed by the Essenes to be the 'Enemy of the Truth'. Across a span of many centuries, the message of the Dead Sea Scrolls speaks directly to our hearts and minds and the hidden knowledge of the 'Sin-fearing ones' provides a vital clue in unlocking the Secret in the Bible.

Foremost among the books of the Dead Sea Scrolls is the Book of Enoch. Eight complete copies were found in the Qumran caves, indicating the importance it held to the hierarchy of the Essene movement. That old writing contained arcane information by deliberate design, preserving in symbolic manner evidence concerning the true nature of the Bible. The very word 'Enoch' means 'initiated',[9] and its mystic meaning was revealed in the biblical years of life given to 'Enoch'. They amounted to three hundred and sixty five, being equal to a solar revolution, and the prominent number of ancient rites. The Book of Enoch was one of the most highly regarded religious writings of early times and its significance will be clarified in later chapters.

The earlier founders of the Essene movement had formulated a definite mystical understanding of some aspects of the Old Testament and they paved the way for a far different understanding of scripture to that presented by mainstream churches today. Until the spectacular discovery of their hidden library, a veil of mystery hung over the Essenes but it is known that members were required to pass through a period of strict probation before attaining full membership and, in particular, were bound by a solemn oath not to disclose secrets imparted to them. A candidate for the society had to pass through a probationary period before he was given the emblems of the order…a special belt and a white apron.

The real test that served to distinguish an Essene from all who more or less closely resembled him was the fearful oath that he took on becoming a member. The oath was a strict promise not to disclose the secrets of the community and there is no certain knowledge of what the substance of those secrets were. In principle, the Essenes objected to oaths, but once taken they were never violated; herein lay the chief disciplinary power of the elders. The Essenes chose to cast a veil of secrecy over what they considered of the highest religious importance and conceal under the threat of death a great mystery. Modern scholarship confirms that in the time of the compilation of the Christian texts, the Essenes possessed a deep understanding of an ancient Secret Tradition that became the key element in the life of Rabbi Jesus.

The Dead Sea Scrolls, which, it is generally agreed, were written by the Essenes, referred to the 'wonderful secret of God' and 'the seven things hidden from men' that were 'created before the creation of the world'. They maintained that the movement of planets affects a person's destiny and the day of birth determines each person's individual character (Horoscopes). Their 'Manual of Discipline' alluded to 'the revelation of the Mysteries, which has been kept in silence through all times eternal'. This hymn, found among the Scrolls recorded:

> Thou hast made me the authorised interpreter of profound mysteries. Then hast given me understanding of thy faith and the knowledge of thy wonderful secrets.

It is undeniable that the Essenes held an assemblage of doctrines carefully concealed from the multitude. First century historian Flavius Josephus from whose records we learnt so much about life in Palestine at the time of his life, stated that he himself underwent the probationary period with the Essenes but then withdrew. After his experience, he wrote that they 'live the same kind of life as do those the Greeks called Pythagorean'. The oath extracted from the initiate before he was admitted into the brotherhood stated that he was not 'to have any secrets from one's brethren and never to betray one of theirs, even at the cost of one's life; to pass on the traditions one had received; never to be a brigand; and to safeguard the secret books'.

The fact that they had 'secret books' is of significance in this study and there is reason to believe the same people who encoded the Secret into the Bible wrote those mysterious books.

What was so special about the Bible?

Moses ben Maimon, the celebrated Rabbi, Jewish theologian and philosopher of Cairo (1135-1204), sometimes called Maimonides, expounded that the Old Testament was not historical but allegorical in its entirety. In an effort to explain its problems, Maimonides wrote:

> Every time that you find in our books a tale, the reality of which seems impossible, a story that is repugnant to both reason and common sense, then be sure that the tale contains a profound allegory veiling a deeply mysterious truth…and the greater the absurdity of the letter, the deeper the wisdom of spirit.

That learned injunction damages the usual affirmation that 'Holy Scripture' is the only book in the world whose oracles contain plain unvarnished truth and recommended silence with regard to the true meaning of biblical texts, particularly the Book of Genesis. This was what the highly-regarded Hebrew philosopher said:

> Whoever shall find out the true sense of the Book of Genesis ought to take care not to divulge it. This is a maxim that all our sages repeat to us, and above all respecting the work of six days. If a person should discover the true meaning of it by himself, or by the aid of another, then he ought to be silent, or if he speaks he ought to speak of it obscurely, in an enigmatical manner, as I do myself, leaving the rest to be guessed by those who can understand me.

The Jewish philosopher confesses to a 'Secret' in the Bible, and others made similar admissions. Clement, for example, who had earlier been initiated into the Lesser Eleusinian Mysteries, said: 'The doctrines they taught me contained in them the end of all instructions…and a great mystery'. Clement, in his book, *Stromata*, openly admitted to the existence of confidential information in ancient times and wrote that the hidden mysteries were not divulged to all, 'But since this tradition is not published alone for him who perceives the magnificence of the word, it is requisite, therefore, to hide a Mystery of the wisdom spoken, which Jesus knew'.

The Mystery that Rabbi Jesus knew holds within itself the answers to the individual seeker's deepest needs and inner longings. Other church writings also established the Secret was known to Rabbi Jesus, such as this passage from the Clementine Homilies:

And Peter said: We remember that Jesus and Rabbi, as commanding said to us, guard the Secret for me, and the Sons of my House. Wherefore also he explained to his disciples, privately, the Secret of the Kingdom of the Heavens.

Indeed, some of Rabbi Jesus' followers expressed surprise to find him using unusual forms of expression with the people. 'Why speakest thou unto them in parables', they inquired.[10] Rabbi Jesus answered them: 'To you it has been given to know the Secret of the Kingdom of Heaven, but to them it has not been given...'

According to Young's Analytical Concordance, the exact sense of the word 'Secret' as used in the New Testament is, 'that which is known only to the initiated'. Here we leaRN that Rabbi Jesus' reply was that of one initiate speaking to another. New Testament narratives revealed numerous traces of a secret doctrine taught by Rabbi Jesus and clearly showed that he and some of his associates were in possession of classified information. Three examples are cited: 'It is given unto you to know the Mysteries'; 'We speak the wisdom of God in a Mystery', and, 'We are stewards of the Mysteries of God and understand all Mysteries'. The Gospel accounts of Rabbi Jesus' ministry therefore provide a number of cases where he taught an open exoteric message (in parables) to ordinary folk and privately instructed associates in a deeper esoteric or secret meaning.

The Bible of ancient Egypt

The earliest known reference to the Secret was found in a remarkable old writing first carved into stone at the dawn of civilization on Earth. That literature is the oldest known to mankind and is erroneously called *The Egyptian Book of the Dead*. The opening passage said this about itself:

'This is a book of exceedingly great secrecy. Let not the eye of any profane behold it... That would be an abomination. Conceal its existence. *The Book of the Master of the Hidden Places* is its name'.

Some call it the Bible of Ancient Egypt but it is much more than that, and in this study, constant references are drawn from *The Book of the Master of the Hidden Places.* However, it shall be called by its now commonly known name, the *Book of the Dead,* so as not to cause confusion as to what book is being quoted.

The *Book of the Dead* is the title generally given to the texts because they were found inscribed on the internal walls of tombs or on papyri rolls resting on or near mummies, and because they were deposited with the dead, that title developed in the late 19th century. The longest papyrus version discovered to date measures 135 feet (41 metres) and is 28 inches (48 cms) high and on many occasions, special papyrus rolls were sealed in a hollow statuette shaped like the deceased's favourite god and placed with the mummy.

Over the last 150 years or so, the discovery of burial chambers holding funerary texts revealed to the modern world the innermost sacred secrets of a select body of ancient Egyptian priests. In those times, the *Book of the Dead* revealed the ultimate secrets of the gods and was carefully hidden beyond the eye of the living for what the priests thought would be forever. They believed that secrets revealed in their sacred writing were visible only to the eyes of the soul of the person buried in that crypt and thus preserved from the eyes of the profane. Chapter 114, for example, states:

> I know it, (the Secret), for I have been initiated into it by the Shem priest, and I have never spoken nor made repetition to the gods…I have entered as a Power because of what I know; I have not spoken to men; I have not repeated what was said or written in tombs…it is a Secret.

Some verses of the *Book of the Dead* were later found in the Pyramid Texts which appeared carved in hieroglyphic form on the inside walls of the burial chamber and anteroom of the pyramid of King Unas, last ruler of the Fifth Dynasty (c. 2345 BC). Some of the 189 chapters are so old they were recorded on the sarcophagus of Queen Khnemnefert who lived around 2700 BC according to Egyptologist's reckonings. Other hieroglyphs state that one particular chapter of the *Book of the Dead* was in existence during the reign of Hesep-ti, about 4266 BC, and was established by Egyptologists as the most ancient documentation of any kind known in the world today.

The most moderate estimate makes certain sections of the *Book of the Dead* more than 6000 years old and archaeological evidence showed that, according to biblical chronology, those writings were in existence before God created the earth. In any case, Egyptologists were justified in estimating the earliest form of the work to be contemporaneous with the foundation of the civilization that came into Egypt thousands of years ago.

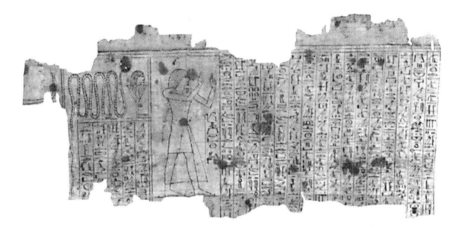

Section of the Egyptian Book of the Dead (Papyrus of RA, c. 1300 BC). The owner of this writing was a scribe and that enabled him to purchase this expensive, richly illustrated papyrus. To the left is a large figure of RA with his hands raised in prayer.

That fascinating, but perplexing, old writing provides an extensive description of systems of various chambers, passageways, halls, temples and gates that were accessed in a complex journey through twelve divisions of an underworld realm of darkness called *duat*. It also records a compilation of prayers, magic spells and incantations, and lists amulets that were to be worn to provide assistance in safely completing the journey. Although used for funerary purposes, some descriptions provided in the *Book of the Dead* are frequently unconnected with the mystical realm and seem to have originally had an entirely different use. In many cases, explanations are far removed from actual meanings of the passage and are presented in a romanticized manner. It is not an easy book to read but sometimes comments on particular heavenly passages show an accurate grasp of a subject matter having an earthly parallel. For example, seven halls are painstakingly described, along with a detailed description of twenty-one vertical columns or pylons. That documentation is significant in this study for those descriptions are directly associated with the Great Pyramid and the Sphinx at the Giza complex.

The elaborate commentary provided in the *Book of the Dead* seems to have been the work of an intensely formal mind, one that devised a number of explanations that fitted a dual purpose. In simple terms, it was written specifically to be comprehended on two different levels of understanding; esoteric and exoteric. Ancient Egyptians believed that the employment of the texts by the soul of the deceased would give them various divine powers that enabled them to secure acquittal at the Judgment. The numerous pictures and symbols were understood to assist the departed overcome the perils that they believed beset the path of the dead. However, those instructions were also used on the physical Earthly plane by the living and were coded initiatory processes used by ancient Egyptian priesthoods, the original guardians of the Secret knowledge. In other words, the deceased persons in the *Book of the Dead* became the living initiates in Egyptian temples. Therefore, the *Book of the Dead* is a secret manual of initiation from the mysterious First Times and describes a series of procedures and passwords to be spoken that purposely have two distinct levels of meaning, one spiritual and the other physical.

The 'Hidden Places' mentioned in the original title are particular underground chambers at the Giza complex and are described allegorically as mystical places in the abode in heaven. Underlying descriptions given in the *Book of the Dead* is the outline of an original priestly ritual used in Egyptian temples aeons ago. That ritual was romanticized by the author (authors, maybe) into a supernatural experience disguised as the pathway to be used by the deceased on the journey to the afterlife. In other words, it was possible to duplicate the trip to the heavenly existence while here on Earth, the purpose being to prove to the living that there was an afterlife that could be glimpsed, or experienced, while living the physical life. Therefore, the *Book of the Dead* records the earthly method used in discovering heavenly mysteries of the hereafter, concealed in words and symbols that themselves were hidden in tombs of the deceased.

The *Book of the Dead* carries some unusual narratives with a curious reference to 'those who live among the stars'. Another passage spoke of a specific knowledge that enabled those in its possession to 'reach the vault of the sky'. The whole of Egyptian theology is clothed in mysterious statements and it will be revealed that its arcane writings and secrets in architecture were originally and purposely intended for a great and noble purpose.

The Pyramid and the Bible

Without the Great Pyramid and the mysterious *Book of Thoth*, there would be no Bible today, simply because the very essence of the hidden information evolved at the Great Pyramid. In church dictionaries, that statement is not corroborated but the result of this work shows the entire primary function of the Great Pyramid was directly responsible for the coming into being of both the Old and New Testaments of the Bible.

The Great Pyramid is supreme among the wonders of antiquity, although now a poor reflection of its original grandeur. Herodotus (c. 484-430 BC), a highly regarded historian who travelled to Egypt in 449 BC, gave the earliest recorded eyewitness description of the structure and other marvels that surrounded it. What today stands as ruins, he saw in something of their original splendour and even then, the unique nature of the complex probably seemed but a distant memory to him. Herodotus is often called the Father of History and the World's First Travel Writer. He was born at Halicarnassus, in Asia Minor, and travelled widely, living first at Samos and later at Athens. Herodotus was the first to carry on research into events of the past and treat them in a rational rather than a mythical manner. He had immense respect for the wisdom of Egypt and was personally initiated by high priests of the temple hierarchy. He spoke of the mystery of the Great Pyramid and what he learnt there with great reverence:

> I impose upon myself a profound silence in regard to the secret of the Mysteries of which I am acquainted. I know the whole course of the proceedings in these ceremonies, but they shall not pass my lips.

There were no guidebooks and few recorded histories in the days of Herodotus. He started on his travels armed with a ready intelligence, a lively wit, and an insatiable curiosity to see, hear and record what was happening in the world, and to learn from others the story of the past. His primary informants were senior members of the high Egyptian priesthood who held the reputation as guardians of superior wisdom. Because of the respect they maintained for Herodotus, they shared with him their age-old Temple knowledge and read to him from records of great antiquity. It was from Herodotus' documentation that the world learnt what upper-level Egyptian priests knew of Egypt's remote past preceding the fifth century BC, and much of that long-silent information is noted in this book.

The thesis provided in this work presents the spiritual side of the Great Pyramid and supports long-held contentions preserved in ancient traditions that it was not planned and built as a tomb for a Pharaoh. Those traditions claimed that the Great Pyramid was a place designed and used exclusively for holy encounters. Whether incidentally, or coincidentally, those traditions also said it was built as a monument for the preservation of wisdom and an everlasting prophet for the future. The Great Pyramid is connected with the same intelligence that fashioned the Sphinx and those creations were not built at random but followed a definite structural plan both above and below the ground. For that reason, this work does not become involved in, or deal exhaustively with, the mechanical, engineering, scientific or other features of the design and structure of the Great Pyramid, except as far as they cast light on its spiritual symbolism and its practical usefulness in accordance to the thesis referred to above.

However, the important point is that whoever built the Great Pyramid was directly responsible for the Secret in the Bible that was subsequently, and intentionally, encoded into the original Torah. The word 'Torah' means 'instruction' or 'guidance' and is used in both singular and plural form. It is the original name of the first five books of the Old Testament, those being Genesis, Exodus, Leviticus, Numbers and Deuteronomy. It is those (now) five books that are of primary interest in this study for therein 'lies hidden in every detail thereof',[11] the concealed secret knowledge.

In any discussion revealing the secret in the Torah, it is vital to mention that it is expressed in its original form as one unbroken scroll, not as a series of five separate books with pages like today, but as a large continuous parchment that was unrolled in one long piece. At what precise time the first part of the Bible was restructured from a single scroll into separate books and called the Pentateuch (Greek, meaning Penta, five) is a question not yet settled. The word Pentateuch was used for the first time in recorded history in a letter to Flora by the Valentinian Ptolemy,[12] variously dated between 150–75 BC.

© Archives de Histore

An ancient depiction of a Torah Scroll.

The importance of the Torah

In this work, it is of utmost importance to refer to the early books of the Old Testament as the Torah and stay with its original Scroll form. In that respect, the Zohar is a document presumed to be of great antiquity and its authorship is ascribed to the Palestinian Tanna Simeon ben Yokai (second century) as it was written in the dialect of his time. Of the Torah, it stated:

> …each word of the Torah contains an elevated meaning and a sublime mystery. The simple take notice only of the garments or recitals of the Torah, they know no other thing, they see not that which is concealed under the vestments. The more instructed men do not pay attention to the vestment, but to the body which it envelops.[13]

29

Only few people know the Secret of the Torah and even less know how it originated. Samuel (d. c. 254), head of the rabbinic school of Nehardea, sent a certain Rabbi Johanan (an Initiate) thirty-nine camel loads of written questions about the Torah in a desperate attempt to discover the Secret hidden within it. His requests went unanswered. Many early presbyters did not question or realize the importance of the Torah and regarded it as nothing more than a collection of symbolic fables. Origen (185-251), one of the shining lights of early Christianity, exclaimed: 'If we hold to the letter, and must understand what stands written in the Torah after the manner of the Jews and common people, then I should blush to confess aloud that if it is God who has given these laws; then the laws of men appear more excellent and reasonable'. Of the Creation narratives in the Book of Genesis, Origen asked, in a fit of indignation:

> What man of sense will agree with the statement the first, second and third days in which the evening is named and the morning, were without sun, moon and stars and the first day without a heaven? What man is found such an idiot as to suppose that God planted trees in Paradise, in Eden, like a husbandman? I believe that every man must hold these things for images, under which the hidden sense lies concealed.[14]

Origen clearly did not believe the account of Creation in Genesis yet millions of people in all ages believed every word of the Bible was unchallengeable, but he was right when he reasoned that 'the hidden sense lies concealed' below the surface. When Paul's unequivocal statement in Galatian's[15] that the Torah's story of Abraham and his two sons was 'an allegory', then little blame can be attached to any Christian who declines to accept the Bible in any other light than that of an ingenious allegory. However, it is more than 'an allegory', that being only a conventional explanation of what it really is.

A modern day printing of the Torah in any language, including Hebrew, is of no value in establishing the Secret in the Bible. All references to the Torah in this book are to the original handwritten versions and the reason for that shall become apparent as this work proceeds. Those particular Torahs are the same letter-for-letter reproduction as the original text and the author of this book was privileged to have had access to a 2000-year-old version for research. There is nothing like it in the history of literature or religion and in that respect, the handwritten Scroll stands indisputably in a class by itself.

For centuries, copies of the Torah Scroll were made exactly in accordance with ancient regulations regarding tradition; namely: written by hand, without vocalization, according to a prescribed arrangement of 49 vertical lines and sections and published by means of dependable materials. It was rigidly forbidden to have pictorial decorations on any Scroll and for 'those who know' (*Zohar*), every detail of the writing (or copying) was laid down to the minutest detail. The lineation, the division into columns and text (7 x 7), the margins and borders, the binding up of the individual parchment sheets into Scrolls by means of thongs,[16] and the division and adornments of letters, were all strictly controlled. Those tasks were undertaken with extreme care, providing painstakingly executed handwritten Scrolls from behind locked doors.

To preserve the Secret, and with loving care and sacred devotion, generations of rabbinic scribes jealously guarded every letter of the Torah Scroll. Detailed rules were laid down in order to ensure that reproductions of the Torah should be free from human error. If one tiny mistake was made, that particular copy was ceremoniously buried, for it carried within it the divine name of God and as such, destruction was forbidden. In the year 50, a Roman soldier desecrated a Torah Scroll and the popular outcry was so great that the Governor had him beheaded.[17] Such was the respect for that extraordinary old text.

The institution of reading the Torah Scroll was indeed very old, and the first reference to a public reading was carried in the Old Testament book of Nehemiah (8) when the high priest, Ezra, read from the Torah at an assembly of people in the year 397 BC. The congregation thereupon obligated itself to the observance of the laws of life and how it was to be lived, as written in the 613 commandments in the Torah. With the rise of Judaism in the 19th century, and the advance of the historical critical approach to the Bible, many Jewish intellectuals saw it, at least in part, as an exclusive moral, political and religious law of one particular body of people. That was probably so with a surface reading, but there is much more to the Torah than that and whileas it was (and is) read as narratives, its deep meaning is *not* at the story level.

The Rabbis 'who knew' had a profound and extensive knowledge of every word, jot and tittle (decoration of letters) of the handwritten Torah. The statement in the Talmud that the Soferim (a specific class of scribes) were so called because they counted every letter of the Torah, expressed only the mechanical aspect of their intense preoccupation with the text. Every word, every expression, was made the subject of intense study, the reason being that they knew, and were preserving, the sacred Secret information originally concealed in those writings.

CHAPTER TWO

THE MYSTERY SCHOOLS:
KEEPERS OF SECRET KNOWLEDGE

The House of the Panthers

In ancient Egyptian records filed in the Alexandrian Library, brief mention is made of a god named Leo who resided on the Pyramid Plateau with fifteen associates. That grouping was called 'Leo-prds' and the short reference to their existence provided the origin of the use of the word Leo as the symbol of a lion. In those times, Leo did not originally describe an animal and it is probable that the leopard of the cat family was named from that group of gods. That animal was originally called 'Panthera Leo-pardus' (Panther Leo-pardus, Leo-pard, Leo-prds) and the name later evolved to 'panther leopard'.[1] Subsequently, the word Panther became a group name or general term for all members of the cat family, large and small, and distinction of the various types was only given in later times.

Similarly, in early history the big tawny yellow-coated cat known today as a lion was called 'Panthera Leo' or 'Leo Panther' (Leo the Panther). When 'leo' was pluralized it became 'leon', and after the Moors attached that name to it around 450, 'panther' subsequently became 'lion' in English. When the titles 'lion' or 'leopard' are found used in writings pre-dating the fourth century, they could be correctly replaced with their original appellation, 'Panther'.

In mythology, the first monster that Hercules exterminated was the Nemean Panther, and from its skin he made a long coat that, when worn, rendered him indestructible. Hercules' costume became the trademark of the descendants of the Leo-prds who were later called Panthers and they carried forward the special knowledge of their forefathers. The Panthers developed a confidential teaching system around the Osiris rites and their name became synonymous with 'secret information'. It was that group who were directly responsible for the advent of all later Mystery Schools and, even today, a family group of people on Earth still carries the Panther knowledge.[2] In early ritual performances, high initiates wore ceremonial costumes fashioned from Panther skins and embossed with five-pointed stars, striking garments that symbolically represented the special wisdom that they possessed.

Later Egyptian priests wore skins of lions, tigers, panthers, pumas and leopards in their ritualistic re-enactment of earlier Panther procedures and the type of fur represented particular levels of initiation. The skin was generally thrown over the left shoulder and swayed with the movement of the body; sometimes it was carefully adjusted over one shoulder and under the other to bring the curve of the chest into prominence. The head of the animal, skillfully prepared and enlivened by large eyes of enamel, rested on the shoulder or fell just below the waist of the wearer; the paws, with the claws attached, hung down over the thighs and, to complete their adornment, a blue or black wig was worn.

Statue of priest Aa-nen wearing the Panther regalia (XVIII Dynasty; Turin Museum)

The wearing of feline skins was obligatory for certain orders of priests, or for dignitaries, performing priestly functions of a prescribed nature. The sacerdotal costume was a survival of the ancient attire of the head of the family and those who inherited or had obtained the right of wearing the Panther skin on certain occasions bore, under the ancient empire, the title of *Oîrû-basit*, 'Chiefs of the Fur'.[3] Wild beast's skins later became the insignia of authority with which priests and princes adorned themselves on great days and at religious ceremonies.

Leo the Lion became king of the animal family and in allegories perpetuated by the Mysteries, Leo opened 'The Secret Book'. The Leo-prds originally developed the Secret concealed in that book and it was eventually encoded into the Bible by a later initiate of their line who thus preserved the Order's ancient sacred knowledge. In later times, those who achieved initiation into the highest Panther Mysteries were awarded the appellation 'Panther', and that title was included into their family and given names. In that regard, Julius Caesar, Emperors Augustus and Tiberius, Rabbi Jesus, Joseph of Arimathea, and Agrippa, who built the Roman Pantheon to the gods, were all recorded in history as carrying the Panther (Panthera in Latin) designation, and that directly identified them as initiated bearers of special knowledge. They were 'versed in all the Wisdom of the Gods'[4] and their understanding of the Bible revealed that for centuries it was read by the uninitiated in a sense contrary to its intent.

Initiation processes

The principles of secrecy and silence are the reasons why the Panther Secret remained concealed for so long. Those virtues constitute the core of all Mystery Schools and were the safeguard of the Institution, ensuring its security and perpetuity. That principle existed in all ancient Mysteries and in some systems of religion. Secret ceremonies were practised and the knowledge revealed to candidates was held in strict confidence. Lucius Apuleius (second century), an initiate into the Mysteries of Isis, confirmed the rule: 'By no peril will I ever be compelled to disclose to the uninitiated the things that I have had entrusted to me on condition of silence'. That secret worship was termed the Mysteries to which none were admitted but those selected by preparatory ceremonies called Initiation, a programmed alteration of individual consciousness. The term 'initiation' was first used by Romans to designate admission into their secret and sacred rites and was derived from the word *initia*, which signified the first principle of a science. The person presiding at the ceremony was called the Mystagogue and revealed and explained sacred matters to the candidate. He was also called the hierophant, the word signifying literally the 'one who makes or conducts an initiate'.

The ceremonies of initiation were time-consuming, and candidates to whom the Secret was eventually revealed undertook long periods of instruction. A planned period of specific teaching was in place for aspirants and they were entranced for periods of varying length…the more advanced the degree for which they had entered the longer and deeper was their entrancement. During that time, various elements of achieving the overall knowledge were gradually released, and every year only a comparatively few were fully initiated into the Mysteries, consequently the number of persons who knew the School's deepest secrets was never at any time large.

Initiation was not obtained by filling out an application form. The full process took many years of the candidate's life and was won by merit, perseverance, discipline, integrity, honour, worthiness and increasing spiritual perception. The Mystery Schools would not initiate a slave or a person convicted of any felony, nor would they accept anyone who was not of sound body and mind. Particularly in later Egyptian Mysteries, circumcision of the candidate was required before admission. He was then given a code-name, a tradition still carried on today in Freemasonry. Initiation was designed for the aspirer to face and undergo a series of ordeals and trials preliminary to admission into higher levels of secret knowledge and the transition to greater enlightenment required dedication and study. Approach to the great mystery was heavily guarded and total ostracism pronounced upon initiates who deliberately divulged secrets entrusted to them. Offenders were often killed, because keepers of the Secret held the power of life and death of those in their custody.

The writings of first century historian, Pliny (Caius Plinius Secundus), graphically described the story of a person called Anaxarchus, an initiate into the Mysteries, who was imprisoned in order to brutally extort from him secrets with which he had been entrusted. So seriously did he take the confidentiality of the Secret, he bit out his own tongue and threw it in the face of Nicocreon, the tyrant of Cyprus. Likewise, the Athenians revered a brazen statue that was represented without a tongue to denote the sanctity with which they regarded their oath-bound secrets. In the Eleusinian and the Bacchi Mysteries, initiates dared not reveal the inner Secret and between the Chaldean and Asian Magi, the same rule applied.

It is doubtful that the Gnostics, Neo-Platonists and medieval philosophers required such an extreme penalty but they, even so in the present Masonic Order, issued the strictest of warnings to the candidate never to reveal the entrusted Secret. Even today in Masonry, the 'Lost Word', or the 'Master's Word', is communicated to the candidate near the ear and in 'a low breath', him again being cautioned to its secrecy. He swears under dire penalties not to divulge the secrets of the Order, although Masons today no longer possess the awesome power of the Ancients.

The secrets that successful candidates learned in the Mystery Schools depended upon the degree through which they passed, but their experiences could roughly be condensed into two results and they formed the core of the revelations they received. Later initiates termed those differing understandings, the Evening walk (to public audiences) and the Morning walk (to select disciples). In the words of Pythagoras, when turning away unsuitable applicants from his own academy at Croton, 'not every kind of wood is suitable for the making of Mercury'. In the earlier degrees, called the Lesser Mysteries, the candidates became acquainted with the human soul, pictured as a little birdman in the system of Egyptian hieroglyphs. The Lesser Mysteries candidates who achieved full initiation in their division did not learn the Secret. In advanced degrees, they became acquainted with the divine soul, and the supernormal character of the instruction leading to that result, they called the Greater Mysteries. The Greater Mysteries allowed candidates to experience the Secret only on one occasion and the instruction involved an external, physical, almost brutal way to the 'end revealing'. That was a daunting and life-threatening experience for them but the Secret in the Bible, however, allows access to the intrinsic element of the Greater

Mysteries in an almost angelic way, and only the highest initiates used the hidden instruction.

It all started in Egypt

The very basis of the Panther's mysterious knowledge was the cause of the Mystery Schools coming into being and looking dEEply into the substance of the Greater Mysteries discloses the core of the Secret in a usable earthly form. That may sound complex but it shall become clear in the following chapters. Ancient writings revealed that the Panther knowledge was introduced into Egypt in the earliest days of mankind, a point gleaned from Plato's *Timaeus* in which Solon (640-558 BC) was told by Egyptian priests of a chronology dating back 9000 years before his time. That presupposed the existence of historical archives in Egypt covering vast periods and Herodotus claimed that priests with whom he was acquainted were indeed in possession of prehistoric records. Herodotus's writings lead his readers to understand that *all* Secret Schools of the ancient world were branches from the original Panther teachings and were channels of other countries through which one basic philosophic principle was disseminated. Herodotus asserted that the Mysteries known to Greek priests were originally derived directly from Egyptian temples. Prominent and learned Greeks, and later some Romans, travelled to Egypt to seek for themselves the Ancient Wisdom of temple priests. Before the development of their respective Schools, both Pythagoras and Plato admitted to having sat at the feet of Egyptian priests in their search for secret knowledge.

A work entitled *Crata Repoa*, or *Initiations of the Egyptian Priests*, was published at Berlin in 1770. It was produced from writings of great antiquity, and professed to reveal the whole formula of initiation used by early Egyptian priests in the subterranean chambers and crypts of ancient temples. According to *Crata Repoa*, the Mystery teachings were divided into seven degrees, the first devoted to instructions in the physical sciences and the second to geometry and architecture. In the third degree, the candidate was instructed in the symbolical death of Osiris, and was acquainted with the hieroglyphic language. In the fourth, he was presented with the book of the laws of Egypt, and became a judge. The instructions of the fifth degree were dedicated to chemistry, and the sixth to astronomy and mathematical sciences. In the seventh and last degree, the candidate received a detailed explanation of all Mysteries, his head was shaved, and he was presented with an ankh-cross, which he was to carry constantly, a white mantle, and a square headdress. To each degree was attached a secret word and a sign.

The secret operations of God

The question may legitimately be asked: 'If those ancient mystical institutions were of such 'great pith and movement', why is so little information available concerning them and the processes of initiation that they claimed to use?' Oral, not written, instruction was the only means of perpetuating knowledge preserved by the cults of the ancient world and, excluding the veiled *Book of the Dead*, no real literature divulged the principles and essential details of Mystery School teachings. However, a peculiar type of literature was dispensed by various later priesthoods for the mystification of the laity or, at best, coded literature beloved by mythologists and cabalists. To understand that curious prose required special oral instruction obtained only by joining one of their Orders, and for a complete unveiling of information, admission into the ultimate inner priesthood by initiation. Great care was taken to see that the mysteries of the Secret, or the secret of the Mysteries, were never revealed to the unqualified. Thus, relatively few people knew the fundamental nature of the Mysteries and that was the main reason why it is so difficult today to find any substantial written records on the subject.

In the Egyptian galleries of the Museum of the Louvre at Paris is the tomb of Ptah-Mer, a High Priest of Memphis, and it bears an inscription, as epitaph, that says: 'He penetrated in the Mysteries of every sanctuary; nothing was hidden from him. He covered with a veil everything which he had seen'. The hierophants were compelled to maintain extraordinary reserve, yet the necessity of excluding skeptics and scoffers from experiments fraught with so much danger to the candidate's life was obvious, while the inadvisability of casting pearls before swine was equally obvious. Nineteen centuries ago, Philo, the Alexandrian philosopher, historian and statesman, recorded these lines about the high respect held for preservation of knowledge given by the system of initiatrix instruction:

O, ye Initiates, ye whose ears are purified, receive this in your souls, as a mystery never to be lost! Reveal it to no profane! Keep it and contain it within yourselves as an incorruptible treasure, not like gold or silver, but more precious than everything besides…for it is the knowledge of the Great Cause, of Nature, and all of that which is born of both.

The initiates used inscrutable language to safeguard their cherished secret knowledge and Plato's words in a letter to Dionysius the Younger served as an example of that old practice: 'I must write to you in enigmas so that if my letter is intercepted by land or sea, he who shall read it may in no degree comprehend it…what is written is unintelligible to fools'.

Symbolism was subsequently developed as the language of the Mystery Schools and a single figure in a drawing or painting could both reveal and conceal particular information. To the initiated, the subject of their School's symbol was obvious, while to the ignorant the figure remained enigmatic. A variety of elements was revealed to the initiate under veiled symbols to which the profane did not have the key and because of the secrecy maintained, they spoke little and acted well. In a book called *The Golden Ass*, Lucius Apuleius of the second century said:

Perchance, eager reader, thou burnest to know what was then said, what done. I would tell thee, were it lawful for me to tell, and thou shouldst know all, were it lawful for thee to hear. Both tongue and ear would be infected with like guilt did I gratify such rash curiosity. Yet since, perchance, it is pious craving that vexes thee, I will not torment thee by prolongation of thine languish.

Those lines are tantalizing but do not reveal a great deal. However, other old writings explain a little more of secrets taught, and constantly expressed a cosmic character to the substance of the Mysteries. Philo frankly disclosed: 'The Mysteries were known to unveil the secret operations of God'. 'In Egypt', wrote Origen, 'the philosophers have a sublime and secret knowledge respecting the nature of God'. From his personal experience, Heraclitus of Pontus recorded these remarkable words: 'The eternal nature of the universe was revealed to me and it became apparent that earth was man's temporary place of abode'.

A number of strange and apparently supernatural phenomena were said to have accompanied many ancient Mystery rituals and advanced initiates jubilantly claimed to have seen living gods themselves. Whether that was the result of religious ecstasy, the use of the Secret, or the co-operation of invisible powers with visible initiators, must remain a mystery. Lucius Apuleius described his initiation into the Mysteries of Isis:

> Hear, then, and believe, for what I tell is true. I drew nigh to the confines of death, and I trod the threshold of Proserpine, I was borne through all the elements and returned to Earth again. I saw the sun gleaming with bright splendour at dead of night, I approached the gods above, and the gods below, and worshipped them face-to-face. Behold, I have told thee things of which, though thou hast heard them, thou must yet know naught.

Seeing the 'sun' shining at midnight is often mentioned in association with the rites of Secret Societies. A year later Lucius was initiated into the Greater Mysteries of Osiris and alleged that at that higher level initiates were 'made acquainted with the divine soul; they were brought into personal communion with the Creator; they stood face to face with the divine'.

A record left by an ancient writer about initiates provided this insight: 'They are made to know the meaning of the riddle of existence'. When Roman Emperor Julian (361-363) spoke of the 'seven-coloured god who lifted souls to salvation through his own nature', he was talking about the very substance of the Secret in the Bible. It was obvious from the foregoing records that the Secret of the Mystery Schools opened the eyes of the subliminal Self and raised initiates to a higher plain of awareness.

The Pyramid connection

A particular trait of the rites of Mithraism was a direct copy of a structural element taken from the King's Chamber in the Great Pyramid. The word Mithra itself evolved from the earlier idiom, 'The Myths of Ra', (Mythra) and incorporated many earlier Egyptian teachings. Mithraic rites were performed in caves that were adorned with two signs of the Zodiac, Cancer and Capricorn. Summer and winter solstices were thus symbolically represented and to support their ritual, two small tunnels were dug up through the walls of the cave to the surface. Those little tunnels were similar in concept to the star (or soul) shafts leading to the external surfaces of the Great Pyramid from the King's Chamber. The initiates believed that those shafts were the gates for the souls descending into this life, or passing in their ascent to the gods - Cancer being the gate of descent, and Capricorn the gate of ascent. They believed those shafts were the 'avenues of the immortals' passing up and down from earth to heaven and from heaven to earth.

Candidates who successfully passed the Mithraic initiations were also called Panthers and were marked upon their foreheads in ochre with the sign of the Egyptian ankh-cross. For some reason, the word Panther was substituted for Lion in the 15th century when printing presses first came into being. Reference to the 'Lion' and the 'Grip of the Lion's Paw' in the Master Mason's degree had strong Mithraic tinges and may have originated from that cult, although once again, 'Lion' was originally 'Panther'. A ladder of seven rungs appears to have been of special significance in the Mithraic initiation rituals and some researchers are of the opinion that the 'ladder' was, in reality, a pyramid of seven steps, like the step-pyramid at Saqqara, at which initiation ceremonies were conducted both internally and externally. It is possible that the symbolic seven-runged ladder of Masonic Mysteries also had its origin in the Mithraic rite. Women were not permitted to enter the Mithraic Order and the refusal to permit women to join the Masonic Order may be based on the esoteric reason given in the secret instructions of Mithraicism.

Probably the most famous of later Mysteries were the Eleusinian, whose rites were celebrated mainly in the village of Eleusis near Athens to honour Demeter. In 1374 BC, the King of Eleusis, Eumolpos, spent seven years at the Great Pyramid in Egypt completing his initiation and, after returning home, started his Mystery School patterned on Egyptian teachings. For the next twelve hundred years, his descendants, the Eumolpidae, presided over the Eleusinian Mysteries as Hierophants.

The rites of the Eleusinian Mysteries were also divided into two different grades, the Lesser and the Greater. While the Lesser Mysteries were mere popular cults, the Greater Mysteries were reserved for an exclusive circle of mature minds capable of rising above the average level of the masses.

Even the Lesser Mysteries required a high reputation for entry, denying admission to persons of doubtful character. In spite of his power, Roman Emperor Nero (37-68 first century) dared not attend Eleusinian Mysteries after he murdered his mother. Likewise, Emperor Constantine (died 337) was refused admission to the Lesser Mysteries after having assassinated his son Crispus and then drowning his second wife Fausta in boiling water. It was the same Constantine who butchered his little nephew, murdered with his own hands his two brothers-in-law, bled to death several men and women, and smothered an old monk to death in a well. Emperor Constantine's application for initiation into the Mysteries was refused on grounds of his 'animalistic nature and carnal lust',[5] and that made him so angry that he destroyed many temples where the Mysteries were taught. The later Christian church sermonized that the destruction was the result of Constantine's conversion to Christianity and subsequently canonized him.

Women and children were admitted to the Eleusinian Mysteries (the Lesser Mysteries only) and at one time, there were literally thousands of initiates. They were famous throughout Greece for the beauty of their philosophic concepts and their high standards of morality that they demonstrated in their daily lives. Because of their excellence, their teachings spread to Rome and Britain and later initiations were given by Eleusinian adepts in both those countries.

The Lesser Mysteries were celebrated in the spring in the town of Agrae, and the Greater, in the autumn, at Eleusis or Athens. It was supposed that the former were given annually and the latter every five years. It seemed those Mysteries began to vary from the Egyptian model as centuries rolled on. Because candidates were bound by unwritten and inviolable oaths, it was difficult to obtain satisfactory information about the changes. Of that great secret institution, Cicero said that he knew, however, that it taught men not only how to live, but also how to die. Aristotle (384-322 BC) said of them, 'You went there not to learn anything, but to have an experience'.

Through indirect channels, nevertheless, some of their secrets leaked out. Their ritual ceremony began with the candidate standing upon skins of animals specially sacrificed for the purpose, and vowed that death should seal his lips before he would ever divulge the sacred truths which were about to be communicated to him. The crux of the revised Eleusinian argument, it seemed, was that man was neither better nor wiser after death than during life. If he did not rise above ignorance during his earthly sojourn, man went at death into eternity to wander about forever, making the same mistakes that he made here on Earth. If he did not outgrow the desire for material possessions here, he would carry it with him into the invisible world, where, because he could never gratify the desire, he would continue in endless agony.

The Eleusinian Mysteries survived all others in a degenerated form and ceased to exist as an institution in 438 when, by a general edict of proscription, they were abolished by Emperor Theodosius (self-styled the 'Great') who destroyed those who did not accept the Christian faith.

Candidates 'buried' alive

A unique insight into the Osiris rites of Egypt is also seen in the study of the Druids, an ancient order of priests in Britain, Gaul and Ireland. Their teachings closely resembled the Bacchic and Eleusinian Mysteries of Greece and were justly designated 'The Druidic Mysteries'. There was much speculation concerning the secret ceremonies Druids performed and getting to the kernel of their innermost rites was not easy. The most striking ceremonial adornment of the garments worn by the exulted Arch-Druid was 'The Breastplate of Judgment' which, the Druids themselves said, possessed the mysterious power of strangling to death any person who made an untrue statement while wearing it. The breastplate was placed around the neck of witnesses to test the veracity of their evidence. An early initiate of the Druidic Mysteries related on his deathbed that admission to their midnight ceremonies was gained only by means of travelling in a mysterious glass boat. Whatever that meant is unknown but was probably associated with the shape of a new moon.

The Druids gave 'themselves wholly to the contemplation of divine and hidden things' and believed in books of secret knowledge that originated at the dawn of civilization. An old tradition maintained they possessed certain sacred writings containing laws and promises as well as predictions of future events. That was possibly the *Book of Thoth*, an ancient Egyptian writing directly associated with the Secret in the Bible. According to Cicero and Virgil, some Mystery Schools taught the doctrine of reincarnation and elucidated that the pains and sorrows of this life were an expiation of prior faults and sins. That idea could have been a later importation from India, with which ancient Greece and Rome had commercial and cultural contacts. However, it was certainly a Druidic principle and they taught people much concerning their belief in the immortality of the soul, transmigration and reincarnation. They borrowed in one life, promising to pay back in the next. They believed in a purgatorial type of lower life where they would be cleansed of their sins, afterwards passing on to the happiness of unity with the gods. They taught that all people would be saved, but that some must return to earth many times to learn the lessons of human life and to overcome the inherent evil of their own natures.

Before a candidate was entrusted with the secret doctrines of the Order, he was taught that if he ever deliberately divulged the Mysteries, he would personally bear the karmatic punishment for his transgression. Those doctrines were imparted only in the depths of the forests and in the darkness of caves. In those secret places, far from the haunts of men, the candidate was instructed concerning the creation of the universe, the personalities of the gods, the laws of Nature, the secrets of occult medicine, the mysteries of celestial bodies, and the rudiments of magic and sorcery. It was understood that the ancient initiations took place only at the two solstices and the two equinoxes.

The Druids were the original and primitive inhabitants of Britain preceding the commencement of the Christian era by many centuries and even then, they knew the Secret. Attesting to that was the most famous of their altars, a great ring of rocks in Stonehenge in south western England, a structure laid out on an astronomical basis and still standing today (in part), a wonder of antiquity. Long before either the Old or New Testaments were written, the Druids had a virgin mother with a child in her arms who was sacred to their Mysteries. At dawn of the 25th day of December, the birth of the Sun God, HU, was celebrated. Like so many early world religions, HU was subsequently murdered and, after a number of strange ordeals and mystic rituals, restored to life. HU was resurrected at the time of the year corresponding to that which Christians today celebrate Easter. Both the cross and the serpent were sacred to the Druids as were the highly regarded symbols of HU who was actually the Druidic Osiris. They believed that HU the Mighty was the first settler of Britain and that he came from a place that the Welsh Triads called the Summer Country, the present area of Istanbul, but of major importance in this study is the knowledge that part of the 'Lost Word' of Masonry is concealed in HU's name.

Instruction into the Druidic Mysteries consisted of three degrees of learning, with each degree made up of seven separate sections (3 x 7 = 21 levels), but few successfully passed them all. The candidate was subsequently 'buried' in a coffin, as were all initiates into the Mysteries. That curious ritual originated in the sarcophagus in the King's Chamber at the Great Pyramid and was part of the ceremonies conducted by the Egyptian Magi in their initiation performances reproducing the death of Osiris. It was an act only, albeit a dangerous one, denoting a symbolic death. The supreme Druidic test, however, was that of being sent out to sea in an open boat. While undergoing the ordeal, many lost their lives and there are peculiar stories relating to that particular part of the ritual. The few who passed the third degree were 'born again' and then instructed in the deep secret and ancient truths that Druids had preserved from antiquity. From those initiates were chosen many dignitaries of the British religious and political world.

The Mystery Schools laid great stress on the evils of suicide, explaining that there was a profound Mystery concerning what they called 'a crime'. Of this they would not speak, but warned their disciples that great sorrow came to all who took their own lives. Maybe the Mystery which they would not discuss is answered in the writings of the wise Tibetan monks. The magnificent and mysterious Tibetan Lamaseries contained many secret and semi-secret volumes detailing the lives of great Sages who lived in them in preceding centuries. Many of the learned statements recorded there, particularly about Karma, were purposely confused, and in others the reader became bewildered, unless a clue be given, by the use of one name to cover many individuals who followed the same line of teaching.

Thus, there was a succession of 'Living Buddhas' and the name 'Buddha' was given to teacher after teacher. The reader must therefore depend upon his or her own intuition to distinguish between the human Buddhas or the original, first Buddha 'the enlightened'. However, in one of those old manuscripts there is a curious story of one called Shankara who, at the age of 33 years and tired of this mortal body, 'put it off' in a cave he had entered. As the legend went, Shankara's Soul was left with 'the burden of a sin upon him which he had not committed'. In other words, because Shankara had committed suicide, his Soul had to suffer for something it had not done. At the same time was added:

> At whatever age one puts off his outward body by free will (suicide), at that age will he be made to die a violent death against his will in his next rebirth.

Neither had his Soul any responsibility for the deed, whether sinful or otherwise, and therefore, it seemed, Karma cannot act unjustly. There is certainly some deep mystery involved in that story, one that no uninitiated intellect could ever unravel, Still then, there it is, suggesting the natural query: 'Who then was punished by Karma…Shankara or his Soul?'…and leaving it to be answered.

Great women initiates

A great deal of discussion exists on the exclusion of women from modern-day Secret Societies but women were once admitted to the Mysteries on equal terms with men and were just as able to learn the Secret as anybody else. In answer to the opinion that Masons today, by excluding women, are following the tradition of the ancient Mysteries, Brother Ward in his book, *Freemasonry: Its Aims and Ideals*, said:

> Now I have actually heard this argument, and let me hasten to say it is worthless, for women undoubtedly were admitted into the Ancient Mysteries. There is abundant evidence that there were women members of the Mysteries of Eleusis. The idea that women were not admitted to the ancient Mysteries is probably because it is generally believed that they were excluded from the Mysteries of Mithra. Even this has been disputed, but it is probably correct, because the Order of Mithra was, essentially, an Order connected with the army. But similar reasons did not operate in the case of other Mysteries. Indeed, numerous monuments testify to the fact that husband and wife often went through the ceremonies together.

That point was substantiated by Bishop Leadbeater, who wrote, 'Women were admitted to the Mysteries and were able to penetrate into the inmost sanctuaries as well as men'.[6] Dudley Wright said in his book *Women and Freemasonry* that, 'there is evidence in days gone by that women were admitted into the Order of Knights Templar', substantiated by the recent discovery of Templar gravestones for women. The full participation of women in the central Mysteries of antiquity went far deeper than was hitherto conceded, and many high profile women were full initiates into the innermost Secret of the Egyptian temples.

The word 'Pharaoh' is generally associated with only men but many women also held the position. All Pharaohs were initiates…they knew the Secret. Queen Hatshepsut was perhaps the most famous example of the lady Pharaohs. Rather than delegating the position, she exercised her royal prerogative and, for 22 years, chose to wield direct authority of the office of Pharaoh herself. Pharaoh Hatshepsut's work enlarged the Egyptian empire to its greatest extent to that date and that degree was exceeded only by her successor. 'At the start of her reign she seemed to have been involved in military campaigns, fighting with her troops in Nubia and elsewhere, but she was generally associated with peaceful prosperity and cultural life'.[7] Pharaoh Hatshepsut was particularly famous for having led an ambitious and successful trading and diplomatic expedition to the Land of Punt. E G Davis, in his book *The First Sex*, said, 'Hatshepsut reigned supreme as Pharaoh, and her long and glorious reign is recognized to have been one of Egypt's finest hours'. A beautiful stone statue of Hatshepsut dressed as Pharaoh was recently uncovered in excavations in Egypt and today stands in the Egyptian Museum at Cairo.

Near Thebes, at a place called Deir el-Bahri, is situated the mortuary temple of Hatshepsut and it also contains the burial chamber of Senmouth, her royal architect who designed the temple structure. The ceiling of her tomb has two astronomical charts and, in one, the cardinal points are enigmatically reversed, making it appear as though the Earth had shifted on its axis. That star map suggested that learned priests kept records for untold periods and the true significance of the chart is currently unknown. There was no mistake on the part of Senmouth, since three other ancient Egyptian documents...the Harris, the Ipuwer and the Hermitage Papyri, all corroborated that curious anomaly.

Other significant Egyptian Queens included Nitocris of the Sixth Dynasty who 'had herself proclaimed Pharaoh in the hope of saving the dynasty', and Queen Khentkaues, the founder of the Fifth Dynasty, who insisted on being called king and was spoken of as king in later records and respected as such. Her tomb was unearthed in 1935 and close by was found 'the remains of a beautiful city'.[8] Consider the mysterious 'Lady of Saqqara':

> The unknown Pharaoh buried at Saqqara is omitted from history. Yet the splendour of her tomb leaves no doubt that she was once a mighty monarch. With her were found the bones of uncountable men, together with the tools of their trade, who were sacrificed and buried with her...craftsmen who would serve the dead woman in the afterlife.[9]

In Helene Bernard's book, *Great Women Initiates*,[10] the beautiful Queen Nefertiti was described as superior to Akhenaton for she was heavily involved in government actions of policy and administration. The last of many female Pharaohs was Cleopatra VII, a Greek queen of Egypt, described by John of Nikia, a seventh century Coptic bishop from Upper Egypt as 'the most illustrious and wise among women...great in herself and in her achievements in courage and strength'. Having given some idea of the ancient foundations of the presence of women initiates in the Ancient Mysteries, it is relevant

that in ancient times Ceres, the Roman goddess of Agriculture, was depicted as 'The Patroness of the Mysteries', Patron being the protector.

Ceres carries two vertical torches, one emanating from the other. In the Secret Mysteries she was represented riding a chariot drawn by winged serpents. This depiction was redrawn from an ancient mural painting found in Pompeii. © Ancient Europe Art Reproductions (AEAR), Italy, 1972.

The decline of the Mystery Schools

Every pre-Christian nation had not only its own particular state religion, but another into which the philosophical elect alone had gained entrance. Many of those ancient cults vanished from the Earth without revealing their inner secrets, but a few survived the test of the ages and their mysterious symbols and teachings were preserved to this day. Few realize the extent to which the ancient Mystery Schools influenced contemporary intellects and, through those minds, posterity. They taught mankind to use and expand his faculties more intelligently, to be patient in the face of adversity, to be courageous when confronted by danger, and to be true in the midst of temptation. Most of all, they learnt to view a worthy life as the most acceptable sacrifice to God, and their body as an altar to Deity.

There were literally scores of ancient cults and they branched off into all parts of the Eastern and Western worlds. Robert Macoy (a 33° Mason), in his book *General History of Freemasonry*, paid a magnificent tribute to the part played by Mystery Schools in the rearing of the edifice of human culture. His summary said, in part:

> It appears that all the perfection of civilization, and all the advancement made in philosophy, science and art among the ancients are due to those institutions, which, under the veil of mystery, sought to illustrate the sublimest truths of religion, morality and virtue, and impress them on the hearts of their disciples. Their chief object was to teach the doctrine of one god, the resurrection of man to eternal life, the dignity of the human soul, and to lead the people to see the shadow of the deity, in the beauty, magnificence and splendour of the universe.

While the ignorant multitudes brought their offering to the altars of various deities, the wise recognised in those marble statues only symbolic concretions of great abstract truths. Renowned philosophers the world over sought to enhance their wisdom through initiation into the sacred rites of Egypt. They humbly and readily admitted that the priests of Thebes, Memphis, Hermopolis, Saqqara, Heliopolis and Giza dispensed a secret knowledge unknown in their own countries and unattainable elsewhere in the world. The enlightened and most illustrious sons of Greece, Thales (700 BC), Solon, Pythagoras and Plato, returned to Greece to establish their own parallel schools and sought to spread the light of the Panther Mysteries among their disciples. With the eventual decline of the purity of original Egyptian instruction, priests, hierophants and keepers of the Temple Secrets disbursed into desert lands and foreign territories, carrying with them their precious knowledge.

Around 172 BC scandals rocked the Egyptian society. Priests were discovered profiteering from exploiting religious beliefs. Fake mummies were created and sold as genuine and cats were embalmed as babies. At that time, it required two months wages to pay for proper mummification of a deceased person and only the rich could afford it. The process was time consuming, entailing the removal of brains and other parts, and drying out the body. At one point, dishonest embalmers were concealing dead Romans in mummified costumes and passing them on to Egyptian families as the correctly embalmed body of their deceased relatives. Excesses of power, abuse of knowledge and personal ambition very often led selfish and unscrupulous priests to Black Magic, just as the same causes led to similar conduct among Christian popes, cardinals and priests.[11] Black Magic subsequently led to the decline of most Mystery Schools, as society shunned the desecration of the Divine Science. Shortly before the commencement of the Christian era (around 50 BC) Roman authorities discovered a secret school of Black Magic of the most revolting kind and that moral pestilence had spread all over Italy. 'More than seven thousand initiates were prosecuted, and most of them were sentenced to death'.

Later on, Titus Livy (Livius; died 17th year of the first century) recorded that another 3000 initiates were sentenced to death during a single year for the crime of poisoning. Livy's writings showed that the Mystery Schools had not died out in his time but by the fourth and fifth centuries, they had lost their primitive grandeur and solemnity. Their rites had fallen into desuetude and degenerated into mere priestly speculations and religious shams.

The secrets of Egypt were later passed on through temples of learning scattered abroad and were consequently embedded in cryptic messages and preserved in symbolic form on stone tablets. Others were secreted into the designs of buildings or structured into particular enigmatic writings, one being the Holy Bible. In the First Degree ritual of the Freemasons, for example, new candidates were clearly told from where their secret teaching derived:

> The usages and customs of Freemasons have ever borne a near affinity to those of the ancient Egyptians. Their philosophers, unwilling to expose their mysteries to vulgar eyes, concealed their peculiar tenets (doctrines, beliefs, etc) and principles of polity and philosophy under certain hieroglyphical figures, and expressed their notions of government by signs and symbols, which they communicated to their priests or Magi only, who were bound by oath never to reveal them.

Their connection and origin to the Mysteries of ancient Egypt was in no doubt. In excavations at Dendara around 100 years ago, British Egyptologist Sir William Flinders Petrie found a 5000-year-old vignette of a carpenter's square and plummet placed on the left breast of a mummy, which often represented the candidate for initiation. Any Mason will quickly recognise those symbols and any member reading the *Book of the Dead* will learn where their most secret passwords originated. The Freemason movement was established as a direct result of Egyptian Mysteries and they, like the ancient Egyptians themselves, developed their own 'systems of morality veiled in allegory and illustrated by symbols'. That instruction was passed along over a 22-year period in ritual form to those nominated and signed into the Lodge as candidates for initiation. When new members joined Freemasonry, they were required to take certain obligations in each degree through which they passed. Those obligations were sealed by kissing the Bible, called in Masonry, *The Volume of the Sacred Law*, a direct reference to the Torah in the Old Testament. Upon entering the Lodge, they were also required to take the following vow of secrecy:

I (name of candidate) in the presence of TMH (The Most High) and in the body of the Charted and Rightful Lodge of Master Masons, regularly assembled and properly constituted, of my own free will and accord, do hereby and hereon solemnly and sincerely promise and swear that I will always hele (hide), and never reveal, any of the secrets or mysteries of, or belonging to, the Degree of Master Masons, to anyone in the world.

Initiates knew that a special knowledge relating to the 'science of the soul' had existed from the earliest days of civilization on Earth, and a gradual unfolding of confidential sacred matters was available to those who wished to apply themselves.

The 'Golden Age'

Today mankind has advanced to the point where satellite photos regularly provide updates on the expanse of the universe and medical science is at a level that the Ancients would never have been able to comprehend. Scientists have now provided answers to matters of which the ancient world had no conception, therefore the Mysteries of the past are not so much Mysteries for the modern world today. Nevertheless, there was still one great hidden Mystery or Secret that only few people knew and from the earliest of times, certain people were instructed in that wisdom and preserved it.

Ancient writings recorded that the Panthers were in receipt of a profound understanding, one that subsequently brought into existence all Mystery Schools on planet Earth. It provided thousands of years of spiritual teaching…but where did they get it? They said the knowledge derived directly from an earlier age when, 'Golden gods and goddesses roamed the Earth, sailed its seas and lived within'. In Egyptian tradition, it was called the 'Golden Age', and persistent priesthood belief maintained that the more learned were taught by gods of great knowledge. Those gods instructed them in the nature of the human soul and the unseen world and set forth how the world came into existence, and much more.

All evidence points to the existence of a very advanced civilization once operating on the Giza plateau, one that came into Egypt in great antiquity. Herodotus recorded that priests of the Temple, 'read to me from a faded papyrus' that said, 'Egypt had gods for its rulers, who dwelt on Earth with men, one always being supreme above the rest'. Who the gods were presents a promise of high secrets waiting to unfold and the next chapter reaches back beyond the historical horizon of the First Dynasty into the uncharted depths of a remote and mysterious past and records what is known about 'the gods'.

CHAPTER THREE

'HUMANS, GODS AND THE DEAD'

The gods of Egypt

When modern academics composed reference books about early Egyptian history, they scrupulously avoided mention of the impressive body of ancient evidence attesting to the celestial rulers of predynastic Egypt. Like all researchers, historians drew their material from recognised ancient sources such as the *Book of the Dead*, the Pyramid Texts, the Turin Papyrus, the Bible, and the records of highly regarded historians, Herodotus, Manetho (c. 305-285 BC), Strabo (c. 24 BC), Diodorus Siculus (d. 14th year of the first century), Pliny (first century) and Iamblichus (250-330). However, the paranormal portion of academia's primary reference material was relegated to myth and only data required to support a particular line of study was used. Those that 'patrolled the earth'[1] are scarcely mentioned by scholastic writers, church leaders and the reputable press, and if scientists mentioned them at all, it was usually to denounce or dismiss them as irrelevant.

Key aspects of Herodotus' writings involved descriptions of advanced beings living on Earth providing guidance and direction to local inhabitants. A generation of scholars examined the form and structure of Herodotus' records and concluded that his constant references to 'gods' was 'full of difficulty and frequently muddled with mythology'. However, in a series of Harvard University Press books called simply, *Herodotus,* the following opinion of Herodotus' records was expressed:

> It happens sometimes that the stories which have reached Herodotus from very distant land and seas, and which he duly reports without necessarily stating his belief in them, do in truth rest on a basis of actual fact.[2]

Not all of Herodotus' records have been publicly released but the picture that emerges from researching what is available is extraordinary and necessitated an examination of his reference sources. They proved to be none other than the initiated high priests of the Egyptian temple hierarchy, the men in charge of the age-old libraries and temple traditions. Of them, Herodotus said:

> That these were real facts I learned at Memphis from the priests of Hephaestus. I got much other information also from conversation with these priests while I was at Memphis, and I went to Heliopolis and to Thebes, expressly to try whether the priests of those places would agree in their accounts with the priests of Memphis. The Heliopolitans have the reputation of being the best skilled in history of all the Egyptian priests. They proved to me that what they said was true.

The priests told Herodotus that sky-gods descended to Earth in 17,500 BC, and that traffic continued until 11,850 BC, after which 'no god ever assumed mortal form'. The priests also told him that Osiris appeared in Egypt about 15,500 BC. Speaking of the great antiquity of the age of the gods, Herodotus remarked, 'They (the priests of Egypt) claim to be quite certain of these dates for they have always kept a careful written record of the passage of time'. Herodotus realised the vastness of the period about which he was writing, for he stated that since the legendary era of the gods 'the sun had changed its usual position four times', probably having in mind the precession of the equinoxes, already noted in an earlier chapter recorded in the tomb of Senmouth.

Additional documentation suggested that gods visited not only Egypt but also other parts of the planet in prehistoric times. History and sacred scriptures of most peoples contain a wealth of material portraying the descent of wisdom-bearing gods to Earth and their life among ignorant humanity. For centuries, the Dogon of Mali in Africa worshipped a pyramid with steps leading up to a square platform on top, where, according to one of their

legends, sky gods landed on each of their visits to Earth in times past. The
Dogon priests spoke of an epoch when gods came regularly 'to play on
Earth' and taught the Elders how to divide and cultivate their land.

The astronomer-priests of Babylon had stepped pyramids, the pinnacles
of which were reserved for sky-beings descending to Earth. The pyramids of
Chichen Itza and Tikal in Central America were very much like those of the
Dogon and Babylonians. Again, their purpose was similar...to provide specific
sites upon which celestial visitors could land. Considering the isolation of
the Old World from the Americas for thousands of years, it is a wonder that
such identical structures and legends should have originated independently.

Egypt also had its flat-topped stepped pyramids, the oldest being the
magnificent example at Saqqara within sight of the Great Pyramid. An ancient
inscription found in the Pyramid Texts uncovered in the Valley Temple of
Unas in the same Saqqara complex read, 'A stairway to heaven is laid for
them so that they may mount up to heaven thereby'. The idea of building
stepped pyramids caught on and at Meidum another one was created, possibly
for King Huni. Similarly, the mystery of the flat-topped sacred mountain of
Gebel Barkal rising 90 metres (300 feet) high near the fourth Nile Cataract
has never been solved. So sacred was the mountain that around 700 BC an
enormous temple dedicated to the god Amun was built on its summit.

The Edfu Building Texts referred to a Company of beings on Earth
called the Shebtui, and Coptic texts called the same group the 'gods of
Egypt' who came from 'the direction of the setting sun'. It seemed that the
Company of gods came into Egypt with a fully developed knowledge of the
sciences needed to build the Great Pyramid. Those suppositions are not
generally accepted today, and shall probably be considered a live heresy in
the field of classic Egyptology. Yet, some answer must be given to the question,
'from whence sprang that extremely advanced knowledge?' From records
available, it appeared to literally spring into existence from nowhere for
there is no evidence of its accomplishments preceding it. Diodorus Siculus
visited Egypt around 40 BC and wrote:

> The Egyptians themselves claimed that their ancestors were strangers who in
> very remote times settled on the bank of the Nile, bringing with themselves

the civilization of their motherland, the art of writing and a polished language. They had come from the direction of the Setting Sun and they were most ancient.[3]

Many may scoff at the idea that Egyptians at the time were suddenly evolved and their consciousness infused with a rare wisdom, but credence must be given to the documentation of ancient chroniclers. Herodotus' records were founded upon stories that endured the dust of the ages in the archives of Egypt and in *Histories*, probably his most celebrated work, he said: 'Thus I give credit to those from whom I received this account of early Egypt...the priests say nothing but what is true...and I myself am persuaded'.

Unusual events are recorded to have occurred in those momentous years, implying the presence of an outside agency. Herodotus distinctly defined his initiated understanding between godly matters and human matters by stating, 'Now, the accounts which they gave me (the Egyptian priests) with regard to mere human matters, and which they all agreed, were the following,' and he then relayed a series of simple earthly issues associated with 'some of the Greeks wishing to get a reputation for cleverness' after learning a number of priestly secrets. That type of basic worldly narrative was in stark contrast to his understanding of the high priesthood's portrayal of celestial visitors: 'They called them gods', he said.

An anomaly in the Book of Genesis

Nearly all great cosmological myths forming the foundation of various sacred books of the world stemmed from Egypt, including the Book of Genesis. Genesis's opening chapter recorded that 'Elohim' created the Earth and Mankind. The word 'Elohim' is plural, its singular aspect being 'Elio'. When the church subsequently translated 'Elohim' into the singular word 'God', the opening chapters of Genesis were rendered incorrect. It may have been feared that had the word been correctly translated, Christians and Jews would have been accused of worshiping a plurality of gods in the face of their repeated claims to monotheism.

An examination of Bible dictionaries, encyclopedias, and commentaries disclosed the plural form of the word 'Elohim' to be beyond the comprehension of their respected authors and editors. *A Dictionary of the*

Bible, edited by James Hastings, recorded that: 'The use of the plural Elohim is difficult to explain'. That reference is representative of efforts made to circumvent the damaging plural word for, in simple terms, the Old Testament originally stated that 'gods' created everything, not a singular God.

Humans, but not human

The term 'gods' is tantalizing, implying that there was something special or different about them. In ancient Egyptian theology they were called the Great Ennead, the original gods of the complex earthly notion of 'First Time'. That group of gods was responsible for the creation of 'the Line of the Immortal race' on Earth and the descendants of that line exist today. The earliest and most significant instance of such a grouping consisted of Atum (the so-called 'bull of the Ennead') and three generations of his progeny: his children Shu and Tefnut, his grandchildren, Geb and Nut and his four great-grand children, Osiris, Isis, Seth and Nephtys. Those nine deities participated in the Heliopolitian Creation Myth, whereby it was said that the Sun-god emerged from the primeval waters of Nun. In fact, there were four pairs of gods and goddesses ruled over by the supreme god, who were the progeny of a cycle of gods. According to ancient Egyptian theology, they were the original gods on Earth, the first gods, and they were responsible for secret information now hidden in the Bible. Bringing with them the sacred and mysterious Benben, the gods of the Great Ennead established themselves at Heliopolis in Egypt, where tradition held that they became planet Earth's first divine rulers.

A green basalt statue of Osiris found at Saqqara, and now in the Egyptian Museum at Cairo.

A green basalt statue of Isis wearing the cow-horn headdress.

It appeared that they had no invasive intent but seemed to have been culture bearers or ones who passed on to the earthly sub-species the seeds of science, culture and philosophy. Those gods behaved like superior human beings, with the same passion and needs, but with some sort of transcendental power. They were depicted as human, but also superhuman, suffering, but also capable of enjoying life. Osiris, for example, had a special liking for fine wine 'that maketh him glad'. They were more ethereal, stronger, more powerful, better fitted to command, to enjoy, and to suffer than ordinary humans. They had bones,[4] muscles, flesh and blood. Indeed, the blood of RA, Isis and other divinities is mentioned in the *Book of the Dead*.[5] When they were hungry, they ate; when they were thirsty, they drank; mankind's passions, griefs, joys and infirmities, were also theirs. Towards the end of Shu's (Supporter of Heaven) life, he was so ravaged by disease that even his most faithful followers revolted against him. RA's health also declined with the passing of time, and 'men perceived his decrepitude; Lo! His Majesty waxeth old' (Inscription in the royal tombs at Thebes). At the end of his rule he was a wrinkled, stumbling old man with a trembling mouth from which saliva ceaselessly dribbled to the ground.[6] Weary words from the age-old Sun-god's own mouth are found verbatim in numerous texts, including the *Fayum Geographical Papyrus.*[7] RA himself said: 'My limbs are decrepit for the first time; I will not go to any place where I can be reached'. Many gods, as the Greek historian Plutarch records, were neither begotten, nor imperishable. They were born, or created, subject to continuous change, aged and physically died.

The idea of inevitable death of gods was expressed in other places as well as this passage in the eighth chapter of the *Book of the Dead:* 'I am that Osiris in the West, and Osiris knoweth his day in which he shall be no more'.[8] That was to say: the day of Osiris' death was predicted, the day when he was to cease to exist on Earth. None of the gods escaped that destiny; for them, as for mankind, the day came when they left and went forth to the earthly tomb. However, whoever they were, they were different, for they carried within them an indeterminable life-principle substance called 'SA'.[9] SA was a mysterious fluid that circulated throughout their bodies and carried with it health, vigour, and life and was sometimes called the 'SA of Life'. The gods were not all equally charged with that fluid; some had more, others less, their energy being in proportion to the amount that they carried. The better supplied willingly gave of their superfluity to those who lacked it, and all could readily transmit it to mankind, the transfusion being easily accomplished in the temples.

The king or any ordinary man who wished to be impregnated presented himself before a god, and knelt at his feet with his back towards the god. The god then placed his right hand upon the nape of the man's neck, and by making 'passes' of an unrecorded nature, caused the fluid to flow from him, and to accumulate in the recipient as a receiver. That rite was of temporary efficacy only, and required frequent renewal in order that its benefit might be maintained. By using or transmitting the SA, the gods themselves exhausted their own supply, and the less vigorous replenished themselves from the stronger ones, while the latter went to draw fresh fullness from a mysterious reservoir called the 'pond of the SA'.

Administering the SA. Drawn by Boudier from a photograph by M. Gayet of a scene in the hypostyle hall at Luxor, taken in 1889. The illustration shows the relative positions of prince and god. The importance of the two vertical snakes on the costume of the kneeling prince are relevant to the Secret in the Bible and become important in later chapters.

The mystical pool of magical fluid was referenced in the Unas Pyramid Texts, but without elaboration, implying only that it was somehow connected with the spiritual body. Divine bodies, continually recruited by the influx of the magic fluid, preserved their vigour beyond the term allocated to bodies of men and beasts. Age, instead of quickly destroying them, was extended but decrepitude was no less irremediable with them than humans and came slowly. Early Egyptian priests referred to 'SA' as 'heka' and described it as some sort of mysterious divine force. It could be invoked both by the earliest gods and by later initiated priests, and was eventually personified as a god called Heka.

A description of the gods

The vexing question is...what did the gods look like? Were they people, creature-beings, figments of later priestly imagination, personalities created out of principles, or even allegorical symbols and ciphers? Ancient hieroglyphs describe some peculiar forms of gods and trying to work out whether or not they were mythological conceptions is intriguing research. Horus, with the head of a hawk, for example; Thoth, depicted with the head of the Ibis; Osiris, the lion; Anubis, the jackal or dog; Bastet, a cat-head; RA (in the Netherworld) shown with the head of a goat; Tefnut, a lion head and Khepra, a peculiar character shown with the head of a scarab beetle...and the list goes on. At the very least, the convergence

A bronze depiction of the hawk-headed Horus from the Saite period. From the Posno collection, now in the Louvre.

of symbolism may have been used to link the early gods with their personal characters. Courage was depicted by the eagle, for example, self-sacrifice by the pelican, cruelty by the buzzard and pride by the peacock. A wolf or dog was always the symbol of the lower mind attached to desire, fierce and cunning.

The constant depiction of superior animal-headed beings in Egyptian art has parallels with other traditions and temple histories. Ancient Sumerian clay cylinder seals record the story of two special emissaries 'clothed like birds, with wings for garments'.[10] In the fragments of some Chaldean tablets found in 1870 is inscribed the Babylonian *Legend of Creation* and in the first column of what is called the Cutha Tablet, a description was given of seven particular human beings 'with the faces of ravens' that came and instructed the local inhabitants with new knowledge. The Chinese have a similar tradition. According to the commentator Kwoh P'oh, in the work called 'Shan Shan-Hai-King',[11] a book written by historiographer Chung Ku from engravings on nine urns made by Emperor Yu (2255 BC), an interview is mentioned with men having two distinct faces on their heads, 'before and behind'. The words recording those strange creatures were so highly valued that Chung Ku, at the time of the last Emperor of the Hia dynasty (1818 BC), fearing that the Emperor might destroy the urns, stole them and carried them out of the country.

Strange Sumerian beings on a bas-relief in the Louvre.

Let the reader also be reminded of 'the winged races' of Plato, and the Popul-Vuh accounts of the first human race who, it was said, 'could walk, fly and see objects, however distant'. It was tempting to wonder whether the oldest surviving Australian Aboriginal Elders' claim of an ancient race long gone who could 'fly over the hills' is in anyway connected to those legends. Weeded of metaphors and allegories what would today's scientists say to those old records of a primordial creation of bizarre species? A men who 'could fly as well as they could walk' but who 'were destroyed' because they were not 'perfect'; i.e. they 'were sexless, like the Kings of Edom'.[12]

The lives of many early churchmen were full of stories of strange creatures and old texts they left behind make fascinating reading. Since many of those narratives are rarely mentioned today, perhaps it is appropriate to record here some words from the records of St Anthony (281–356), the Egyptian-born founder of Christian monasticism. He claimed that, while alone in the desert, he encountered a strange being of small stature that flew away after a brief conversation with him. He described the creature as, 'a satyr, a manniken with a hooted snout, horned forehead and extremities like goat's feet'. St Jerome (347-420), author of the Roman Catholic Vulgate Bible, supported the story that happened before he was born:

> Let no man scruple to believe this incident, its truth is supported by what took place when Constantine was on the throne (died 337), a matter of which the whole world was witness. For a man of that kind (satyr) was brought alive to Alexandria and shown as a wonderful sight to the people. Afterwards his lifeless body, to preserve its decay through the summer heat, was preserved in salt and brought to Antioch that the Emperor might see it.[13]

Captain Cook and his companions landed on Easter Island in 1774 and described stone carvings of humans with hoof-like feet as the 'most extraordinary thing'. A collection Cook took back to London was subsequently displayed at the British Museum in 1872 and included several amazing figurines of human-faced birdmen and birdwomen with wings or fins. The mythologies of many nations also contain extraordinary accounts of educating gods who 'came out of the sea'. Certain shamans among the American Indians told of holy men dressed in bird's feathers and wampum that rose out of the blue waters and instructed them in arts and crafts. Among the strong legends of priests of the Chaldeans was that of Oannes, a partly amphibious creature who also came out of the sea and taught savage peoples along the shore to read and write, till the soil, cultivate herbs for healing, study the stars, establish rational forms of government, and become conversant with the sacred Mysteries. Among the Mayas, Quetzalcoatl the Saviour-god issued from the waters and, after instructing the people in the essentials of civilization, rode out to the sea on a magic raft of serpents to escape the fierce god of the Fiery Mirror, Tezcatlipoca.

There are many other legends to the effect that long before the appearance of humans there existed various races or particular species of composite creatures that, it seemed, were destroyed by a superior race. The temples of antiquity preserved their own historical records and possessed information concerning the pre-historic world that was never revealed to the world at large. According to one set of records, the human race evolved from a species of creature that partook somewhat of the nature of an amphibian, for at one time it was said that primitive man had gills of a fish and was partly covered with scales. To a limited degree, we could say the human embryo demonstrates the possibility of such a living condition. Because of the theory of man's origin in water, the fish was looked upon as the progenitor of the human family. Some old versions of the Bible recorded that Noah 'had upon his chest, scales, which he kept hidden'. The Book of Jasher (2: 3) further recorded that Noah was 'the father of those who go down into the deep and occupy themselves in much water'.

While the Teutonic dwarfs were far best known, it should not be imagined that dwarfs were invariably of Middle Europe, for Easter Island preserved a legend of a clan of large-headed dwarfs. Egypt also had dwarf tribes, living in 'the Land of Shades', where tradition held that the living came into close contact with the souls of the departed. It was inhabited by the Dangas, hordes of half-savage dwarfs whose grotesque faces and wild gestures brought fear into all those who encountered them. In excavations, Sir William Petrie found skeletons of two Danga dwarfs who were at one time eagerly sought after as household pets by Pharaohs of the Memphite dynasties. The Dangas reminded Herodotus of the dwarf-god Bes, one of several monstrous-looking deities who, surprisingly considering his appearance, became the special guardian of expectant mothers and an expert in make-up.

A limestone statue of the six-toed dwarf Khnumhotpû, superintendent of royal linen. Dwarfs were court favourites of the Pharaohs who amused themselves by collecting and displaying the ugliest and most deformed creatures. Many dwarfs accompanied their master into the tomb (Drawn by Faucher-Gudin from a photograph taken in a crypt by Emil Brugsch-Bey, c. 1895).

But if it be Nature and the physical law of evolution that was creator of all now on Earth, why could there be 'no such abyss' when the Globe was covered with waters, in which numbers of monstrous beings were generated? Moreover, arguing from the standpoint of Science, do not our newspapers of the 1800s occasionally furnish us with details of peculiar specimens? A two-headed child was reported, and several cases of animalistic-type bodies with human heads. It is relevant to mention the records of a dog-headed baby born in the USA in 1869, being maybe a throwback to an earlier race mentioned by Herodotus: 'It is here, in eastern Libya, where the dog-headed men are to be found'.[14] An example of a girl born in Australia in the 1960s with a single eye in the middle of her forehead reflected the giant of classical myth, Cyclops.

St Augustine, writing some 800 years after Herodotus, recorded similar peculiar races and claimed that he preached the Gospel to some of them. He was credited with a scientific leaning towards the doctrine of Evolution and as recognizing the origin of species. But some of his species were truly singular, and, in Augustine's mind, were variations from Adam, who he believed was father of them all. In all soberness and tinged with a breath of skepticism with respect to some, he thus philosophized:

> It is reported that some monstrous races of men have one eye in the middle of the forehead; some, the feet turned backward from the heel; some, a double sex, the right breast like a man, the left like a woman, and that they alternately beget and bring forth; others are said to have no mouth. They tell of a race who have two feet but only one leg, and are of marvellous swiftness, though they do not bend the knee; they are called Skiopedes, because in the hot weather they lie down on their backs and shade themselves with their feet. Others are said to have no head on their shoulders. What shall we say of the Cynocephali, whose doglike head and barking proclaim them beasts rather than men? But we are not bound to believe all we hear of these monstrosities. But who could enumerate all the human births that have differed widely from their ascertained parents? No one will deny that all these have descended from that one man, that one first father of all. Accordingly, it ought not to seem absurd to us that as in the individual races there are monstrous births, so in the whole race there are monstrous races; if they are human, they are descended from Adam.[15]

That proves then, that if Nature will still play such freaks now that she has been settled for ages in the order of her evolutionary work, weird monsters were a possibility in her opening program...a possibility which may have even existed once upon a time as a law, before she sorted out her species and began regular work on them. Some of those abnormal beings may still be roaming the planet today for, in 1997, a search was conducted for a tribe of tailed people seen in a remote part of an island off the coast of Irian Jaya. On

25 October 1997 the Jakarta Post reported: 'We received information about them (tailed beings) from people living near the tribe'. The tailed tribe reportedly roam an isolated part of Serui Island, off the northern coast of Irian Jaya, Indonesia's easternmost province, said Rangga Wuwung, a Ministry of Social Services official.

The Bible too, recorded some curious people…a baby born with 'red skin entirely covered with long hair', for example, and races with 'six fingers and six toes'. It also recorded 'there were giants in the earth in those days'[16] and that narrative directly involves the Secret in the Bible.

Giants on Earth

In 1757, the King of Denmark, Christian VI, commanded the Royal Society of Sciences at Copenhagen to publish a two-volume series of books called *Travels in Egypt and Nubia*. That volume was written by Frederick Lewis Norden after seven years extensive research in Northern Africa and included a series of remarkable illustrations 'hand-drawn on the spot'. Norden and his team compiled a comprehensive record of 'the antiquities of Egypt, enlarged with observations from ancient and modern authors' that included some remarkable information, much of which was revealed throughout this book. Norden gave this account of a belief current in Egypt at that time:

> There runs amongst the people that inhabit Egypt at present, a tradition, that there were anciently in the country, giants; and that they raised, without much difficulty, the pyramids, the vast palaces, and the temples, whose remains occasion at present our admiration.

That conception of the primitive Egyptian world was clearly expressed by the ancient temple scribes and their principal hieroglyphic texts confirmed the tradition that the first generations of gods were giants. Osiris, the great and powerful 'son of God', was a giant 'in the nature of flesh'.[17] A papyrus of Ramesside times fixed the height of Osiris at seven cubits,[18] and a phrase in a Ptolemaic inscription placed it at 'eight cubits, six palms, and three fingers'.[19] Taking the accepted length of a cubit as 17 inches, the height of Osiris was between 10 feet 6 inches and 12 feet 6 inches, and all members of the Ennead, including Isis, were of comparative height.[20]

A 16ᵗʰ century BC hieroglyphic carving showing a sacred 'djed' pillar being raised by a giant with the help of smaller workers.

Historical records, scripture and fragments of philosophical and scientific work; in short, almost every record that has come down from antiquity, contains references to giants. Here again, we come into collision with science, which denies that man has ever been much larger than the average tall and powerful man now met with occasionally. Nevertheless, giants have not been left without their witnesses, and ancient records furnished the needed proofs. It was noted by archaeologists that the older the excavated skeletons they have found, the large, taller and more powerful was their structure. This report from the mid 1800s said:

> All those bones found in the Department of the Gard, in Austria, Liege etc...those skulls which all remind one of the negro type...and by which reason of their type might be mistaken for animals, have all belonged to men of very high stature.[21]

In English history, Geoffrey of Monmouth believed a race of giants originally inhabited Britain, the last two being Gog and Magog, whose statues stand in London's Guildhall today.

Documentation furnished by ancient presbyters also recorded the existence of giants on Earth at that time. Tertullian (died c. 220) elatedly recorded that a number of giant skeletons were found at Carthage while he was living there. A newspaper story in 1858 reported that a 'sarcophagus of giants' was found that year on the site of that very same city (Carthage). As to other ancient writers, the records of Philostratus spoke of a giant skeleton twenty-two cubits (over 30 feet), as well as another being 'only' twelve cubits (17 feet approx.) seen by himself on the promontory of Sigaeum. That skeleton may not have belonged to the giant killed by Apollo at the siege of Troy, as believed by Protesilaus, but it was that of a giant.

According to the records of Philostratus,[22] a man called Messecrates of Stira, in Lemnos, described the remains of a giant he discovered as 'too horrible to behold'. Plutarch, the 'encyclopaedist of antiquity',[23] declared that a person called Sertorius saw the tomb of Antaeus, the Giant; and Pausamias vouched for the actual existence of the tombs of Asterius, Geryon and Hillus, son of Hercules, all giants, titans and mighty men. Giants featured prominently in the records of first century historian, Pliny. He spoke of a giant in whom he thought he recognised Otus, the brother of Ephialtes,[24] and of Gabara, the ten-foot tall Arabian giant who lived in the days of Emperor Claudius. In a Greek work called *Les Volcans de la Grece*, was written:

> In the neighborhood of the volcanoes of the Isle of Thera, giants with enormous skulls were found laid out under colossal stones, the erection of which in every place must have necessitated the use of titanic powers, and which tradition associates in all countries with the ideas about giants, volcanoes and magic.

The bones of similar human creatures over ten feet tall were found in South-Eastern China. According to paleontologist Pei Wen-Chung those bones were 3000 years old. At Agadir in Morocco, hunting weapons of a large size were found that indicated its user was at least 13 feet tall. A human skeleton 17 feet tall was discovered at Gargayan in the Philippines and the Aztecs today still talk about 'white-haired giants' existing in their ancient history.

Recent discoveries in Australia and New Zealand produced further evidence of gigantic beings once living on Earth. In the seaside town of Timaru on New Zealand's South Island during the 1960s, skeletons 12 feet in length were found and this author knows of a cave in outback Queensland preserving human skeletons 10 feet in length, laid out on ledges hewn into the walls. The locals call it the Cave of the Giants and it is now protected from unwanted entry by a steel door fixed into the rock-face. Ironically, just four hours drive east from the Cave of the Giants is another, smaller cave, holding the skeletons of a pigmy tribe, wrapped and bound in kangaroo skins that preserved their bodies in an excellent, almost mummified condition.

The books of Genesis, Jasher and Enoch make ongoing references to giants once living 'in the earth' and the story of giant-killer David is one of the more memorable Old Testament stories. The Bible stated that the Nefilim was one of six races of giants and because they were mentioned both sides of the flood, they obviously survived. The interchanging or overlaying of the name 'Nefilim' to 'Guardians' determined the 'Guardians' were also considered giants by ancient authors. The *Book of the Dead* said that the 'Guardians' were keepers of the Secret (Spell 12) and that is the Secret being revealed in this book. The Egyptian term for 'gods divine' was Neteru, which translates to 'Guardians'. That was also the term by which Sumer was at one time called: 'The Land of the Guardians'. In early Greek translations of the Old Testament, the term Nefilim describing the giants[25] was rendered 'Guardians'. The suppressed Book of Jasher[26] recorded that a particular race of giants wore 'shoes of iron and brass'[27] and dwelt 'in the land...in a great city...a royal city', and the normal populace exclaimed:

> ...we cannot stand before this people, for they are stronger, and in stature we appear unto them as dwarfs; the sons of Anun (Anak, in some translations) are giants; lo...! We shall never be able to go in and possess their land.

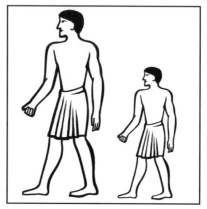

Giants in scripture; this is a comparison of size. There are six races of giants recorded in the Bible; King Og of Bashan was 'of the remnant of them'. His bed was 13 feet long (Deut. 3: 10-11).

Thus, the books of Genesis, Jasher and Enoch record the existence of giants variously called Nefilim, Guardians or Watchers and the difference in their names was probably a simple traditional overlay of titles used by different races of people for the same body of beings.

Sumerian clay tablets spoke repeatedly of a knowledge given to the people by a race called the Anunnaki. That plural word had a striking similarity to the singular word in the Book of Jasher, 'the sons of Anun' and it may be that 'the sons of Anun', as a group, were called the Anunnaki. They came from 'The Land of the Guardians' and it appeared that the Anunnaki was another name for 'Guardians'.

The highly regarded Book of Enoch provided references of 'great giants whose height was three thousand ells', an exaggeration, meaning simply a great height. That old scripture contains enlightened knowledge so dangerous to Christian teachings that it was banned as heresy by the fourth century church.[28] It was further denounced, cursed and finally condemned in explicit terms in the fifth century Apostolic Constitutions (vi: 16). St Augustine said it was 'too old' (Ob Nimiam Antiquitatem) to be attached to Christian writings and became uncomfortable for the church to have around. It was then 'lost' for 1400 years but resurfaced in 1773 when three copies were found preserved in an Ethiopian Christian church by Scotsman and Freemason, James Bruce. Orthodox Christian scholars then claimed that it was a post-Christian writing because of similarities to large numbers of *New Testament* terminologies. However, the discovery of eight more copies of Enoch among the *Dead Sea Scrolls* in 1947 established that it was in existence long before the time of Rabbi Jesus and Judas Khrestus.

The Book of Enoch was believed written sometime around 150-120BC (*Lakeland Bible Dictionary*) and was the most popular scripture for at least 300 years, particularly among early presbyters. It recounted the intriguing story of a company of heavenly messengers called Watchers who were commanded to visit Earth to develop order among a degenerate mortal race. An undeveloped culture of 'helpless ones' existed that 'feasted on dead substance evaporating, raw flesh and foul smelling worms…and tear these things with their teeth, and dwell after the manner of four-footed beasts'.

The Watchers were to 'fashion a colony…and raise them up in industry, weaving and making clothes and otherwise producing; raise them up in virtue, wisdom, love and benevolence, and little by little ye shall teach them to live on fish food, and other kinds of food'.[29] However, the Watchers yielded to temptation and consorted with the 'good-looking daughters of men'[30] who were 'redolent of the monkey, and had a way of making their labia protrude like we have observed in orangutans'.[31] Those originally 'holy, spiritual, eternal beings…lusted after the flesh…as do mortal and perishable creatures'[32] and their illegal sexual encounters with the 'daughters of men' produced a race of 'giant sons' who were called the Nefilim in the Old Testament.

The Line of the Mortal race

The 3000-year-old Ethiopian text, Kebra Nagast, referred to the enormous size of babies produced from the sexual unions of humans with the so-called fallen angels. It records how 'the daughters of Cain with whom the angels had conceived…were unable to bring forth their children, and they died'. It also describes how some giant babies were born by what could be called forced Caesarean section, 'having split open the bellies of their mothers they came forth by their navels'.[33] 'And they had become very large; twice the size of men of the day. But they were without judgment of little sense, and hardly knew their own species. And they mingled together, relatives as well as others; so that the idiocy and disease were the general fate of the tribes of men'.[34]

The Watchers' sexual involvement with earth women was in flagrant contravention of their mission as well as the divine order, and their indiscretion caused them to be bound to Earth. That may have been the 'fall' recorded allegorically in the opening passages of the Book of Genesis for that body of beings forfeited their spiritual state and fell in their level of consciousness. The Most High (the name given to God in the Book of Enoch) chastised them, saying; 'From this time forward, never shall you ascend into heaven…Earth will bind you'.[35] Continuing, the Most High said:

Now the impious offspring who have been born of spirit and of flesh, shall be called upon Earth "evil spirits", and on Earth shall be their habitation. Evil spirits shall proceed from the seed of their flesh…their evil spirits…shall oppress, corrupt, fall, bruise and cause trouble upon Earth. [36]

That remarkable narrative recorded the commencement of 'the Line of the Mortal race' on Earth, and, like 'the Line of the Immortal race' emanating from the divine Ennead, their line still exists today, 'and thus has it been from the beginning of the world'.[37] 'And these two peoples have lived on the Earth from the first, and even to this day, are two races of the seed and blood of old'.[38]

The deciphering of old texts provides an insight that reveals the origin of circumcision on Earth. The women of the time expressed concern about mating with the 'descendants' of the Watchers and 'cried out with fear, saying; O Lord, how shall I bring forth for thee, and not unto the carnivorous sons of darkness?'

And it came to pass that the Lord spoke to them and said; Because thou hast brought forth in pain, and yet called on my name; behold I will be unto thee as a shield and protector. For I will put a mark on them so thou shalt know them when they come naked unto thee; By this sign shall the tribes and their descendants be known until the end of the world; circumcision shall be the measure of my chosen. And the Lord commanded the male, old and young to be circumcised, that women might not be deceived. And they circumcised one another, old and young; for it was the testimony of the Lord'.

That was probably the start of the custom of arranged marriages, developed to either support the legend of Osiris and Isis or to legitimize the practice.

© A. C. Bushby 2003

This is probably the earliest depiction of circumcision on Earth. It was carved in stone in a passageway in the tomb of Miraroka at Saqqara, Egypt, thousands of years ago.

The descendents of 'the Line of the Mortal race' were once 'in heaven, but the Mysteries had not yet been revealed to you'.[39] In other words, those of 'the Line of the Mortal race' did not know the Secret and thus the means of reinstating their earlier higher level of consciousness that allowed them to return to the immortality of Heaven.

Three gods in one

In the folklore of various nations, and particularly in Egyptian hieroglyphs, certain insects were given special significance as gods. Among American Indians, for example, is the legend of a 'Spider Man' whose web connected the heavenly worlds with the earth. Moreover, the old Secret Schools of India symbolised certain gods who they referred to as Spider Gods and their supreme God was, at one time, designated, 'The Great Spider'. A scorpion was often portrayed as the great betrayer, the butterfly as an emblem of metamorphosis, and the bee a symbol of industry. The beehive was found extensively in Masonry, it being a reminder that in diligence and labour for a common good, true happiness and prosperity are found. However, the insect that had received worldwide veneration and consideration was the scarab beetle, king of the insect world...and it is the very essence of the Secret.

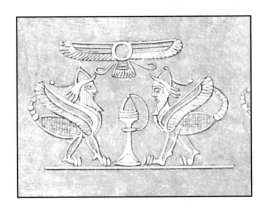

The Scorpion-men of the mountains of Mashu. There were several other representations of the same subject in Assyrian literature.

The Egyptian scarab is one of the most remarkable symbolic figures ever conceived in the mind of man. It was evolved by the erudition of the priest craft from a simple insect that, because of its peculiar habits and appearance, symbolised the resurrection of the soul. The following passage concerning this belief appeared in the Egyptian book of initiation, the *Book of the Dead*:

> And behold, thou shalt make a scarab of green stone, which shall be placed in the breast of a man, and it shall perform for him 'the opening of the mouth'...

The Egyptian god Khepra was symbolised by the head of a scarab and he also signified the resurrection of the soul and new life at the end of the mortal span. Khepra was portrayed as one of the three important aspects of RA, the great god of the Sun. The mummy cases of the Egyptian dead were nearly always ornamented with scarabs and usually one of those beetles, with outspread wings, was painted on the mummy-case directly over the breast of the dead body. The finding of such great numbers of small stone scarabs indicated that they were a favourite article of adornment among the early Egyptians, both men and women. Khepra, the scarab-headed aspect of

RA was often symbolised riding through the sea of the sky in a wonderful ship called the Boat of the Sun. But Khepra is also something else.

A vignette from the Book of the Dead shows veneration being paid to the scarab god, Khepra. The platform-topped pyramidal stand is reminiscent of the top of the Great Pyramid. The Papyrus Ani stated that the scarab beetle was 'one of the emblems of the Creator'.

Early Egyptian priests believed that RA and Khepra personally arrived on Earth in a mysterious 'secret object' called 'Akka'. That object was later renamed 'Benben', a term deriving from an Egyptian word meaning 'seed' or 'essence'. It is repeatedly recorded in traditional Egyptian history that the Benben 'came from the sky' and it became the most esteemed object of the time. The Great Ennead of Heliopolis constructed a square hewn stone column in the centre of a protective temple complex and placed the Benben upon its summit. The principal structure in that compound was called 'The Palace of the Ancient One' or sometimes, 'The Palace of the Old Man', the dwelling place of RA while he lived on Earth as King of the gods of Egypt.

The name Benben was subsequently applied to the pyramidion or apex-stone (cap-stone) on top of pyramids, tombs and obelisks and in a symbolic sense was always associated closely and directly with both RA and Khepra. The ancient priests became famous for their privileged access into the sanctuary of that powerful, mysterious and sacred object and its specially built temple became the site where the earliest religious concepts of humans on Earth crystallized in pre-historic time. Later Egyptian priests held the strong belief that their primary gods personally arrived on Earth in the Benben and, for many centuries, revered the intriguing object as the life creation force. The secret that the celestial phenomenon held is central to our exposition and will be later shown to transcend human limitations.

Many Egyptian gods symbolically appeared to represent the great forces of the universe, the sky (e.g. Nut, Shu), stars, earth, and the River Sin-Hor, now called the Nile, was originally named after combining the names of Sin, the Moon-god with Horus, the Solar-god.[40] Whenever a holy power was felt, a divinity was recognised by Egyptians and that power could irradiate from a cult object (Djed Pillar), a holy city, or a holy conception. Therefore, when Khepra is shown in ancient hieroglyphs with the body of a man, the head of a beetle and the wings of a bird, it is not probable that such a creature walked the earth in that form.

Egyptian 'Magicians'

The fact remains that there was once a body of beings on earth who were superior to the bulk of the populace and succeeding priests always referred to them as 'gods and goddesses'. The celestial visitors had knowledge of secret wisdom that Egyptian priests claimed had been personally passed on to them for preservation. From the earliest times, the Panther priests constantly claimed to be proud guardians of a transcendental knowledge so profound as to be incomprehensible to all but the most exalted intellect. They said it was so potent as to be revealed with safety only to those in whom personal ambition was dead and who had consecrated their lives to the unselfish service of humanity.

They had no doubt that they would live eternally and were renowned throughout Egypt for their high wisdom, proficiency in magic arts and prophecy. They were called 'Magicians' (Isis was also called a 'Magician') and they were the original Magi, the latter word simply being an abbreviation. The Magicians were high initiates who could 'evoke the most formidable deities from beyond the confines of the universe'.[41] Later Persian initiates adopted the 'Magi' name after initiation in Egypt and were amalgamated into their own mystic fraternity. A Magician (Magi) was not one who conjured up tricks or pulled rabbits from a hat, but a high-ranking priest serving the truth of the earliest Egyptian religion and fiercely guarding their age-old Secret. With the needs of posterity foremost in their minds, the sages of old went to inconceivable extremes to make sure their celestial knowledge was preserved. They engraved and symbolised upon the face of stones, and concealed vital information within some of their colossal images, each of which was a technical and geometric marvel in itself. Mute testimonies they were of the lost arts and science of Egyptian priests of antiquity and concealed, their deep wisdom has remained for thousands of years.

The word 'priest', as understood today, is somewhat misleading, for the Egyptian sages were highly conversant in complex detail, not only with religious ideologies, but with the study of celestial bodies, mathematics, architecture and scribal matters associated with sacred hieroglyphs. There were groups of priests with specialist knowledge, including 'hour priests', whom many Egyptologists today interpret as astronomers. There was also a very strong association between serpents and the ancient Egyptian priests, and that curious tradition involved the innermost mystery of their religious worship. They were in receipt of special knowledge and were active in initiating new candidates into their most secret mysteries after years of compulsory training. Believing that they alone held the Secret of ever-lasting life, they sought to pass the knowledge silently on to new initiates. They were highly civilized, intelligent men and were, in their own fashion, scientists, as judged from their work. The issue of priestly secrecy and the passing along of oral tradition was discussed at length in a book called *From Fetish to God in Ancient Egypt*. The author Sir Wallis Budge said:

> It is impossible to think that the highest order of the priests did not possess esoteric knowledge which they guarded with the greatest care...each priesthood possessed a Gnosis, a 'superiority of knowledge', which they never put into writing.

They believed every human consisted of a natural body, a spiritual body, a spirit, a form and a name. All aspects were bound together inseparably, and the welfare of any single one concerned the welfare of all. From the well being of the spiritual parts, it was necessary to preserve from decay the natural body, and certain passages in the Pyramid Texts showed that a belief in the resurrection of the soul was carried into the earliest human dynasties.

The most ancient spiritual traditions maintained the idea of three classes of people. The Essene community consisted of three types of members...the postulants, novices and initiates. Rabbi Jesus' followers consisted of hearers, those under instruction and the baptised. Plato, in his 'Republic', discussed a society composed of an ascending scale of bronze, silver and golden souls. The Celtic Druids were divided into three classes, and narratives attributed to Paul in the New Testament referenced three basic human elements...body, soul and spirit. A similar triad existed in early Egyptian society. The fact that ancient Egyptian priests divided the inhabitants of the universe into three classes, 'humans, gods and the dead', was sufficient indication that gods were not looked upon as so very different from the dead, and the dead no different from the living.

The priests of Egypt had various magic spells that they believed could prolong life, alter fate, assist in love and romance and combat any number of physical and mental afflictions. Other types of religious objects one may cite almost at random were stones carrying written divine decrees safeguarding their bearers, busts of ancestors in houses and numerous special objects and modes of dress surrounding childbirth. From ancient texts, we know OF magical cures for illness, calendars of lucky and unlucky days, the avoidance of the evil eye, divination through dreams and various rare practices such as letters written to dead relatives who were thought to hold a grudge against the living. Some of their 'legitimate' magic spells survive in the Pyramid Texts and the *Book of the Dead*. Mystical performance was clearly a significant aspect of an Egyptian priest and the recent remarkable discovery of a shaft tomb of such a priest highlighted the basis of their craft. That particular tomb was of the late Middle Kingdom (c. 1700 BC) and was excavated from beneath the Ramesseum in western Thebes. It contained a curious mixture of 'religious and magical artifacts', including a statuette of a woman wearing a lion mask and holding two snake wands; an ivory clapper; an unusual lantern; a section of a magic rod; a black mirror; a female fertility figurine; a bronze cobra wand and a box of papyri inscribed with a wide range of religious, literary and magical texts. That single collection of equipment clearly demonstrated the vast spectrum of strategies that were involved in priesthood rites, enabling an individual priest to draw on the power of the gods using a wide variety of means and for a number of different purposes.

In the ancient initiatory rituals of the Egyptian Mysteries, later priests subsequently disguised themselves with facemasks and appeared as composite creatures looking like the hieroglyphic images of their earlier gods. They used birds, animals and reptiles as emblems of the various deities, often creating forms of grotesque appearance and assigning to them imaginary traits, habits and places of domicile, all of which were symbolic of certain truths carried through from the past. A hierarchy of priests continued to 'stand in' for, or 'act as' the earlier original gods and painstakingly cared for their images. In return they believed the gods took up residence in the images and showed their favour to the priest and hence to humanity. They saw themselves as the lineal descendants and living representatives of the famous original gods and the special bearers of the cosmic Secret. They painstakingly showed the initiates how each one of them could, correctly using the Secret knowledge, personally get in touch with those gods who they believed were now living in the afterlife.

Summary of the gods

Egyptian annals record that 'the gods' were twice as tall in stature as the natives. Professor WB Emery, in his book *Archaic Egypt*, said:

> ...towards the end of the fourth millennium BC we find the people known traditionally as 'The Followers of Horus' apparently forming a civilized aristocracy or master race ruling over the whole of Egypt. The theory of the existence of this master race is supported by the discovery of the late pre-dynastic period in the northern part of Upper Egypt which were found to contain the anatomical remains of a people whose skulls were of greater size and whose bodies were larger than those of the natives, the difference being so marked that any suggestion these people derived from the earlier stock is impossible.

On penetrating into that mysterious world, one finds evidence of a widespread belief that the early gods of Egypt were a master race of giants who carried within them a supernatural substance called SA. They 'came with books of magic',[42] and the possibility exists that one of the six races of giants recorded in the Old Testament built the Great Pyramid.

CHAPTER FOUR

BIBLE WRITTEN SPECIFICALLY TO PRESERVE THE SECRET

In 1992, the international media released news that 'the first ten books of the Old Testament are fiction', and the ecclesiastical world reacted with shock, quickly dismissing the claim as 'outrageous'. Those books are: Genesis, Exodus, Leviticus, Numbers, Deuteronomy, Joshua, Judges, Ruth, Samuel (1 and 2, combined as one) and Kings (1 and 2, combined as one) and it was Professor Thomas Thompson of the Marquette University in Milwaukee who publicly announced to the world that the Bible was untrue. The findings of Professor Thompson, one of the world's foremost authorities on biblical archaeology, centred on the city of Jerusalem, and his conclusion has the backing of world experts, including the British Museum.

From the chronology of dating provided in the Old Testament, the 'city of Jerusalem' (first mentioned in the Bible at Joshua 10:1), was first overrun and set on fire by Judah[1] but only in part, and finally sacked by David, the second King of Israel in 1009BC.[2] During 1011-1004BC, its great temple was built; in 970BC it was plundered by Shislak and in 884BC by the Philistines and Arabs in the days of Jehoram; in 808BC by the Israelites and in 710BC it was besieged by Sennacherib.

Within that scriptural dating lies a fatal weakness, one that discredits the whole of the Old and New Testaments as books of history. Decades of archaeological analysis by Professor Thompson and his team provided incontrovertible evidence that Jerusalem was not in existence at the time the Bible dating says it was. Extensive excavations and investigations of major sites in Palestine produced no historical or archaeological evidence whatsoever to support the existence of Jerusalem until a much later period in time.

Based upon a synthesis of ancient Egyptian records, evidence from excavations and surveys, and absence of archaeological remains, Professor Thompson concluded that Jerusalem became the capital of a regional state in the course of the 7th century BC, and not 500 years earlier as biblical chronology dates it. Jerusalem was then only a small self-governed village, one of around one hundred that developed throughout Palestine during that time, each with a population of around two hundred people and a village head addressed as lord (spelt with a small 'l', see Genesis 18:3 for example).

Textual analysis revealed major Old Testament problems that rested around conflicting dates given for various biblical events that were in serious disagreement with comparative dates given for the same event. That made the narratives internally inconsistent with themselves and Professor Thompson's fieldwork provided physical evidence to support a human origin to major books of the Bible. Discrepancies in the genealogies, standing alone, provide a series of superabundant errors in each successive period of the Old Testament stories and in some areas, an enormous time-gulf of four centuries is identified.

The plain intention of Exodus[3] for example, is to describe the Israelites as having dwelt in Egypt for 430 years. That violently conflicted with other passages that assigned around 120 years to the same event. Those contradictory narratives dramatically reduced the period of the sojourn in Egypt by a staggering 310 years. That did not include 400 years of missing time between the closing of the Book of Genesis and the opening of the Book of Exodus. Such vast timeframe discrepancies provided huge areas of doubt and experts agreed that everything recorded in the Torah 'opens itself to the suspicion of having been formed artificially'.[4] Thus the church knew that the recorded sum total of just four generations from Jacob's children to Moses[5] accounted to three centuries of time less than the major Exodus[6] description of the same event. That mistake of time is fatal to every word of the Torah when read at a surface level.

The church admitted that stories in the Torah were 'fictitiously projected backwards',[7] a statement that supported another learned opinion that said, 'we are not able to speak of any portion of the Torah as history'.[8] So dramatic are the time variations in the opening books of the Bible its inaccuracy is 'fait accompli' and that factual error carries deeply into the New Testament. Simply put, the fundamental structure of the chronological sequence of events portrayed in the Old Testament is false.

In his book, *The Early History of the Ancient Israelites*,[9] Professor Thompson also provided evidence that major Old Testament characters Moses, Jacob, and Abraham are mere fictions. His research also provided proof that kings, Saul, David and Solomon did not exist in actual historical reality, the sources for the biblical stories being derived from strands of ancient oral tradition consisting of folktale, legend and saga, built up around very remote and unknown folk heroes. Those stories were transmitted orally for centuries in a form not unlike the party game, Chinese Whispers, in which a sentence is passed around a room in a whisper and ends up distorted beyond recognition.

The *Encyclopedia Biblica* (1914), in its article on 'Names', confirmed Professor Thomson's findings, saying that names of Old Testament patriarchs are 'artificial and originally had some special meaning'. That explains why the names and the stories associated with Abraham, Isaac, Jacob, Moses, Solomon and David appear only once in the recorded history of mankind and that is in the Bible. There is no historical knowledge of those people existing in the records of antiquity that cover a period of time extending into thousands of years.

The implications of Professor Thompson's research are staggering, and for those who accept his findings, the traditional perception of God is immediately demolished and the Old Testament, like the New Testament, becomes a product of purely human endeavour. However, even though the Torah is unhistorical, it is still a divine writing and therefore it is fundamental to understand what it really is, and how it came into being.

What was really on Mount Sinai?

Establishing the true origin of the Torah strikes right at the heart of the history of biblical religion and theology, not only for the Jewish faith, but also for the Christian dispensation. The church constantly maintained that the original Torah was 'divinely-revealed' to Moses while alone with God on the summit of Mount Sinai. However, information recorded in detail around 100 years ago presented an entirely different view about the origin of the Torah, and supports the findings of Professor Thompson.

The mountain now called Mount Sinai did not receive that name until the fourth century and it was 'derived from that of Sin, the Moon-god'.[10] It was so-named by a handful of Greek Christian monks who travelled to the 'Wilderness of Sin'[11] around that time and established a small sanctuary that subsequently developed into St Catherine's Monastery. The mountain Moses was said to have climbed was called Mount Horeb in oldest Bibles, not Mount Sinai. The word 'Horeb' simply meant 'desert', hence the 'mountain in the desert'. That mountain is today called 'Serabit' and sits on the plain of Paran, some distance north of what is now called Mount Sinai. The religious authorities agreed by stating, 'the formation of Jewish Law occurred on the sacred mountain of Horeb'.[12] Therefore, Mount Sinai recorded on maps today is not the mountain upon which the church said the Torah was given to Moses.

In the third chapter of the Book of Exodus,[13] the mountain was first called Mount Horeb, then, strangely enough, renamed Mount Sinai in the ninth chapter of the same book.[14] Later in the story, it was again called Mount Horeb.[15] Mount Sinai referenced in this work was Mount Horeb and not the Mount Sinai marked on modern-day maps in the southern area of the Sinai Peninsula. The pious old monks who originally trekked there and named that particular mountain Sinai, simply went to the wrong mountain.[16]

To disentangle the strands of church tradition that claim the receipt of the Torah from God was an historical reality, it is necessary to discuss that mountain further. What was originally called 'The Egypt Exploration Fund' was set up in Britain in 1891, its exclusive purpose being to provide funds to promote excavation work solely 'for the purpose of elucidating or illustrating the Old Testament narrative'.[17] In other words, funding was available for research teams to travel to Egypt and conduct excavation and research work in areas that would help establish the Old Testament stories to be true. What was soon to happen, however, proved the exact opposite.

At that time, William Flinders Petrie, a professor at the University College in London, applied to the new funding body to finance an expedition into the 'Exodus area of Egypt'. That was approved and in January 1904, Petrie and his team were in the peninsula area of Sinai. What Petrie discovered was of a truly profound nature and little was publicly mentioned of the find. In relation to the church's view of the origin of the Torah, it was probably the most damaging discovery ever made and related to Mount Horeb/Sinai.

On the plateau near the summit of the mountain, Petrie and his team discovered ruins of ancient habitation in the form of carved vertical stone columns and extensive shaped and inscribed rock remnants of a major formation of some sort. They cleared away rubble and sand that had accumulated over the centuries and found on top of Mount Horeb/Sinai remains of an enormous temple complex. At the 1998 Nexus Conference in Sydney, Australia, a lecture presented by author Lawrence Gardner, described Petrie's temple discovery in detail. Here is (in part) what Gardner relayed:

> Set within an *enclosure* wall was an outer temple built over an expanse of 230 feet (approx. 70 metres). This extended outwards from an inner temple cut within a great cave in a mountainside. From the various cartouches, carvings and inscriptions it emerged that the temple had been in use from as far back as the times of Pharaoh Sneferu, who reigned about 2600 BC and whose immediate successors are reckoned to have built the pyramids of Giza.

> The above ground part of the temple was constructed from sandstone quarried from the mountain and it comprised a series of adjoined halls, shrines, courts, cubicles and chambers, Of these, the key features unearthed were the main Sanctuary, the Shrine of the Kings, the portico court, and the Hall of the goddess Hathor (to whom the whole complex was dedicated). All around were pillars and stellae denoting the Egyptian Kings throughout the ages, and certain Pharaohs such as Tuthmosis III were depicted many times on standing stones and wall reliefs.

> The adjoining Cave of Hathor was carved into natural rock, with flat inner walls that had been carefully smoothed. In the centre stood a large upright pillar of Pharaoh Amenemhet III, the son-in-law of Esau. Also portrayed were his Senior Chamberlain and his seal bearer. Deep within the cave, Petrie found a limestone stele of Pharaoh Rameses I – a slab upon which Rameses surprisingly describes himself as 'The ruler of all that Aten embraces'. Also

found was an Amarna statue-head of Akhenaten's mother, Queen Tiye of Egypt, with her cartouche set in the crown.

In the courts and halls of the outer temple there were numerous stone-carved rectangular tanks and circular basins, along with a variety of curiously shaped bench tables with recessed fronts and split-level surfaces. There were also round tables, trays and saucers together with alabaster vases and containers, many of which were shaped like lotus flowers. In addition, the rooms housed a good collection of glazed plaques, cartouches, scarabs and sacred ornaments designed with spirals, diagonal squares and basketwork. There were magical wands of an unidentified hard material, and in the portico were two conical stones of about six inches and nine inches respectively in height.[18]

Lawrence Gardner was of the opinion that what Petrie discovered on Mount Horeb-Sinai was the fabled alchemical workshop of Akhenaten and the 18 dynasties of Pharaohs before him…a temple laboratory where fires roared 'and the smoke thereof ascended as the smoke of a furnace'.[19]

The church contends that Moses lived about 1400BC, but around 1000 years before the time ascribed to him, there was, on the wide plateau near the summit of Mount Horeb/Sinai, an enormous temple complex. That information completely devastates the biblical account of a person called Moses climbing the mountain and being alone with God, and establishes it as a fictitious narrative. The crucial issue is that the priesthood occupied the summit of Mount Horeb/Sinai and that knowledge puts an entirely different light on the matter of the origin of the Torah. Therefore, the evidence of modern archaeological discoveries conflicts with the church presentation, and an account in the suppressed Book of Jasher reveals yet another version. In summary, Jasher records that 72 priests met at the temple on Mount Horeb/Sinai and wrote the Torah using the Babylonian Code of Hammurabi as their exemplar.

The Torah does not present itself as a complete literary production of any one person, let alone a man called Moses. It contains an account of Moses' death and tells the story of his life indirectly and in the third person. The presence of anachronisms, the strange use of different Hebrew names for God, the diversity of style and vocabulary, and the existence of duplicate and contradictory accounts of the same event, all serve to postulate that the Torah was a composite work assembled from a variety of traditions. Each tradition betrays its own peculiar literary style and phraseology, and displays variant religious and theological outlooks. However, there is no doubt about the great antiquity of some traditions, particularly the story of the flood.

The books of Moses unhistorical

The discovery of the temple disintegrates the teaching that Moses was the author of the Torah and the church knew that, for around 100 years ago, on June 27 1906, an Ecclesiastical Decree was officially established by the Bible Commission that said, in part:

> These books have not Moses as their author, but are compiled from sources for the greater part later than the Mosaic age.

The church itself regarded as untenable the view that Moses wrote the Torah and freely conceded that the creation of the five most important books of the Bible was:

> no longer attributed to the personal authorship of Moses, but ascribed to a much later period in the history of Israel, probably the 9th - 5th century BC.[20]

The modern church conceded that Moses never wrote the books of the Bible that it maintained for 2000 years that he did. Up until the late 1960s, millions of Bibles carried the words, 'The Books of Moses' in their Subject Index and page headings when they referred to the writings of Genesis, Exodus, Leviticus, Numbers and Deuteronomy, but those words have been deleted from bibles printed since then. Allowing for the huge variation of time quoted above (500 years), ultra-orthodox Christian experts brought the creation of the Old Testament forward by around 1000 years, a vastly different period to what they claimed up until two decades ago. The latest archaeological and geological evidence destroys any credibility the church places on the Bible as a book of history.

In meticulous stone records Egyptian priests kept over vast epoch of times, the name Moses was never recorded and his physical existence was unknown. Mankind knew nothing externally of him or events attached to him in both the *Old* and *New Testaments*. The Exodus is a major event in the Bible but growing controversy has surrounded its factuality. The description of the departure of the Israelites from Egypt took four decades in which Moses played a significant role. In thousands of Egyptian inscriptions that survive, however, nothing is recorded that relates to the mass-exodus of 600,000 men and their families. Many people found it inconceivable that such a significant *Old Testament* episode and the dramatic disasters associated with it, could have struck as well organised a people without their recording them, particularly the River Nile turning to human blood. The church admitted that vital *Old Testament* references to Moses were later interpolations, stating that 'the last eight verses of Deuteronomy, which speak of the death and burial of Moses, are assigned to another author'.[21]

That a man called Moses was the author of the Torah is today seen as a generalization, as is the inspiration of the Book of Psalms to David and the so-called Wisdom Literature to Solomon. The basic proposition underlying the tradition that Moses was the first legislator and, as such, responsible for the original legislature of ancient Israel is known and officially accepted by the church hierarchy to be untrue. In spite of the differences in nature and chronological background between the various books of the Torah, a common legal law can be discerned in them that was traced back to around 2250-1750 BC and to the Mesopotamian king, Hammurabi.

In Egyptian Mysteries, a high initiate was called a Mese, Muse or, in some translations, Mose. The plural of that word was Muses or Moses. The great Alexandrian Library was known as the 'Museion' simply because it was the 'place where the Muses meet', the Muses being the high initiates into the Mysteries. When Freemasons refer to 'our Grand Master Moses', they are referring to the ancient Egyptian 'Grand Master Muses'. Thus, subsumed in the figure of Moses is the real inspiration behind the Torah, a work overseen by an initiate into the secret Mysteries, one with 'the wisdom of the Egyptians'.[22] The name of Mese or Muse was probably also associated with the Meses of RA, the name used in the Royal Titulary of eleven Egyptians rulers in the 19th and 20 Dynasties; Ra-Meses, all initiates.

The author of the Torah

The real truth is that 'the Torah…received its form at the hands of Ezra',[23] a high priest and scribe. In the records of Manetho, he had the Egyptian name of 'Osarsiph the Muse' and had passed through all initiatory degrees with honours, reaching the rare and culminating degree of a Panther Adept. All instructed Egyptians believed in the power of names for they possessed magical value for them, and Osarsiph adopted the name, Os-Ra, an abbreviated combination of Osiris and RA. In later ages, and as languages evolved, it took the variant form of Ez-ra, just as the name of the goddess Asherah was applied to represent a female version of RA ('a she Ra').The Egyptian Magi had an awareness of a mysterious power behind magical names, formulae, amulets, talismans, pictures and statuary, woven into and around the performance of particular ceremonies accompanied by secret utterances of hidden names and words.They were called 'passwords' and are still used in Mystery Schools today.

Ezra (400 BC) lived at the end of a period today called the Babylonian Exile. The earlier transplantation of Jews from Palestine to Babylonia took place some 70 years before his time[24] and followed a tactic of deportation of peoples to Mesopotamia arising out of the old tendency to make Palestine a buffer state against Egypt and deter attacks from the south-west.The forcible removal of peoples was also used to promote the colonization of unpopulated areas in certain parts of Babylonia. It was only after Cyrus captured Babylon and his kindly policy of repatriation for captive peoples, that Jews were allowed to return to Palestine.[25]

Ezra then triumphantly led a large number of people out of Babylon and, complete with the Secret and a great treasure for the Temple, arrived safely at Palestine some five months later. Upon his arrival, he associated (or reunited) himself with the then governor of Judaea under Artaxerxes, Nehemiah. Nehemiah was credited with rebuilding much of Jerusalem after the Exile and writing one of the later books of the Old Testament that carries his name. However, from available records, the chronology of that period is quite confused and some believe that Nehemiah arrived in Jerusalem after Ezra.

Over many years, Nehemiah built up a considerable collection of old documents, a personal library of some substance:

'And the same things were related both in the public archives and in the records that concern Nehemiah; and how he, founding a library, gathered together the books about the kingdoms and prophets'.[26]

Subsequently, Nehemiah offered his library to Ezra, saying, 'if therefore ye have need thereof, send someone to fetch them unto you',[27] and Ezra came into receipt of Nehemiah's collection of books. Since those books were written at earlier and different times, it is difficult to form an adequate opinion as to their exact nature and extent, and impossible to know what they said or who wrote them.

They found a mysterious old book

In the Old Testament book of Kings, a high priest named Hilkiah made an intriguing discovery: 'I have found an old book of laws in the house of God'.[28] Its origin was unknown, but around 400BC it was considered...

> ...so very old that our modern antiquarians might ponder over its pages an indefinite time, and still not quite agree as to the nature of the fabric upon which it is written. It is the only original copy now in existence. The most ancient Hebrew document on secret learning (the Siphrah Dzenioutha) was compiled from it and that at a time when the former was already considered in the light of a literary relic. One of its illustrations represents the Divine Essence...like a luminous serpent proceeding up to form a circle; and then, having attained the highest point of its circumference, the ineffable Glory bends back down again.[29]

The recorded existence of an illustration of the 'Divine Essence' some 2400 years ago is stunning, and reveals that whoever originally wrote or compiled that extraordinary book was the highest of Egyptian initiates. It was probable that it was originally an ancient top-secret Temple manuscript of indeterminable age and exclusive to the most trusted Pyramid priests. The 'fabric' it was written upon was unidentifiable to the high Hebrew priesthood and, from the description given, it is evident that it had a long preceding existence. That old document was originally called The Book of O, but was renamed the Book of God in later times. It was the original work from which the Sepher Yetzireh (Book of Creation) and parts of the Torah were derived.[30] The significance of what was written in that book is paramount to the Secret in the Bible and its importance shall be addressed later. The 'old book' was subsequently read aloud to King Josiah who then called together the elders of Judah and Jerusalem…

> …and he read in their hearing all the words of a book of a covenant which had been found in the house of YHWH. And the king stood by the pillar and made a covenant before the Lord, to walk after the Lord and to keep his commandments and his testimonies and his statutes, with all his heart and all his soul, to perform the words of his covenant that were written in this book; and all the people joined in the covenant.[31]

That is the oldest known reference in mankind's available recorded history to the now-called 'Book of Laws', the laws or commandments of how life was to be lived, like the earlier laws of Hammurabi.

From internal evidence, it is possible to determine that the Book of Jasher was compiled from the Book of God. The oldest known version of Jasher in the world is held in the secret Archives of the Vatican under the title, The Essene Book of Genesis.[32] It was also in Nehemiah's collection of books that subsequently passed into Ezra's hands and was of vital importance in the structure of the Torah, particularly Genesis. That specific document existed well before Ezra's time and it was interesting to see how Ezra dealt with the information carried in it.

Before Ezra assumed the role of religious leader of the Jerusalem community, he was apparently an important person in Babylon. Scholars held the differing opinions that he was either an Egyptian or Persian functionary in charge of Jewish affairs. That indicated he had considerable knowledge of religion and had achieved prominence in his society, thus earning the respect of the general community. Manetho's *Aegyptiaca* recorded that Ezra received candidates into the secret rites of Osiris, highest of the Panther rites of Egyptian Mysteries. He was a man of extraordinary learning, patience and status. Though he had the power to 'appoint judges and magistrates',[33] he took care not to encroach on political matters. He was called a 'scribe of the law of the God of Heaven'[34] and a 'scribe of the commandments of the Lord'.[35] The frequent biblical references to Ezra's involvement with the book of the 'law of God'[36] confounded church analysts for centuries but it was the same mysterious 'old book' found in the house of God.[37]

The book of Ezra forms part of the Old Testament and was originally attached to the books of Chronicles and Nehemiah. However, there are three other ancient writings carrying the name of Ezra, and the Fourth Book is the one of interest in this inquiry. It is the most profound and touching of the Jewish Apocalypses and that particular writing was purposely excluded from the canon of the Old Testament at the 18-yearlong Council of Trent (1546-1564). Importantly, it records the saga of how Ezra wrote the vital writings of the Bible, and introduced the Secret knowledge into them.

How the Torah came into being

Ezra preached to the rabble that he had seven visions with the 'Most High' in which he claimed that he was told to write down in a scroll 'the Secret of the times' and preserve it in a 'hidden fashion' for the future. The 'Most High' said to Ezra:

> Thou alone hast been found worthy to learn this secret (secretum hoc) of the Most High...therefore write all things that thou has learnt in scrolls, and put them in a secret place, and thou shalt teach them to the wise of the people whose hearts thou knowest are able to comprehend and keep this secret.[38]

Ezra, by saying that he had spoken personally with the 'Most High', inferred that what he was to write would contain a truth the people would believe was implicitly revealed to him, a theologically certain truth, thus to be a sacred book, the word of God. He said that he was told to...

> Go thy way, assemble the people and tell them not to seek you for forty days. But do prepare for yourself many writing tablets, and take with you Saraia, Dabria, Selemia, Elkanah and Osiel, these five, because they are equipped for writing swiftly; and (then) come hither, and I will light the lamp of understanding in your heart, which shall not be extinguished until what you are about to write shall be completed. And when you shall have finished, some things you shall publish, and some you shall deliver in a secret manner to the wise. Tomorrow, at this hour, you shall begin to write.[39]

Ezra took the scribes the 'Most High' commanded and went into the wilderness, probably to the temple on Mount Horeb/Sinai, and remained there[40] until they completed their scribal task:

> And the Most High gave understanding to the five men and they wrote what was dictated in order, in characters they knew not…And so they sat forty days: They wrote in the daytime and at night did eat bread…but as for me (Ezra) I spoke in the day and at night was not resting.[41]

That statement recorded the first written reference to the spirit of the Secret in the Bible. Ezra clearly stated that he dictated words he wanted recorded to scribes who wrote down what he said, 'in characters they knew not'. In other words, they used a type of script or alphabet previously unknown, and it may have been that particular narrative that caused the church to suppress the Fourth Book of Ezra. Nevertheless, there is more to that remarkable episode. Ezra said:

> So in forty days were written ninety-four books. And it came to pass when the forty days were fulfilled, that the Most High spoke to me saying: "The twenty-four books that thou has written, publish, that the worthy and unworthy may read: but the seventy last books you shall keep, to deliver them to the wise among the people: for in them is the spring of understanding, the foundation of wisdom, and the stream of knowledge. And I (Ezra) did so.

The twenty-four books recorded by Ezra were the twenty-four books that eventually made up the Old Testament and read openly 'by the worthy and unworthy' in churches and synagogues. The number twenty-four was the ordinary reckoning of the original Old Testament books (5+8+11). In the Jewish Talmud (and the Midrash), the Old Testament was regularly termed 'the twenty-four holy Scriptures'. Another reckoning was twenty-two[42] being accordant with the number of letters in the Hebrew alphabet. Origen, Epiphanius and Jerome also claimed there were twenty-two Old Testament books. The conflicting total seems to have been originally obtained by combining the books of Ruth with Judges, and Lamentations with Jeremiah, thus reducing the number of books to twenty-two while maintaining the full complement of writings.

Where are the missing books of the Bible?

The vexing question that arises is: 'Where are the other seventy books that Ezra and his scribes wrote?' Moreover, 'What did they contain?' The secret knowledge in those books was obviously placed by Ezra on a higher level than the new knowledge secreted into the Torah known today. So precious was their nature, they were kept hidden by the initiated priesthood and guarded from public circulation. It was probable that the seventy texts came into the possession of the Essenes or, more likely, the original possessors of those secret books were the founders of the Essene sect. If that was the case, the missing books may be amongst the Dead Sea Scroll collection today.

Ezra frankly recorded that he and five scribes wrote the important books in the Old Testament and by claiming he personally had visions with the 'Most High', he boasted of an illustrious origin to his new collection of writings. As Ezra employed the ancient collection of Nehemiah into the composition of this work, and having the services of five scribes, the question to be asked is: 'How far is the Bible, in the strict sense, factual?' That question is beginning to overshadow all other aspects of Old and New Testament studies and this work provides the complete answer. The immediate relevance of the church account of the writing of the Old Testament for the present discussion was that its own texts emphatically and explicitly represented Ezra and his scribes as the authors of its sacred scriptures. That led to the ultimate and supreme question: 'Wherein, then, does lie the divine uniqueness of Israel's religion?'

Ezra made the manner of receiving 'divine' communication fictitious and supernatural so he and his fellow priests could assert to the simple people of the time that the Torah came directly from God himself. That was conceived 'so as they may indeed see but not perceive',[43] and implied that the Torah was revealed from Heaven. The Secret part of it most certainly was, but not in the manner people were led to believe, and they were not told the substance of the mysterious information it carried. The extreme divergence and inconsistent nature of the chronology of Ezra's new compilation was irrelevant to him. To Ezra, there was no harm in adding, diminishing or introducing fictional innovations into the stories, for he was creating a new and 'divine' revelation. For example, he used the *Book of the Dead* as his source for the famous story of the 'parting of the waters' in the Book of Exodus. The first obstacle of RA on his journey into the afterlife was to cross the Sea of Reeds…a long body of waters made up of a series of adjoining lakes. Symbolically he had the blessing of his guardian god to cross by parting its waters. The words 'Red Sea' in older Bibles were an inaccurate translation and in most modern Bibles they are now correctly translated, Sea of Reeds. The Ten Commandments of the Bible also had their origin in the *Book of the Dead*. The Commandments were not original codes of conduct invented for the Israelites, but were simply newly stated versions of the ancient pharaonic confessions from Spell No. 125.

The stories in the Torah had their major weaknesses and deficiencies…but they also held some extraordinary surprises. In the Book of Numbers, for example, 'light' was given as a numerical value of 186,400, being the physical constant of the 'speed of light'.[44] Astronomers knew that the 'families' of the House of Israel gave the proportions of the 360-degree circle of the heavens.[45] However disfigured is the wording of the Torah, it is still full of remarkable knowledge, even in the 'husk' that first met the eye of the reader. Under the outward veil or cloaking, however, is to be found the substance of a deeply concealed beauty, hidden below its structure. The visible architecture, notwithstanding its apparent symmetry, is unable to stand the criticism of cold reason. There is, however, more wisdom concealed under the fables of the Torah than in all the science in the literature of this world.

One of the main objects of raising the biblical inconsistencies is to establish through the developing disclosure of the Secret that the Torah has no historical meaning but mystical significance alone, and that the true literal meaning was spiritual. In other words, the Torah of the Bible must be seen as purely figurative, and therefore destitute of all historical meaning. Orthodox Jews talked constantly about the 'heavenly essences' of the Torah and they had very good reason for doing so. Passages of narrative that say something unworthy of God, or are senseless and contradictory, abound but that does not matter. Allegorical sentences that are used in passages to cast doubts on the literal sense, render the whole verse suspect, but Cabalists do not care. Many biblical critics set aside major areas of Torah text as being of questionable value, but they are only looking at a surface reading. However, the problems with a surface reading, whether absurd or reasonable, clear or confused, do not reflect the under-meaning of what it was really written for. Based on the major problems previously described, it is apparent the scribes who wrote it did not take the framework of the Torah too seriously. Ancient Rabbis agreed, and expressed the opinion that 'had the Torah simply been intended as a series of literal narratives, the authors would have been able to compile a better book'.

Had Ezra not said that his new Scroll was the work of God, it would have held no power over the people and by 'super-naturalizing' it, he facilitated its heavenly character which became its most powerful means of expression. The people of Palestine were so primitive that they were in urgent need of laws regarding morals and especially hygiene, and those laws were detailed in the list of 613 commandments. Most of the populace were slaves and Mixtures, a body of sub-normal humans with animal characteristics, many of which lived in caves and brayed out sounds like an ass's cry. It is recorded in the Books of the Kings that those backward people 'ate their own dung and drank their own urine', burned their own children as offerings, consumed the heads of asses, devoured dove's dung as food and boiled and ate their own children. Such were their depraved beliefs that stray dogs entering the city were tried and could not be put to death until the result of the trial was determined. A dog found guilty was eaten. Such was the mentality of the greater number of people and when Ezra said his collection of new writings was 'inspired' by God, they believed him.

It was after the enlightened Ezra had written the new Scroll that the tradition of the 'Torah reading' was instituted. Since the numerous laws carried within it could not be learnt at one hearing, it became necessary to provide regular instruction in teaching them. Ezra is recorded as firstly having publicly read to small gatherings of people 'day by day, from the first day to the last day, he read in the book of thE law of God'.[46] He was relaying words and stories as written on the new Torah Scroll. On a surface level, it contained ancestral traditions, remnants of tribal memories, updated legends and folklore, fictitious narratives, a mass of interwoven allegories, some cultural elements, and a description of Hebrew ceremonial practices from early days. Nevertheless, that surface reading concealed the Secret and to reveal it to certain people, the Rabbis established particular requirements. The earliest Jewish conditions governing the choice of those suitable to be initiated into the deep truth hidden below the words of the Torah were thus formulated.

The simple people looked upon the 'miracles' in the Torah with awe and accepted the stories at face value. Ezra had invested his volume with certain 'divine' attributes by virtue of which it was regarded as sacred and given by God. He and his scribes had simply added, cut, rearranged and reinterpreted some of the already existing material in Nehemiah's library and, importantly, the Book of O. From that assorted material they created a new entity, rewritten from a Jewish point of view, reworked in accordance with latest viewpoints, and creatively expanded. The world now had a sacred writing, one that was given the name 'Bible' 900 years later, and the Panther's cosmic Secret was in it.

CHAPTER FIVE

WHY JESUS STOLE THE TORAH

The Babylonian Talmud and the rare 'Aquarian Gospel of Jesus' describe in detail the travels of Rabbi Jesus into Egypt and his participation in the Mystery initiations at the Great Pyramid. There, he learnt the Secret and major ceremonial elements of Rabbi Jesus' initiatory process are recorded esoterically in the New Testament, particularly in the Gospel of Mark. A common appellation for Jesus in the Talmud was Yeshu'a ben Panthera, Panthera being the Latin equivalent of Panther. The fact that he knew the Panther Secret was supported not only by his Talmudic name but also by particular Gospel statements, and that knowledge ultimately caused his downfall.

The initiation into the Egyptian mysteries was, of all systems practised by the ancients, the most severe and impressive. The Greeks at Eleusis imitated it to some extent, but they never reached the magnitude of its forms or the austerity of its discipline. The 'learning of the Egyptians' was imparted in those mysteries, and as Clement of Alexandria recorded, the more important secrets were not revealed even to some priests, but to a select number only.[1] A 'Word' of surpassing value and claiming a profound veneration was revealed at that final stage of enlightenment. That became the mystical 'Lost Word' of Masonry because it was something that only highest initiates knew. In biblical terminology, it was known as the 'Word of God' and was passed on 'through prophets or patriarchs'[2] or 'revealed to individuals through visions'.[3] In the New Testament, it was also called 'the word of life',[4] and was known to Jesus.

The Egyptian priests were very jealous of their 'magic' lore (secrets) and did all they could to prevent written evidence of their Secret being removed from the country. However, ancient rabbinic texts recorded several traditions of Rabbi Jesus bringing written confidential information out of Egypt, and provided substantial details of the peculiar means whereby it was done. Jesus was said to have circumvented the Egyptian's protective vigilance by some subterfuge as that which was handed down in the story in the Palestinian Gemera:

> He who scratches on the skin in the fashion of writing is guilty, but he who marks on the skin in the fashion of writing, is exempt from punishment...Rabbi Eliezer said to them: But has not Jesus brought 'magic' out of Egypt in this way? Surely he learned sorcery by such writing.

Rabbi Eliezer defended the objection that the marks on Jesus' skin were 'scratches', or, as recorded in another version of the story, 'letters cut upon the body'. Those statements implied that permanent tattoos were strictly forbidden but the marks on Jesus' skin were not of that nature. They were presumably not letters proper, that being the writing of letters or words, for the discussion was not as to writing, but distinctly to 'marks' that were similar to writing. That suggested some sort of diagrams of sigils, or drawings of some kind and referred directly to the fundamental nature of the Secret in the Bible.

In summary, Jesus had travelled to Egypt and received the highest possible level of initiation in the Egyptian temples. There he learned the ultimate Secret, and with the inscriptions that he needed to unlock the secret knowledge drawn on his skin, returned to Jerusalem, now needing only a physical Torah Scroll to publicly demonstrate the Secret that it held.

Most opportunely for the development of this inquiry, was the recent publication of a curious ancient writing called 'The Narrative of Joseph of Arimathea'. That very concise old document is given only brief treatment by church historians in the construction of their exhaustive dictionaries and encyclopedias. However, for this premise it brought the Secret right into the entire New Testament story of Jesus and shed new light on what the Gospels really are. Therefore, it compelled the setting forth of the substance of the whole matter as it was found recorded in that writing.

As with all Christian writings, there is dispute as to the likely date of its composition, but general academic belief is that it dates to sometime around the beginning of the third century. The genesis of the story behind the writing was obviously much earlier and what was recorded in that document failed to capture the attention of most researchers of the New Testament. The manuscript generally related to a fascinating account of the only Torah Scroll at Jerusalem being stolen and, because of that, the Rabbis were in a state of despair. That is significant in our study because it was Rabbi Jesus himself who was charged with stealing the Torah. A woman named Sarra publicly accused Rabbi Jesus of the theft and the Jews said to her: 'We believe you', for they held her as a prophetess:

> At the fourth and fifth hours they went out and found Jesus walking in the street. Towards evening they obtained a guard of soldiers. They came to Jesus and saying, "Hail Rabbi". They took Jesus to the High Priest who examined him. Jesus was held captive upon Sarra's word.

> On the next day, being Wednesday, at the ninth hour, they brought him (Jesus) to the priest's hall and asked, 'Why did you take away the Torah Scroll?' He was silent.

The story of the missing Torah found parallel accounts in traditional Rabbinic and Jewish literature and one of the most persistent charges of the Jews against Rabbi Jesus was that he learnt 'a magic secret' in Egypt. That statement puzzled the MiNd of Gospel researchers for centuries and the overriding importance it assumed in Jewish tradition was one bit of evidence supporting the fact that it may have actually happened.

The 'Toldoth Jeschu' also recorded that Rabbi Jesus learned 'something special' in Egypt, but its main feature was the description of the robbing of the Torah Scroll by a 'strange device' from the Temple of Jerusalem. That 'strange device' may have simply been a cunning manoeuver, for in the several variants of the story, we see the evolution of the tradition whereby Rabbi Jesus was said to have outwitted the guardians of the Torah Scroll.

Summarising Jewish documents, Rabbi Jesus had stolen the Torah Scroll and was about to reveal the highly confidential Divine name of God, the

'Word' and, more importantly, the Secret in the Bible. He said so himself:

> Nothing is covered up that will not be revealed, or hidden that should not be
> known. Therefore, whatever was said in the dark shall be heard in the light,
> and what was whispered in private rooms shall now be proclaimed from
> the rooftops.[5]

The attempted disclosure of age-old secret information blatantly violated
the Ancient Rule of the Order of High Initiates of the Mystery Schools and
offended the priestly line, 'for one is wholly forbidden to reveal their mysteries;
rather one must keep them secret in silence'.[6] For that reason he was arrested
by the Sanhedrin, charged, and tried.

A passage preserved in the Babylonian Gemara demands close attention,
for it may have provided the spirit of the original charge against Rabbi Jesus.
It ran as follows (in part): 'That thou shalt not have a son or disciple who
burns his food publicly, like Jesus the Nazarene'.[7] The main point of the
accusation is contained in the word 'publicly'. It was the doing of something
or other 'in public' which apparently might not only have been tolerated
privately, but which was presumably the natural thing to do in private. The
main burden of Christian tradition was that Jesus taught the poor, the outcast,
the oppressed, the sinners, to all of whom, according to rabbinic law, the
mysteries of the Torah were not to be expounded. Those so-called 'ignorant
and unclean' persons were 'Amme ha-aretz' (men of the earth) and the Secret
in the Torah was not for them. It was evident that the whole point of the
story of 'burning food publicly' had to do with some scandal or breaking of
the established rule or order of things, or with paving the way for doing so.
From the Jewish record, Rabbi Jesus was challenged because 'he burnt his
food publicly', that is to say, he was about to renounce openly what he had
learned in Egypt.

The chief priests were the key figures in the Sanhedrin and they were
probably former high priests or members of the priestly aristocracy. According
to Josephus, they were 'the leading men of the people, the leading people of
Jerusalem, the powerful and the dignitaries', and at court trials, they sat in a
half circle facing each other. Before them stood two scribes, one writing
down what was said in favour of the accused, and the other what was said

against him. The Gospels said that high priests 'questioned' Jesus about 'his teachings'[8] and he assured them that he did not intend to damage the Torah; 'Think not that I have come to destroy the Torah...I came not to destroy, but to complete'.[9] He wanted to reveal the great mystery it held.

The Sanhedrin had good reason to bring Jesus to trial for he blatantly stole their most valued document, thus preventing them from keeping the Passover and partaking in the consumption of the obligatory four chalices of wine. Not only had they lost their Torah, but also access to the very sacred Secret it contained. 'The chief priests accused him of many things',[10] found him guilty and sentenced him to die by stoning for attempting to make public the fundamental nature of the hidden Mysteries.

The early church knew the real story of the death of Rabbi Jesus, confirmed in an ancient document titled the Arethas Codex. That writing appeared to have had at least two previous titles but in its current form, it purported to be the work of presbyter Clement of Alexandria. That writing stated that Rabbi Jesus, 'In his sixty-third year of his age he was stoned to death'. Another early presbyter also confirmed Rabbi Jesus was killed by stoning. Writing about 198, Tertullian of Carthage rhetorically addressed the Jews stating, 'ye stoned him'.[11] Tertullian spoke of the stoning of Rabbi Jesus not as the invention of an enemy, but simply as a genuine piece of accepted church history. It should be clear from the above quotes that the study of the New Testament is in an exciting phase but also a particularly difficult one for the church. Rabbinic records confirmed the church accounts and stated that Rabbi Jesus was stoned to death by a person called Pinhas at a place called Lud.[12] Both Talmuds[13] contain a precise description of his death that, in both cases, was appended to the following passage from the Mishna, 'and to bring him forward to the tribunal and stone him. And thus they have done to Jesus at Lud, and they hanged him on the day before Passover'.[14] Full details of the stoning of Rabbi Jesus were revealed in *The Bible Fraud* and that book presents a new set of circumstances in any matters associated with researching the origins of the New Testament.

CHAPTER SIX

EGYPTIAN MYSTERY SECRETS
CIPHERED INTO NEW TESTAMENT

In 1610, the Bible was edited by an initiate into the ancient Mysteries and additional secret information was encoded into both Old and New Testaments. The editor was Sir Francis Bacon (1561-1626) and he knew the Secret of the Panthers. He was a man of many talents, a lawyer, linguist and composer, and mastered every subject he undertook: mathematics, geometry, music, painting, astronomy, classical drama and poetry, philosophy, history, theology and architecture. He was a man of many aims and purposes, the father of modern science, remodeler of modern law, patron of modern democracy, and possibly the reviver of Freemasonry. His life and works are extensively documented, and his intellectual accomplishments widely recognized, particularly in academic circles.

At the age of sixteen, he moved to Paris 'direct from the Queens Hand' and there studied Egyptian, Arabian, Indian and Greek philosophy with particular attention paid to ancient sacred Mysteries and their Ritual Rites. He personally recorded that while in Paris he created a secret cipher system that could be inserted into a document without arousing suspicion. While living in Europe, Francis Bacon was initiated into the mysterious Order of the Knights Templar and learnt their very special secret. An ancient document recorded that the true history of early Christianity was known to the Knights Templar, having originally been 'imparted to Hugh de Payens by the Grand-Pontiff of the Order of the Temple (of the Nazarene sect), one named

Theocletes, after which it was learned by some Knights in Palestine'.[1]

Before Bacon returned to London, he travelled to France, Italy, Germany and Spain and completely devoted himself to the study of law. From his understanding of secret information he had learned during his initiation, he conceived the idea of reactivating various Secret Societies and in 1580 founded the secret 'Rosicrosse Literary Society' at Gray's Inn. Later in the same year, he founded the Lodge of Free and Accepted or Speculative Masons, also at Gray's Inn.

On June 25 1607, Sir Francis Bacon was appointed Solicitor-General and Chief Advisor to the Crown. He presented new ideas to the Government for the Reformation of the church and was officially instructed to commence restructuring the Bible. Research in the Records Office of the British Museum revealed original documents still exist that refer to important proceedings associated with Sir Francis Bacon's involvement with editing both Old and New Testaments. They revealed that he personally selected and paid the New Testament revisers who completed their task under the instructions of Bacon's long-time friend, Dr Andrews.

© Photography; Thomas L. Lithgow, Esq.

Portrait of the editor of the Bible, Sir Francis Bacon.

The first English language manuscripts of the Bible remained in Bacon's possession for nearly a year. During that time, 'he hammered the various styles of the translators into the unity, rhythm, and music of Shakespearean prose, wrote the Prefaces and created the whole scheme of the Authorized Version'.[2] Regarding the months of editing, Bacon's biographer, William T. Smedley, said:

> It will eventually be proved that the whole structure of the Authorised Bible was Francis Bacon's. He was an ardent student not only of the Bible, but also of early manuscripts. St Augustine, St Jerome, and writers of theological works, were studied by him with industry.[3]

At the completion of editing, Sir Francis Bacon and King James 1 had a series of meetings to finalise editorial matters associated with the new Bible. It was at that time that King James ordered a 'Dedication to the King' to be drawn up and included in the opening pages. He also authorized the phrase 'Appointed to be read in the Churches' to appear on the title page. That was an announcement clarifying that King James had personally given the church 'Special Command' for that particular version of the Bible to be used in preference to the vast array of Greek and Latin Vulgate Bibles current at the time. His reason was personal, for King James had previously instructed the revisers to 'defend the position of the king' in their restructuring of the texts. In their translation of 1 Peter 2:13, for example, they changed the phrase 'the emperor, as supreme' to 'the king, as supreme'. Because the King James Bible was written to support the authority of a king, the later church often referred to it as the one from 'authority', and it came to be presented as if officially 'authorized'. In subsequent revisions, the word 'authorized' found its way onto the title page and later still was printed on the cover, giving King James' new Bible a false sense of authenticity.

Concealing special messages

Sir Francis Bacon was a master of concealing secret information in his writings and his methods were found in the Bible. Bacon took delight to hide his words, to the end they might be found out, and stands a self-confessed

Teacher of Concealed Principles. He stated that he went down the 'same road as the Ancients but had something better to produce' and spoke of 'two methods of writing, one 'reserved', the other 'open'; one for disciples, the other for the multitude…one shall be oral, and Traditional; the other matter Reserved to a Succession of hands, being Secret Wisdom'.[4] It was a time of severe repression and of harsh government, and free speech was impossible. Able men could only dissemble and speak in allegory. 'If they had expressed their opinions openly they would have been sent to the Tower and the Block'.[5]

Cryptography, or the art of writing in cipher to conceal the meaning of what was written from all except those who possessed the key, may be traced to remote antiquity, possibly to the Spartans. Kings and Generals communicated their messages to officers in distant provinces by means of a pre-concerted cipher, and the system was employed wherever there was a desire or a necessity to conceal the meaning of a written document. Aponas, an astrological writer of the 13th century, revealed some old ciphers that were used originally by Cabalists, and among others, a particular alphabet called 'the passing of the river' which is referred to in some high degrees of Masonry.

The most famous of all later literal cryptograms is the famous bilateral cipher described by Bacon in his *De Augmentis Scientiarum*. Sir Francis originated the system while still a young man in Paris and that particular cipher required the use of two styles of typeface, one an ordinary face and the other especially designed. The differences between the two fonts were in many cases so minute that it required a powerful magnifying glass to detect them. Today, the knowledge of that simple system of ciphers would no longer serve any purpose of concealment due to modern computerized forms of printing and easy detection. Originally, the cipher messages were concealed only in italicized words, sentences or paragraphs, because the italic letters, being more ornate than Roman letters, offered greater opportunity for concealing slight but necessary variations. Sometimes the special letters varied a little in size; at other times in thickness or in their ornamental flourishes.

Alphabets secretly adjusted were not entirely satisfactory, however, for although they rendered unintelligible the true nature of the writings, their very presence disclosed the fact of concealed information. Through patience or persecution, the keys to those alphabets were eventually acquired and the contents of the documents revealed to the unworthy. That was not satisfactory and necessitated employment of more subtle methods of concealing divine truths. The result was the appearance of cryptic systems of writing designed to conceal the presence of both the message and the cryptogram. Thus having devised a method of transmitting their secrets to posterity, Sir Francis Bacon and other initiates like him, encouraged the circulation of certain documents specially prepared through incorporating into them ciphers containing the deepest secrets of religion, mysticism and philosophy. Thus, medieval Masons and Rosicrucians disseminated their secrets throughout the land unsuspected by 'the uninstructed world',[6] since volumes containing those cryptograms could be subject to scrutiny without revealing the presence of the hidden message.

During the Middle Ages scores of 'concealed authors'[7] and members of secret political or religious organizations published books and letters containing codes and ciphers. Secret writings became a fad; every European court had its own diplomatic cipher, and the intelligentsia vied with one another in devising curious and complicated cryptograms. Some were as simple as writing words of a sentence backwards. The literature of the 15th, 16th and 17th centuries was permeated with ciphers, few of which have ever been decoded. Without a key, the works are unintelligible, except by the art of the decipherer or one skilled in literary matters. Many liberal churchmen used cryptograms, fearing excommunication or a worse fate should their research become suspected. Had they failed to conceal their discoveries under complicated cipher, they faced the possibility of persecution as heretics. Some ciphers were so intricate that they may forever baffle attempts at their decipherment. In those susceptible of a solution, sometimes the 'a's and 'b's need to be exchanged; at other times only every other letter was counted; and so on.

Instances of strange pictorial ciphers abound in Masonic and Rosicrucian art and any picture, drawing or emblem with other than its obvious meaning, may be considered a pictorial cryptogram. The example reproduced here is a secret watermark used by a London Masonic printer sometime around

1636. It shows the familiar Masonic emblem of two vertical columns Jachin and Boaz,[8] and their significance, use and mystical meanings that were highly respected by Masons. In that stylized watermark version of the columns, the letter 'G' occurred in the left-hand pillar. That was 'symbolic of the Divine Architect'[9] and denoted God. The letters 'GG' that appeared between the two pillars signified '(G)RAND (G)EOMETRICIAN', and those who know the Structure of Freemasonry will be aware of its meaning, although it seems to be only associated with Scottish Rite.

Ciphered Masonic Watermark from History of the Sabbath (Heylen), London, 1636

Kenneth Mackenzie, in his *Royal Masonic Cyclopaedia*, observed 'an emblem comprises a larger series of thoughts than a symbol, which may be said rather to illustrate some single, special idea. An emblem is a picture or sign representing principles, or a series of principles, recognizable by those who have received special instructions'. In Masonic symbology there is scarcely a pictorial cryptogram in which two vertical pillars do not figure prominently. A foremost symbol of the Rosicrucian fraternity appears to be the Pelican wounding its breast with its beak, and feeding its young with its blood. In addition to the simple pictorial cipher, there is the more technical form in which, for example, words or letters are concealed by the number of vertical stones in a wall, by waves on the surface of water, or by the length and order of lines used in shading. The Great Seal of the United States of America is probably the best-known example of a pictogram concealing numerous hidden meanings that include the Eye of Horus as the capstone of the Great

Pyramid. The shape, height or proportion of a structure or the folds on a person's garment were all used to conceal definite figures or characters that could be exchanged for letters, words or impressions by persons acquainted with the code. The key necessary for their decipherment sometimes accompanied pictorial cryptograms.

A figure may point or look towards the vital aspect of the cipher or carry in its hand some implement disclosing the system of measurement used. Michelangelo's 1510 fresco of the Sibyl of Tarquin on the Sistine Chapel ceiling in Rome depicted two identical 'assisting genii' looking over the Sibyl's right shoulder and was one of many of his pictorial cryptograms constantly revealing that Jesus had a twin brother. There are also frequent instances in which the cryptographer purposely distorts a figure in his drawing by placing the right hand in place of the left, the sun rising in the West, or a battle shield on the wrong arm of a warrior, or by employing some similar artifice. The much-discussed sixth finger on the Pope's hand in Raphael's 'Sistine Madonna' and the sixth toe on Joseph's foot in the 'Marriage of the Virgin' by the same artist are cunningly concealed cryptograms.

A particular pictorial design with dogs, rabbits and archers is found over the address, 'To The Christian Reader', in the 1612 edition of the Authorized Version of the King James Bible. That identical design is also found in the folio edition of Shakespeare and connected both books. However, it is the 1612 quarto edition of the Authorized Version of the Bible that is of most interest, for on the title-page of the Genealogies are two complex head-piece designs both of which were used by Sir Francis Bacon in previous books he wrote and published in 1593 and 1594. The selection of those designs was not made by chance but was deliberately chosen to create similitude between certain books and mark their connections with each other. Most noticeable was the light and dark capital A's (A.A) in the lower design which was also used on several Shakespeare quartos and elsewhere. That direct connection between the Bible and the Shakespearean plays is long overlooked AnD the fact that hidden ciphers appeared in both the King James Bible and the Shakespearean plays arrested attention. Those writings contained cryptographically concealed information that is purposely encoded into the actual text and is still there today.

What the Mystery Schools knew about Jesus

Scores of volumes were written to establish that Sir Francis Bacon was the real author of the plays and sonnets popularly ascribed to William Shakespeare. An impartial consideration of those documents cannot but convince the open-minded of the verisimilitude of the theory of Bacon being author of the Shakespearean plays. Those enthusiasts who for years struggled to identify Sir Francis Bacon as the true 'Bard of Avon' might long since have won their case had they emphasized the most important angle. That was, Sir Francis Bacon, the Knights Templar, Masonic and Rosicrucian initiate, wrote into the Shakespearean plays the secret teachings of the Fraternity of the Rose Cross, the 'Lost Word' of the Freemason Order, and major clues to unlock the hidden story in the Gospels. A sentimental world, however, disliked giving up a traditional hero, either to solve a controversy or to right a wrong. Nevertheless, the Bacon/Shakespeare controversy, as its most able advocates realize, involves the most profound aspects of science, religion and ethics; he or she who solves its mystery may yet find therein the key to the supposedly Lost Wisdom of Antiquity.

Initiates believe the coded symbols in this drawing reveal that Sir Francis Bacon was the true author of the Shakespearean Plays. A caption attached to this drawing said: 'O give me leave to pull the Curtain by. To a brother who has been taught to read, the verses disclose the identity of Shake-speare'. From Peacham's 'Minerva Britannia' (1612).

Abundant proof exists that Sir Francis Bacon was concerned in one way or another with the production or editing of the Shakespearean Plays. He redrafted the original Nine Degrees of the Templars into Thirty-Three, and chose Thirty-Three as the highest degree of initiation simply because 33 was the numerical signature of 'Bacon':

B	A	C	O	N	
2	1	3	14	13	= 33

Thus, 33 became his personal cipher number, and whenever it appeared in the Shakespearean Plays, the Gospels or the Old Testament, a cleverly concealed cipher could be discovered associated with it. In the 'First Part of King Henry the Fourth', for example, the word 'Francis' appeared 33 times on one page. To attain this end, obviously awkward sentences were required, such as: 'ANON FRANCIS? No Francis, but tomorrow Francis; or Francis on Thursday; or indeed Francis when then will; but Francis'. Here we see one example of the concealed use of the mystical number 33 in the Shakespearean Plays.

The Masonic order of degrees was subsequently divided into 33 symbolic sections (33°). The number 33 was then used in a variety of Mystery Schools and it was probable that Bacon's cipher number coincided with an old Cabalist teaching. The Torah employed the Divine Name 32 times in the Creation story at the beginning of the Old Testament book of Genesis. Of that, Cabalists said that through those 32 paths, the soul descended to be clothed in the physical body and the 33rd path was the ultimate return to stand before God's presence at the end of life on Earth.

Sir Francis became heavily involved in the redevelopment of both Freemason and Rosicrucian Mystery Schools. It was suggested that he created his own Secret Society, by the agency of which he carried through his works, but it is difficult to find any concrete evidence that such a Society existed. Books came from his pen at a rate which, when the truth is revealed, will literally 'stagger humanity'.[10] He made translations of ancient classics and histories and his 'Good Pens' (other writers) wrote books under his direction. He saw them through to the press, and every book published under his direction carried his favourite secret cipher, stylized light and dark capital A's, side-by-side (A.A).

The double 'A.A' was Sir Francis Bacon's hidden signature cipher for 'AthenA', known in Mythology as Pallas Minerva, Athene or Athena, which meant Virgin. The letters making up PALLAS MINERVA, ATHENE OR ATHENA, VIRGIN numbered 33, and she was the esteemed Goddess of Sir Francis Bacon's Mystery Schools. The initiates dedicated themselves in her honour and vowed to uphold her ideals.

Athena was the Goddess of Wisdom and usually depicted in art wearing a helmet and holding a spear in her right hand in readiness to strike at a serpent near her feet. She was known as the 'Spear-shaker' among the ancient Greeks because when the morning rays of the sun glinted on the spear, the common people were in the habit of saying smilingly: 'Athena is shaking her spear again'; hence her name, 'Spear-shaker'. She was the Goddess to whom the Rosicrosse Brethren swore allegiance when they were initiated in the Secret Literary Order, the Knights of the Order, and Francis Bacon was the head of the Spear-shakers. Side by side with the Rosicrosse arose the Lodge of the Freemasons and the College of the Rosicrucian Fraternity, which persist to this day.

In both Masonic and Rosicrucian rituals, there was a certain point in learning where the candidate was challenged by a 'spear-shaker' who menacingly threatened the candidate to the chest, shaking and pointing a spear or a sword at him. The design on page 33 of Henry Peacham's *Minerva Britannia* (1612) shows a hand holding a spear as in the act of shaking it. It represented the great secret of Francis Bacon's life and gave the clue to the construction of the word, 'Shakespeare'. That volume is full of literary devices that would amply repay a careful study, but it established that the word, 'spearshaker', when reversed, became 'Shakespeare'. The 'spearshaker' also received a mention in Bacon's restructuring of the New Testament. In the final narratives of the Gospel of John, Jesus was prodded in the side by a spearshaker.

Both Masons and Rosicrucians threateningly 'shake spears' at the candidate during the trials of his initiation. 'It was Francis Bacon's secret symbol to represent that he was 'The Spear-shaker's' representative known by the name of Shakespeare. Thus the 'Spear-shaker' wrote under the name of Shake-speare and was Sir Francis Bacon'.[11]

© Cambridge Photo Archives.

Athena, the Goddess of Wisdom, holding her spear.

Sir Francis Bacon used the first and last letters of Athena's name (A.A) as headpieces to subtly mark particular books connected with the Secret Orders of the Rosicrucians and Masons. 'In these books Francis Bacon had the opportunity to secrete his personal secrets which he dare not write openly about'.[12] There were many different designs of the 'A.A' cipher and numerous books that bore the coded signal were connected, including the Authorised Edition of the King James Bible and the Shakespearean Plays.

> One 'A' was printed light and the other 'A' dark to indicate that while there was much open and straightforward in the designated book, there was also much in the shadow which could only be discovered by searching.[13]

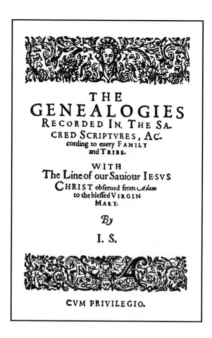

Hidden Information. This is the title page of the 1612 edition of the New Testament. The design at the head of the page was also used on the title-page of the first edition of Venus and Adonis, 1593, and the first edition of Lucrece, 1594. Note the use in the lower panel of the light and dark 'A. A' secret cipher that indicates hidden knowledge. The same design was used on several of the Shakespearean quartos and elsewhere.

Jesus in the Shakespearean Plays

The full name that Francis Bacon constructed to appear on title pages of his writings was 'William Shakespeare', and was created (maybe) without reference to him of Stratford, who possible bore, or had assigned to him, a somewhat similar name, possibly Shakspur. There was good reason to suspect that was exactly what happened, for Sir Francis Bacon created a superstructure of numbers built up on the exact spelling of the words 'William Shakespeare'. Anybody looking closely at Bacon's clues will see also the year 1623 was specially selected for the issue of the complete volume of the plays, because of the extraordinary relations which the numbers composing it bear to the combined names William Shakespeare and Sir Francis Bacon. Simply put, the total number of letters of the two names added up to 33, Bacon's cipher number (WILLIAM SHAKESPEARE; SIR FRANCIS BACON = 33 letters). It is not surprising then, to note that the letters of the year 1623, when written in words, also adds up to 33 (SIXTEEN HUNDRED AND TWENTY THREE YEARS = 33 letters). The chances of that letter/word/number combination happening by chance, according to mathematical experts, are 4.8 million to one. The intriguing relationship of numbers is also carried through to the year 1561, in which the birth of Francis Bacon was registered and, curiously enough, to 1564 and 1616, the reputed dates of the birth and death of the Stratford man.

The Shakespearean plays and the 'authorised' Bible of 1611 contain hidden messages about Jesus, Mary Magdalene and the substance of the Gospel story. Sir Francis knew the secret of Christian origins and concealed his knowledge in both the Shakespearean Folio of 1623 and the New Testament. His biographer said:

> And whosoever would understand the Lord Bacon's Cypher let him consult that accurate Editione in Latine, Anno 1623 (*Advancement of Learning*) for the form of the Letters of the Alphabet, in which much of the Mysterie consisteth.[14]

Sir Francis Bacon's secrets of the Mysteries were encoded in a system of letters and numbers that revealed to the initiated the presence of concealed information. The hidden information of the Knights Templar, Masons and Rosicrucians was purposely encoded into those texts by Sir Francis, and several of his complex and revealing ciphers were decoded in *The Bible Fraud*.

Solving the riddle of Solomon's Temple

It is intriguing to note that throughout Bacon's writings he constantly wrote the word *Kings* in italics, and appears to be directing attention towards the Book of Kings in the Old Testament, now separated into two individual books (1 and 2). The author of the Book of Kings was Ezra, an initiate into the sacred Mysteries, and he purposely ciphered special passages into that document revealing publicly unknown secrets of the Ancients. Of vital importance was his reference to Moses' 'bronze serpent',[15] a curious object with direct relevance to the Secret in the Bible. Because Ezra and his scribes had embodied certain secret literary devices into the Torah, ancient priests admonished their disciples never to translate, edit or rewrite its contents. The 'bronze serpent' in the Book of Kings was one of those devices and Francis Bacon knew that.

It was from the Book of Kings that many Masonic references and symbols were drawn, with most originating from the extensive description of Solomon's Temple.[16] In Masonry, the Temple of Solomon played a fundamental part and was integral to the very essence of their craft. There was a time when every Masonic writer subscribed with unhesitating faith to the theory that Masonry was first organised in the Temple of Solomon; that there Solomon, Hiram of Tyre, and Hiram Abif presided as Grand Masters over the Lodge that they had established; that there the symbolic degrees were instituted and systems of initiation were invented.

However, no archaeological evidence was ever found that attested to an historical existence of such an ornate structure as was recorded of Solomon's Temple in the Bible, and Masons themselves now generally agree that the description was allegorical. Some biblical analysts suggested that Solomon's Temple was in reality a stepped ziggurat like that of Bel (Baal) at Babylon or perhaps a three-staged pyramid similar to those uncovered at Ur, the biblical home of Abraham. Curiously enough, in the foundation of the pyramid of Bel, there was an empty lidless sepulchre similar to that found in the Great Pyramid at Giza. Supporters of Bel believed that it was the actual resting place of their god who promised that one day he would return to earth as Saviour of mankind, but, like the Great Pyramid, no corpse or treasure was ever found.

Concealed in the writings of Francis Bacon is a ciphered clue that when unlocked and associated with a little-known ancient tradition, revealed that Solomon's Temple may have once existed and possibly remains today. In his aptly named book, *Advancement of Learning*, Bacon mentioned the words 'King's Temple' seven times on page 33 in chapter seven. That is significant, and the importance of the use of numbers 7 and 33 determined that he was referring to a code known only to initiates. The number 7 was the most important number in religious literature, and that may have originated with the mysterious layout in the Book of Thoth. The hidden knowledge in Thoth's book is revealed in later chapters and involves another of Bacon's works, *The Wisdom of the Ancients*. That book, published in 1619, was an allegorical interpretation of hidden truths contained in ancient myths. The total number of letters in the title remarkably added to 22, a number representing the amount of letters in the Aramaic language, the number of chapters in the Book of Revelation, and the number of major Arcana cards in a Tarot pack.

Ezra's secret message revealed that the 'King's Temple' that Sir Francis Bacon was drawing attention to was the famous Temple of Solomon. It stood (in biblical terms) for 33 years in pristine splendour and that number is the clue enabling the hidden information to be deciphered. Likewise, King David was made to rule 33 years in Jerusalem and Gospel writers had Jesus Christ crucified in the 33rd year of his life, those numbers again drawing attention to deeper truths. The Hall of Pillars in Solomon's Temple consisted of seven columns, a symbol taken from the earlier description of a Hall of Pillars in the *Book of the Dead*. The black and white chequer-work style of flooring of a Masonic Lodge represented the 'ground floor of King Solomon's Temple' and that chessboard-type pattern was also described in the *Book of the Dead*. Wherever possible, Masonic Lodge buildings were built aligned due east and west being oriented to the same direction as the biblical description of Solomon's Temple.

The name of King Solomon is not recorded by Herodotus or Plato, or by any earlier writer of standing, and, like Moses, appeared originally and only in the Bible. It is extraordinary that the Jewish nation, over whom the mighty Solomon had reigned in all his biblical glory, and with a magnificence scarcely equalled by the greatest monarchs, spending nearly 'eight thousand millions'[17] of gold on a Temple, was overlooked by historians. Not only with Solomon, there was no proof of the 12 tribes of Israel having ever existed, and Herodotus, the earliest and most accurate of historians, never mentioned the Israelites at all.

The best-informed Masonic writers agreed that the biblical description of Solomon's Temple was 'veiled in allegory and clothed in symbols' being, maybe, a fanciful description to hide the fact that Ezra was talking secretly about a real Temple at Giza. New Testament writers also knew that the Old Testament stories were not historical but allegorical, having symbolic meaning only.[18]

It is possible to divided the name Solomon into three syllables: SOL-OM-ON, symbolizing SOL (The Sun) upon his golden throne; OM, the sacred chant to the Sun; and ON, the biblical city of the Sun, called later, in Greek, Heliopolis. Therefore, Solomon may have originally derived from the term 'solar-man' or 'solar-men', worshippers of the Sun-god, and a spectacular clue to the location of the original Temple arose from that scenario. There is another less likely possibility and that involves a combination of the names Sol and Amun (Solamun). The origin of Amun was 'a moon' and the word Solamun was a combination of the Sun and Moon, light and dark. Bible writers subsequently personified the Solar-men (or Solamun) as Solomon, and he became the mythical King of an earthly nation.

Sir Francis Bacon learnt many truths from his initiation into the Knights Templar and coded much of his understanding into Psalm 46 of the Old Testament, the Gospels, and the Shakespearean Folio of 1623. It is difficult to approach any phase of his life without being confronted with what appears to be evidence of careful preparation to reveal, yet conceal, secret information. That observation does not result from imagination or prejudice. Much of his coding was centred directly on his personal cipher number 33, being intentional and having a cryptic meaning that concealed specific information he wanted discovered later. Hidden in the Shakespearean Folio of 1623, in Bacon's favorite cipher system he called 'The Capital Initial Code', is found 33 consecutive letters on page 330 (the zeros being irrelevant in ciphers, for the primary number is harmonic) that spelt out: TEMPLE OF SOLOMON HIDDEN UNDER PYRAMID. That information provided the first of three clues to the history and whereabouts of the celebrated golden Temple and the full story soon unfolds. Directly associated with the Temple of Solomon, and also found in 33 consecutive letters (on page 33) are the words, JESUS CHRIST, INITIATION, GREAT PYRAMID.

CHAPTER SEVEN

THE LOST HISTORY OF THE PYRAMIDS

Not half the truth is known about the Great Pyramid and its immediate environs, and to fully comprehend the profundity of the Secret in the Bible, it is imperative to bring forth new and untold knowledge about the primitive Pyramid Plateau. For many centuries, prehistoric Egypt sustained a spectacular civilization and amidst its splendid ruins, crumbling mummies, ancient curses and empty sarcophagi, the major fundamentals of their hidden knowledge is recoverable.

To understand why exclusive information is concealed in the Torah, it is crucial to analyse what is recorded in historic texts about early Egypt, for many of those old documents provide contradictory information to the traditional story expounded in academic circles today. From what was written thousands of years ago, it is shown that the modern-day portrait of pre-Pharaonic Egypt is distorted by overwhelming emphasis on the study of existing crumbling ruins and exotic carvings, and not intriguing narratives of the early historians, including Herodotus' special section headlined, 'The Gods, and whence They sprang'. For example, the physical environment of Heliopolis, Saqqara, Memphis, the Delta and surrounding regions are not the 'total' picture presented today. In 460 BC, Herodotus said of the area:

> I observed that there were sea-shells upon the hills, and that salt exuded from
> the soil to such an extent as even to injure the pyramids; and I noticed also
> that there is but a single hill in all Egypt where sand is found, namely the

hill above Memphis; and further, I found the country to bear no resemblance either to its borderland Arabia, or to Libya…nay, not even to Syria, which forms the seaboard of Arabia.

Herodotus asked the priests if the Nile Delta was originally an inlet of the sea, subsequently filled by the silt brought down by the river during the annual inundation. The priests answered in the affirmative and added that the whole region above Memphis lying between the two ranges of hills, at one time formed a gulf to the sea. Aristotle[1] added that the Red Sea, the Mediterranean and the area now occupied by the Delta, once formed one sea. The Egyptian priests told Herodotus that, 'the sea came almost to the Fayum, and except the province of Thebes, and the whole country was a pestilential swamp'.[2] 'The Mediterranean once reached to the foot of the sandy plateau on which stand the pyramids, and formed a wide gulf where now stretches plain beyond plain of the Delta'.[3] To conclude, the tradition of the ancient Egyptian priesthood and the research of historians reveals that the pyramids at Giza today were originally built by the edge of the Mediterranean Sea.

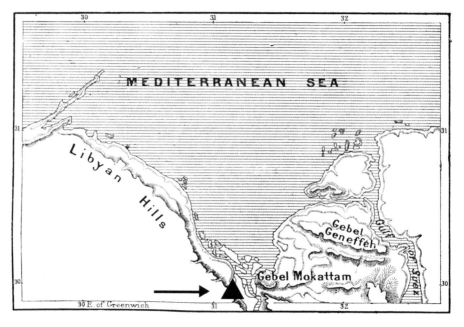

This old map shows the mouth of the Nile before the formation of the Nile Delta. The location of the Great Pyramid is marked.

When Norden visited the Pyramids some 2100 years later (mid-1700s), there were still seashells on the Pyramid Plateau. He was surprised to find in the sand, 'a great number of shells and petrified oysters, which is so much the more surprising, as the Nile never rises high enough to cover this plain; besides that, though it should reach thither, it could not be considered as the cause of them, since this river neither carries, nor has throughout its whole course, any shell-fish. Although there are no shellfish in the Nile, yet they abound in the Red Sea. It might be asked, from whence come these shells such as one finds on the Pyramids themselves?'[4]

Norden's comment that shells were attached to the pyramids revealed that at one time the pyramids were sitting in the sea. Some researchers advanced the possibility that sea-shells provided evidence that the Great Pyramid was erected before the Deluge…a theory substantiated by much-abused Arabian traditions, supported by narratives in the *Book of the Dead* and by a curious watermark running around the Great Pyramid two-thirds of the way up its faces.

The Pyramid Builders

The *Book of the Dead* recorded that the god Thoth was designer and builder of the Great Pyramid and those words were carved into stone at the very dawn of civilization on planet Earth. Elements of that same story were also found in the Pyramid Texts that dated to around 2450 BC and presented in a context that suggested that they were exceedingly old even then. Orthodox Egyptologists, however, constantly insist the builder of the Great Pyramid was Pharaoh Khufu (Cheops in Greek) and that he built it as a tomb specifically for himself. This they state as a fact. It is curious, however, that among all documents that offer evidence to the life and times of Khufu (Cheops), nothing is presented that conclusively links him with the construction of the Great Pyramid. In fact, the opposite applies. A stele in the form of a huge stone scarab symbolizing the god Khepra was found during excavations near the Great Pyramid in June 1954. The inscription carved upon its back stated that Cheops was buried near the south face of the Great Pyramid.

That artifact supported what Egyptian priests told Herodotus 2400 years ago: '...the Nile water was introduced through an artificial duct and surrounds an island where the body of Cheops is said to lie'. Although Cheops may have wished to have been interred in the Great Pyramid, he never was.

A century ago, AP Sinnett, a British journalist and one of few Europeans ever to become a pupil of a Himalayan Mahatma, left some extraordinary notes about what he had learnt during his research trip to the Great Pyramid. He said that documents he witnessed recorded that Pharaoh Cheops simply restored some external portions of the Great Pyramid, closed secret chambers and left his cartouche. That information is supported in the writings of Herodotus but later Egyptologists used that account of renovation work as evidence that Cheops actually built the entire Pyramid. Herodotus cited specifically that the stones Cheops used were, 'none of them less than thirty feet in length...that only polished stone was used...fitted together with the utmost care'. That was a description of the huge white casing stones that faced the pyramid, not the smaller stones that made up the main internal body of the structure. The sort of contrast made between the sizes of the stones indicated that Cheops restored the external facing of the Great Pyramid.

It seems certain that he did effect repairs and was also responsible for the construction of several small royal pyramids to the east of the Great Pyramid, often debased in shape and faulty in proportion. That information is recorded on a stele belonging to his relatives, and the smaller mastabas and some temples surrounding the Great Pyramid were conclusively linked to Cheop's period.

The missing pyramid

So much of Egyptian history is riddled with confusion that it is sometimes hard to know what to believe and the following information introduces an intriguing question: 'What are the ancient eyewitness references to a substantial fourth pyramid at Giza?' The recorded existence of such a structure imparts new knowledge that has the ability to alter everything written in modern times about ancient Egypt and directly affects the Secret in the Bible. Norden gave this remarkable first-hand account of a mysterious black pyramid:

> As to the fourth pyramid it is some one hundred feet more than the third. It is without coating, closed and resembles the others, but without any temple like the first. It has however one particular deserving remark; which is, that its summit is terminated by a single great stone, which seems to have served as a pedestal...the fourth pyramid has been made, upwards above the middle, of a stone more black than the common granite, and at least as hard. Its summit is of a yellowish stone. I shall speak elsewhere of its top, which terminates in a cube. It is, moreover, situated out of the line of the others, being more to the west...it makes a series with the three others.
>
> These four great pyramids are surrounded by a number of others that are smaller; To the west of the first pyramid, we find a great number of others, but all likewise ruined. Opposite the second pyramid, there are five or six of them, which have all been opened, and in one, I have observed a square well, thirty feet deep.[5]

That extraordinary personal description of a fourth major pyramid at Giza, and numerous previously unknown smaller ones, immediately negates the modern-day presentation of the Sphinx and the three familiar pyramids being the original extent of foremost structures on the Giza plateau. Surprisingly, there are additional accounts of Egypt's Black Pyramid and what is recorded of its existence and subsequent demise provides for a complete reinterpretation of all Egyptian religious history currently before mankind.

Ancient confirmation of a Black Pyramid at Giza is found in the most unexpected tradition...the Sacred Legends of the New Zealand Maori. In 1926, Maori Elder and Legend-Carrier, Hohepa Te Rake of Rotorua 'permanently recorded Maori Sacred Legend' in a series of interviews that were subsequently published in a book called *Maori Symbolism*. The report included a substantial description of building the Egyptian pyramids and revealed new information confirmed in historical records. To the ancient Maori such traditions were a sacred trust successfully transmitted from one generation to the next for thousands of years. Hohepa Te Rake moved to prevent the knowledge of his people passing into oblivion, and made the Sacred Legends publicly known. Of particular significance was the belief that Maori forebears laboured on pyramid-building projects under a leader called Parao.

Maori Sacred Legends concerning the pyramids are extensive (40,000 words) and only a brief summary is given here. They state that originally only two pyramids were built at Giza, one White and dedicated to the Sun, the other Black, and dedicated to the Moon. Iamblichus in the fourth century also mentioned a Temple of the Moon (Sin) at Giza and the reverence that it once held.[6] According to the Maori, the basic sub-structure of many pyramids was of blocks made artificially in moulds in somewhat the same manner as concrete building blocks are made today and then faced with glossy casing stones.

Maori tradition maintained that the blocks were made from an aggregate consisting of sand, solid mud from the Sacred River, and rushes and reeds mixed together in a large oblong rectangular bath from which the mixture was run into the moulds the size of blocks required. When the blocks had shrunk and set hard to the satisfaction of the Overseers, the moulds were removed and, by means of rollers and levers, placed in position close to the setting-moulds. The mixing platforms were on the pyramid themselves, and moved upwards as work progressed. The remains of such a structure called Tammaz were recently found in northern Ethiopia and its mud-like blocks were still discernable.

The Pyramid tradition of the Maori claimed that the White and Black pyramids were built on a square-cornered cube-shaped base similar to Assyrian pyramids, and the sloping superstructure now visible of the Great Pyramid is the upper section only (See reconstruction on The Master Plans on final pages). It was believed that the vertical surfaces of the lower section were covered with exquisitely decorated facing stones and Maori legends give special descriptions of that beautifying face-work.

The Maori scheme of historical reckoning is called Jubilees, each Jubilee being a period of forty-nine years (7x7). The Maori regarded their Sacred

Legends in the same way as ancient Israelites regarded the Torah and their tradition extended back approximately 340 Jubilees (17,000 years). The time occupied building the two original pyramids was three Jubilees (3x49 years), being two Jubilees less than the similarly designed Sun and Moon pyramids in Mexico and Peru.

Of special interest in Maori traditions are references to large vertical square-cornered, cube-shaped ornate stone structures used as temples, the same size top and bottom and around half the height of the Great Pyramid. They were built on the Giza Plateau and elsewhere and vines were trained to grow over their walls. Maori Legend recorded that later in time, a new pyramid at Giza was built over one of those cube-shaped structures and the records of Herodotus supported Maori tradition.

The discovery of curious objects

When Arab writer Masoudi spoke of the Great Pyramid, he called it the 'Eastern' pyramid, a standard descriptive phraseology for structures on the Giza Plateau at that time. Another ancient manuscript recorded an extensive description of curious objects found in the 'Western' pyramid. In the 14th century, some old Arabic and Coptic manuscripts were discovered in a Cairo library, which a particular geographer and historian, Muhammed Taki Al-Makrizi, reproduced in detail into his own work called 'Hitat'. The documents he found may have been the tenth century writings of Masoudi, as there was some indication that he was the original author of the recovered manuscripts. In 'Hitat' was recorded evidence of the discovery of striking relics in a pyramid at Giza:

> Then the builder had put thirty treasury chambers of coloured granite into the Western Pyramid. They were filled with rich treasures with instruments and picture columns, of precious stones, with equipment of fine iron, like weapons which do not rust, glass you can fold without breaking, with strange charms and lanterns, various kinds of simple and mixed medicines and with deadly poisons…and corpses of the soothsayers, in sarcophagi of black granite, and beside each soothsayer lay a book, in which were written all his magical arts, his life's story and the works he had accomplished.[7]

The 'Western Pyramid' at Giza at that time was the Black Pyramid and the discoveries were things undreamt of in those times…non-corrosive iron and plastics. The 'thirty treasury chambers' were not found in today's Western-most pyramid, Mycinerus, for detailed records revealed that it was opened in 1196, thoroughly searched, and its solitary chamber razed. The only discovery of importance in that pyramid is discussed in a later chapter.

The reference to 'glass you can fold without breaking' is of particular interest. Persons believing that the pyramid builders worked only in stone and knew nothing of clear plastic or glass need to study the treasures of Tutankhamun (Tut Ankh Amun) on display in the Egyptian Museum in Cairo. The exquisitely carved handles of two pure-gold bladed knives were crafted from a solid translucent glass-like substance. Ancient Egyptian priests told Herodotus that the Great Pyramid had hidden within it 'machines of transparent metal…in secret chambers…of stately architecture…with odd types of mechanical artifacts that could never be understood at first glance…strangely designed…to stifle one's imagination'. Although those records were written in the remote past, the priests who read them out to Herodotus believed them to be true, 'and I can only repeat the account given to me' (Herodotus).

Norden commented that the fourth pyramid was stepped with black stones to its upper levels and topped off near the summit with yellow stones to the level of the platform upon which sat the huge cube-stone. Scalloped into the four vertical faces of the cube-stone was the depiction of a human-headed ram facing east, creating a type of mini-Sphinx structure sitting high on the Giza Plateau. What was originally standing on top of the cube-stone was unrecorded but using a combination of old records and associating them with a series of later events at Giza, it is possible to determine what was displayed upon its upper platform and that will be discussed later.

A record of the destruction of the Black Pyramid was found in Masonic literature and revealed that work commenced in 1759 and took ten months to complete. A Scottish faction of the Masonic movement motivated by the possible discovery of hidden treasure was responsible for its demise. They took the initiative to dismantle the structure with the support of the English Freemasons who were promised a share of proceeds from any discovery to finance the expansion of their movement. The black stones were sold to help finance the operation[8] and some are seen in buildings in Cairo today. They measured 2'9" square and were identified as originally being quarried about 16 kilometres SWW of Giza. The square floor-base of stone can still be seen approximately 100 metres up the sandy rise west of Mycinerus' Pyramid, and identified on the 2001 satellite photo of the Giza Plateau. Dimensions currently available determined that the Black Pyramid was 159'6" high, and the cube-stone on top was 5'8" in all its measurements.

This satellite photo shows the square outline of the remains of the Black Pyramid. The external stone enclosure common to pyramids is also still in place.

Other pyramids

The Pharaoh to whom the construction of the middle Giza pyramid is attributed was Khephren (Fourth Dynasty: 2720 BC to 2560 BC) and that was probably historically so. Khephren's pyramid is vastly inferior to the Great Pyramid both in design and in construction and appears to be only a crude copy of the original. Its interior layout is simple, unsophisticated, and void of the complex design elements found in the Great Pyramid. Khephren 'was accused of sacrilege, of cruelty and extravagance', and was bitterly disliked by the populace, as was Cheops. The hatred towards him commenced when he ordered the closing of a special temple dedicated to the great Sun-god RA and prohibited the offering of sacrifices. He forced all Egyptians to work for him and it seemed that he compelled them to build his pyramid. This premise suggests that Khephren's pyramid was constructed over a cube-shaped temple on the Giza Plateau and that provided the substructure similar to the exposed core of the pyramid of Medum. Egyptian priests told Herodotus that 'one pyramid was built to great opposition' and it seemed that it was Khephren's pyramid, for he purposely built it over the esteemed Temple of the Solar-men. That is the missing Temple of Solomon and its location is shown on The Master Plans (See end of book).

Both Herodotus[9] and Manetho preserved the knowledge that the smaller Giza pyramid, known today as Mycinerus, was built by a woman called Nitokris (also known as Rhodopis), the last queen of the VI dynasty. Some Egyptologists maintained that Nitokris simply ordered its completion by adding the costly casing stones, for Mycinerus died before he finished his project. After Nitokris, tradition was silent, and the history of Egypt remained a mere blank for several centuries. However, whatever was the truth during that time, the fact remained that ancient tradition maintained that there were originally only two pyramids at Giza...one to Sin the god that some believed presided over the Moon, the other to Horus of the Sun...and the river that ran by was named Sin-Hor after them.

The 'great number' of smaller pyramids to the west of the Great Pyramid that Norden described are not there today but it seems that they were associated with Star-worship. From the beginning of the IVth to the end of the XIVth dynasty, more than 1500 years, the construction of pyramids of all sizes was a common State affair, provided for by the administration and secured by special services. Princes and princesses belonging to the family of Pharaohs constructed personal versions, each one sized according to their private resources. They were all built to ancient specifications from 'a Book descended from Heaven to the north of Memphis' (Heliopolis) and one, faced with alabaster stone, is recorded as being demolished in 590 BC. From what it was possible to uncover about the lost history of the Pyramid Plateau, it seems that Sun, Moon and Star-worship were all practised at the complex at various times in its ancient past.

The pyramids of later times were of no major interest in the proposition being developed in this work, for the core of the story is concerned mainly with the Great Pyramid. That is the largest of all pyramids; the most perfect mathematically and geometrically, containing major design elements missing from others that were specific in establishing the Secret. The Great Pyramid was the heaviest and most precise structure known on Earth, and so old that its origin became lost in the shadows of time. It is probable that it was the first structure ever built on Earth, and while traditional Egyptologists contend that it was a tomb, modern archaeological evidence leans strongly towards a much greater purpose or purposes. Today's accumulation of data indicates that the Great Pyramid alone enshrined a lost science…and what is currently known of that inexplicable ingredient relates directly to the Secret in the Bible.

Ancient descriptions of the Great Pyramid

The earliest known name for the Great Pyramid was Khûît, the 'Horizon', and later it was known as 'Adoni', a pure Hebrew word meaning literally 'my Master'. As a significant word in the higher degrees of Masonry, it was translated 'a most excellent Master' and was the origin of the title, 'Rabboni'. That description arose in the first century school of Hillel and was originally given to only seven wise men who were pre-eminent for their understanding of the secrets of the Great Pyramid.

There was apparent mention of the Great Pyramid in the Old Testament and a number of other references in various biblical writings. The author of the Book of Isaiah spoke of an 'altar to the Lord in the midst of the land of Egypt' and Jeremiah talked of 'signs and wonders in the land of Egypt even unto this day'. The books of Isaiah and Jeremiah were composed much later than generally claimed and are now dated to the period around the reforms of Ezra and Nehemiah, that being in the latter years of the fourth century BC.

Herodotus recorded that each of the structure's four perfectly triangular faces of highly-polished blocks were so finely joined that those joins could scarcely be seen at close range, making the Pyramid appear as one solid piece of white stone. He said there was no apparent entrance or exit visible from the outside. In a biblical writing called the Pastor of Hermas, there is a reference to an opening in the Great Pyramid:

> ...and in the middle of the sand, he showed me a great white rock, which had risen out of the plain, and the rock was higher than mountains and angular so as to be able to point to the whole world; but that rock was old, having a hole hewn out of it, and the hewing out of the hole seemed to me to be recent.[10]

Contributors to the *Oxford Dictionary of the Christian Church* dated that writing 'around 100 BC'[11] and attributed its authorship to Hermas. That record revealed that an attempt to enter the Great Pyramid was made around 300 years after the time of Herodotus.

An inscription on a stele of Pharaoh Pi-Ankhi revealed that the capstone or pyramidion had been removed from the top of the Great Pyramid before his personal visit to the area around 750 BC, leaving just a flat, square top 'like a platform'. An eighth century record said that the external lining was still in place up to the platform and a radiant segment of seven horizontal bands of spectrum colours ran unbroken around the uppermost levels of the structure. Engraved vertically down the bands of colour were seven curious inscriptions, positioned in the centre of the top band and dropping down each face to the bottom or seventh band. Apart from the Egyptian priesthood's ancient tradition and the legends of Arabic people, evidence that the upper section of the Great Pyramid was once painted was historically established when chunks of casing stones with one rusty-coloured surface were found around its base early in the 19th century. Subjected to careful chemical and spectrographic analysis at the Sorbonne University at Paris, it was determined that the casing stones examined had once been covered with a layer of paint made from an iron oxide base. It was known that ancient Egyptians used anhydritic iron oxide to make the colour red, and yellow was composed from hydrated iron oxide. Blue was made from powered azurite, lapis or copper carbonate, and green from malachite. Therefore, it was probable that the stones the French analysts were studying were originally painted either red or yellow. Scientists claimed that the colouring on the facing of the stones was not caused by chemical recomposition of the stone itself, but by an external application of a product.

Nothing but the finest and whitest limestone was used on the Great Pyramid and that was extracted from the quarries of Turah, just 16 kilometres from Giza. Two-hundred-year-old records revealed that those quarries were almost as fascinating as the monuments made out of their material:

> The extraction of stone was carried on with a skill and regularity which denoted ages of experience. The tunnels were so made as to exhaust the finest and whitest seams without waste and the chambers were of an enormous extent; the walls were dressed, the pillars and roofs neatly finished, the passages and doorways made of a regular width, so that the whole presented more the appearance of a subterranean temple than of a place for the extraction of building materials.[12]

In the early 1800s, the mines were reopened, and by 1870, work by the Cairo masons destroyed the greater part of the ancient remains formerly existing under the Turah district, completely changing the original character of the mines.

Stone cutters in the Turah quarries dressing limestone blocks for repairs to the White Walls of Memphis (Drawn by Faucher-Gudin, from 'Rosellini', Monumenti civili, pl. xiviii. 2).

The entire white limestone casing was eventually stripped from the Great Pyramid to provide masonry for Cairo's oldest mosques and fortifications. The Mosque of the Sultan Hassan (dated around 1290) was a fine example of the use of the original external covering of the Pyramid, for it had been entirely built from the casing–stones plundered from the Great Pyramid. However, a small amount of those once–brilliant stones are still around the base of the north wall today, and it was calculated from their size that they each weighed between 15 and 20 tons. Those massive blocks were six-sided, approximately three metres thick (around 9 feet), and cut to within 0.01 (1/100th) of an inch. They were perfectly honed and held together with a type of white cement stronger than the blocks themselves. That cement was apparently reduced to the consistency of paint but held the stones together with such tenacity that the rocks split rather than the joints separate.

© Rudolf Lehnert c. 1920

A photo of the Pyramids at Giza around 1890. Note the closeness of the River Nile to the Great Pyramid in the right foreground. Today the Nile is more than 5 miles away.

Symbols once carved on the Great Pyramid

Several ancient documents stated that the casing-stones were originally inscribed with symbols containing 'a peculiar sort of wisdom'.[13] In an old scroll preserved in the Bodleian Library, Abou Balkhi, an astronomer-astrologer of the eighth century recorded this tradition:

> Two of those (pyramids) exceeded all the rest in height, being 400 cubits high, and as many broad, and as many long. They were built of large blocks of stone, and so well joined together that the joints were scarcely perceptible. Upon the exterior of one structure (The Great Pyramid) was inscribed every charm and wonder of physics.

Masoudi (tenth century), another Arabian author, related similar information, even more circumstantially, and said:

> On the Eastern or Great Pyramid, built by the ancients, the celestial spheres were inscribed, likewise the positions of the stars and their circles, together with the history and chronicles of past times, of that which is to come, and of every future event. Also one may find there the fixed stars and what comes about in their progression from one epoch to another…and images made of their forefathers' creations.

The relevant words are those that referred to symbols predicting or foreseeing future events and the inscriptions of 'charm'. Those prophetic words related directly to the Book of Thoth and anything associated with Thoth's work was associated with the Secret in the Bible. During the research for this book the author spent time in the Mosque of the Sultan Hassan in Cairo in an attempt to find a section of casing-stone that still preserved part of the inscriptions once on the outside of the Great Pyramid. The task was made difficult by the fact that it was the holy month of Ramadan and unrestricted access to the Mosque was denied.

Multi-coloured pyramids

Because there are still panels of white casing stones to be seen high up on Khephren's Pyramid, it is generally thought that the whole pyramid was once entirely white like the Great Pyramid. However, only a section of the 'facing, of which about one-fourth exists from the summit downwards, is of white limestone'.[14] Herodotus added to the account: 'For the basement the builder employed the many-coloured stones of Ethiopia'. The lower levels were faced with various shades of red and grey stones, 'with a low polish, which, at a distance, reflects the sun's rays' and two courses of coloured stones were still 'in situ' when Vyse was there in 1837.[15] The surviving higher-level casing stones on Khephren's pyramid are irregular, jagged, thin and ill fitting, and establishes the inferior construction of that pyramid compared to the Great Pyramid.

According to Herodotus[16] the external casing of Mycinerus' Pyramid was 'built half its height of the stone of Ethiopia'. That was red or rose coloured granite, and many blocks still exist upon, and around, the pyramid today. Diodorus[17] stated that the layers of red granite extended up to the fifteenth course while Professor Petrie calculated that there were at one time sixteen lower courses of red granite. The upper levels were finished with white limestone. 'The beauty and richness of the granite casing dazzled all eyes, and induced many visitors to prefer the smallest of the pyramids to its imposing sisters'.[18]

Part of the reinstated external casing stones (arrowed) on the northern face of the third pyramid, Mycinerus. Note the damage made by forced entry into the structure. A granite sarcophagus found in the pyramid was lost off the coast of Spain in the vessel taking it to England.

The destruction of extraordinary structures

Herodotus commented that Egyptians so detested the memory of particularly Cheops and Khephren that they would not even mention their names or acknowledge their association with the pyramids. 'Hence they commonly called the pyramids after Philition, a shepherd who at that time fed his flocks about the place'.[19] In a book written by George Ivanovich Gurdjieff entitled *Meetings With Remarkable Men*,[20] the author related that he once obtained a map of 'pre-sand Egypt' complete with the Pyramids and Sphinx in place. Yet, that picture of a green Giza plateau had another side.

Around the year 1200, an Arab writer, Abd'el-Latif, compiled a concise record about Cairo and its environs. He was a doctor from Baghdad who taught medicine and philosophy in Cairo. He visited Giza, spent time inside the Great Pyramid, studied the Sphinx in detail, which, he said, was originally called Naampku, and preserved his observations. Abd'el-Latif affirmed that around the entire area, substantial ancient stone structures were extensive and wrote: 'It requires a half-day's march in any direction to cross the visible ruins'. It would be conservative to suggest that a person would march five kilometres an hour and if half-a-day was established at four hours, then, around the time of Abd'el-Latif's visit some 800 years ago, there existed monumental stone ruins covering a 20 kilometre radius around the Great Pyramid.

In 1737, English traveller Richard Pococke, visited Egypt and recorded the damage to monuments in his book, *Travels in Egypt*, saying: 'They are every day destroying these fine morsels of Egyptian antiquity, and I saw some of the pillars being hewn into mill-stones'. The profound change in the landscape is a matter of public record. However, of more than 90 pyramids that remain at 12 major sites up and down the Nile, those at Giza and Saqqara are the largest. Visible for miles across the desert, they overshadow the smaller structures built around them, but those pyramids were never stand-alone structures but part of a whole geology of pyramids, temples and mastabas. Excluding the complex at Giza, remaining today between Giza and Saqqara are only four Old Kingdom step pyramids, one Old Kingdom king's mastaba, and twelve Old Kingdom 'true Pyramids' (cased). Herodotus not only referred to the 'vast field of ruins at Memphis' but to the existence of an extraordinary temple to Isis in the area, 'well worthy of notice', but no longer existing.

The last two and a half centuries witnessed devastation in that same area on a scale that is scarcely believable. No one tried to officially measure the extent of the loss, but perhaps 99% is not far from the truth. Three influences from the modern world largely determined the fate of ancient ruins, particularly those in the precinct of Cairo: Economic modernization, population pressure, and the outside world's fascination with Egypt and its illustrious past. Economic transformation began early in the nineteenth century and quickly hit hard at archaeological sites. A number of ruins became quarries for building stone, but the main damage came through a nationwide move to quarry ancient settlements for agricultural fertilizer, sometimes on an industrial scale, and lasting for 270 years. In that brutal way, countless ancient sites of major historical significance were ground into dust and removed forever from the face of the earth.

An Egyptian government department was set up to protect antiquities in 1858, but its vision was long restricted to art treasures and monuments. At the same time, the desire for buried treasure among the local population was inflamed by worldwide passion for collecting Egyptian antiquities. Official agreements led to a number of conspicuous monuments (including three obelisks) being exported to Europe and North America, but their loss was nothing to the methodical looting of sites, sometimes under official licence. Desert cemeteries where ancient artifacts were often remarkably well preserved were prime targets. The theft and export of antiquities, although by no means suppressed, is today no longer a scandal…there is much less to steal.[21]

It was difficult to think that pyramids of considerable dimensions could have disappeared without leaving traces, especially when enormous masses of masonry still mark the sites of similar monuments that were most injured. The crumbling ruins of smaller pyramids around the mummy-pits at Saqqara provide examples of just how much rubble is associated with a crumbling pyramid. The remains of those Giza pyramids, including the Black Pyramid, were removed before the advent of photography in the 1840s, for they do not appear on any of the oldest photos of the Pyramid Plateau currently available. Many Pharaohs themselves were responsible for the destruction of earlier monuments and pyramids. Rameses II had little respect for the works of his predecessors, and demolished a part of the pyramid of Medum in order to procure cheaply the materials necessary for the buildings he restored to Heracleopolis.

A crumbling pyramid; the entrance to the Pyramid of Unas at Saqqara (Drawn by Boudier, from a photograph by Emil Brugsch-Bey, circa 1890).

Strange construction processes at Giza

By and large, modern pyramidologists forced to choose between regarding the records of a supernatural construction of the Great Pyramid as fact or fiction, have chosen to treat them as fiction. However, mankind is left with some extraordinary ancient records providing fascinating narratives relating to unusual procedures in place in the development of structures in Egypt.

An intriguing tradition handed down by pre-Christian Egyptian priests stated that the Great Pyramid was built from the top down. They told Herodotus:

> The upper portion of the Pyramid was built first, then the middle, and finally the part which was lowest and nearest the ground.

Such a construction process conjured up mental images of peculiar antigravity devices lifting and moving stones and operated by people of an unknown nature. However, the Great Pyramid *was* built from the top down and an upcoming chapter expands upon that aspect of its development. While discussing rock and antigravity, an ancient Arabic papyrus recorded one method of moving weighty stones: 'they put sheets of papyrus on which were written secret things beneath the stones and struck them with a rod. Whereupon the stones moved through the air by distance of one bowshot. In this way, they eventually reached the Pyramids'.

One of the most intriguing accounts of building the Great Pyramid was that given by Herodotus. He said: 'I perfectly well remember that the interpreter who read the writing to me (the hieroglyphic descriptions) said that 'they had a machine'. Recorded some 2400 years ago was mention of 'a machine' that related to a much early period and the Old Testament book of Joshua[22] spoke of a 'machine' that stopped working.

Herodotus also mentioned 'engines resting on the stones'. Diodorus Siculus recorded a similar description of raising stones 'with engines on top…and stones sitting on…imaginary heaps of earth'. Academics supposed that engines had not yet been invented, and referred to those references as 'being too absurd to take any notice of'.[23] But it 'was a time when the Gods ruled on Earth; later they handed over the kingship to earthly rulers'.[24]

Whatever the truth of those old writings can be personally assessed by the reader, but it seems that the use of sound in moving blocks of stone was known and mastered by the Ancients, including Tibetans. Rumour suggested that a Swedish museum holds a film taken in Tibet of stone being raised up from the ground and moved into position exclusively by the sound of long *ragdon*-trumpets. Swedish traveller, Sven Hedin, recorded the event early in the 20th Century (c. 1929-31) and the film footage is believed to still be in existence. An interesting ancient Sanskrit script in the Indian temple of

Hoysalesvara read: ' Some day man will know how to lift the bull without effort, and easily hitch the twelve wheels to the carriage which will carry 2000 elephants, strength in one strength, 10,000 horses, speed in one speed, and then man will be able to travel up to the sun in a vessel'. An ancient Egyptian hieroglyph translated by Wallis Budge at the British Museum in London spoke of a 'vessel' among the presents given to the Queen of Sheba 'where-in one could travel by air'.[25]

On 25 September 1952, GR Josyner, director of the International Academy of Sanskrit Research in Mysore, India, shocked the world when he revealed that Indian manuscripts several thousand years old recorded the existence of various types of aerial vessels called 'vimanas'. Six thousand lines of lucid Sanskrit recorded intricate details of the choice and preparation of metals suitable to build different types of aircraft for both civil aviation and warfare. Eight chapters in the 'aeronautics' manuscript provided detailed descriptions of craft that flew in the air, travelled underwater or floated pontoon-like on the water's surface. Some 500 stanzas told of qualifications and training of pilots and detailed on-board equipment such as cameras, radios and a type of radar. The scrolls were preserved in monasteries centuries before the Wright Brothers made the world's first 1000 ft (305m) powered flight at Kitty Hawk in 1903. Coronation Press of Mysore published the manuscripts in book form in English in 1973, and gave the public a certified record of flying machines on Earth thousands of years ago.

Just what is the Great Pyramid?

The prime question regarding the Great Pyramid, no matter what theory one favours about itS age, was why was it built at all? Standard textbooks insisted it was nothing more than a gigantic tomb for a megalomaniac Pharaoh, yet no mummy, hieroglyphic inscriptions, or treasure was ever found. The interior system is so unusual that its construction appears to have been designed completely and purposely for a specific reason. It provides a complex system of passages and chambers found nowhere else on Earth except within the confines of the Great Pyramid and are so mathematically precise that it had to have been pre-determined by the designer. The geometry is too perfect to have been accidental, being constructed to within fractions of a degree. The optometrist's precision of the Great Pyramid demonstrates a fully developed grasp of mathematics, astronomy, geography, navigation, engineering, architecture and complex building and structural techniques at an estimated time of construction without a demonstrable period for the learning of those complicated sciences.

To many, it appeared strange that anyone should go to such an enormous amount of effort to build an imposing structure around a few empty chambers and a curious single, empty, lidless coffer. Stranger still was the manner in which the coffer was built. Among the reasons why the sarcophagus in the Great Pyramid is a veritable miracle in stone, and the profoundest single object in the world, are the spiral markings of drills used to hollow out its interior. To bore out granite thus, as a carpenter bores out wood, requires not only a drill of extreme hardness and toughness, but a machine permitting overhead pressure ranging from one to two tons. That the craftsmen who built the Great Pyramid had and used such drills was established by the evidence of the character of the work done, for in no other way could the existing drill markings in the floor of the sarcophagus be made in that once-solid block of stone. It is an interesting fact that the cubic capacity of the coffer is the same as the biblical 'Ark of the Covenant', that mysterious chest that was said in the Bible to have performed a series of supernatural acts. The situation became even more confused when Egyptologists noticed an unusual phenomenon in the empty sarcophagus. When a hand was placed in the coffer, a bright violet glow appeared around it, shimmering as the hand was shaken. Later experiments showed that the light intensified with sound resonance.

The layout of the Great Pyramid represents a very serious piece of work; nothing is out of place. It is complex, stark and exacting, giving a strong impression that it was built as a device for something specific. The overwhelming opinion is that it had a strict function and a particular design purpose. The Grand Gallery, for example, is a corbelled passageway of unparalleled dimensions, a magnificent piece of architecture being literally perfection in stone, its precision causing great scholars to shake their heads in disbelief. Built in seven vertical overlapping stages, its walls close in ever more at each stage of its height, a breathtaking and unusual sight. The austerity of the Great Pyramid's interior presents a forbidding and haunting atmosphere, particularly with the underpowered electric lights now operating within it. The whole of that gigantic structure is impressive and the precision of its overall construction is daunting. It is interlaced and crisscrossed with perfectly built corridors, chambers, channels and halls, and is void of any ancient hieroglyphic inscriptions, unlike the Unas tomb with its mass of carvings preserving the name of Unas in oval cartouches at the centre of inscriptions.

AP Sinnett, in his book, *Collected Fruits of Occult Teaching*, provided a tantalising clue to why the Great Pyramid was built:

> I have gathered a hint to the effect that, although no doubt from the beginning used as and designed to be temples or chambers of initiation...the Great Pyramid, for one, certainly containing other chambers besides the three that have been discovered...one purpose of the Great Pyramid was the protection of some tangible objects of great importance having to do with the occult mysteries. These were buried in the rock, it is said, and the pyramid was reared over them, its form and magnitude being adopted to render it safe from the hazards of earthquake, and even from the consequence of submergence beneath the sea during the great secular undulations of the Earth's surface.[26]

In context of Sinnett's theory of underground crypts below the Great Pyramid, the possible X-raying deep below the Pyramid proper assumed great importance in the last 30 years, but could not successfully proceed because technology was not capable of probing the extensive distance to reach the centre of the Great Pyramid due to the sheer size of the complex.

Inside the Sphinx

The great monument called the Sphinx is more than an emblem of the Egyptian nation, it is the archetype of antiquity whose image stirred the imagination of painters, photographers, poets, songwriters, adventurers and tourists for many tens of centuries. Stoic beholder of ancient Egypt's passing civilizations and eternal sentry of major aspects of the Secret of the Giza plain, the Sphinx is, like the Great Pyramid, directly linked to the Torah of the Bible. Looking at the tired old edifice, one can only feel sorry for it as it struggles against the ravages of time and the unforgivable encroachment of the modern noisy city.

Today it gazes directly at two American fast food outlets just 300 metres in front of its huge paws, a sad reflection upon city planning, and one that removed the dignity that the Sphinx once held. The decay of the Sphinx was brought into the public domain when a lump from one shoulder fell off in 1988, and turned what was once a symbol of enigmatic wisdom of the past into a symbol of its vulnerability. The Sphinx, like the pyramids, is now stripped of its original beauty and perfection and one can only be appalled at its condition and the sorry state of its immediate environment.

Looking down the Plateau to the Sphinx. Its state of deterioration is apparent, showing the veneers of ancient and modern restoration masonry.

Only with a clear understanding of what transpired in the precinct over the centuries would it be possible to understand a major problem associated with that giant stone creature. The Sphinx is set in a hollowed-out enclosure that, when left unattended, fills with shifting sand to its neck every few decades. Herodotus did not mention the Sphinx in his writings, for it was possible at that time the monument was completely covered in sand. The first evidence of sand clearing was recorded in stone symbols in the now-called Dream Stella that Thutmosis IV had erected between the Sphinx's paws. His inscription recorded that the Sphinx was buried up to its neck in sand in 1400 BC and his documentation provided evidence of the first known attempt to preserve the dignity of the massive monster. The implication of the Thutmosis Stella was that he freed the Sphinx from the sand and thereby became Pharaoh. Mud brick walls inscribed with his name survived in remnants in the precinct and confirmed that Thutmosis IV had provided the necessary work force for the undertaking.

Ancient sources again attested that the Sphinx was cleared of sand for a second time in 500 BC when it may also have been painted. In the Roman period (30 BC–second century), the desert had again encroached upon its precincts and further clearing was undertaken. At that time, the floor of the area around the sanctuary was paved in stone and an altar built between the Sphinx's paws. The fact that Roman restorers did not violate the original Old Kingdom stones suggested they respected the older masonry and its original structure.

The Sphinx covered in sand with the Great Pyramid in the background. In the foreground is the Temple of the Sphinx also partly covered in sand. Note the stone steps arching over the sand heading towards the top of the back of the Sphinx. The huge split across the rear of the back of the Sphinx was later repaired with concrete, and contains a removable hatch. The head of the Sphinx shows remnants of its once-painted red face (Drawn by Boudier, from a photograph by Emil Brugsch-Bey, circa 1890).

In 1925, the Sphinx was again covered to the top of its back. The Egyptian Antiquities Service engaged Emile Baraize to clear the area and move the sand deep back into the desert. After a massive eleven-year project, hundreds of workers and their camels, under the guidance of Baraize, once more freed the Sphinx from constantly moving sands, and at the same time removed large alluvial sand and sea-shell build-ups against the bases of all pyramids. It seemed strange that no excavation report of the massive undertaking could be found, but it was recorded that the 'beard of divinity' was discovered in the sand.

It is a little-known fact that the temples of Luxor and Karnak were also at one time beneath the desert sands, and even in the years 1900-1920 there were portions of Luxor upon which native mud-houses had been built without any suspicion that beneath them existed huge and magnificent ancient temples. The columns of the Temple of Luxor, over eighty feet in height, were at one time entirely beneath the surface of the sands that had accumulated and all needed to be removed basketful by basketful to unearth and uncover the beautiful temples beneath.

The head of the Sphinx, as we see it today, is badly damaged. Napoleon's canon-master, Mamelukes, was often blamed for the defacement, but that was erroneous. Earlier drawings of the Sphinx in the Egyptian Library indicated that the damage occurred in the 14th or 15th century. Vandals hammered steel rods or chisels of some sort into the top of the nose and under its right nostril, then levered off the nose.

There is general and growing support for the view that the Sphinx and the Great Pyramid are far older than orthodoxy will currently accept. Egyptologists are not in complete accord themselves and present the current theory that the Sphinx was built by Pharaoh Khephren at the same time he built the middle pyramid. Their conclusion was established from the recovery of an intact statue of Khephren found in a pit in the Valley Temple near the Sphinx. However, there is a variety of opinion opposing that belief and many researchers treat that view as purely circumstantial. Writing shortly before his death in 1934, Sir Wallis Budge, then Keeper of Egyptian Antiquities at the British Museum in London, had no hesitation in recording that the Sphinx was much older than generally thought. He said: 'The Sphinx was thought to be connected in some way with foreigners or with a foreign religion which dated from pre-dynastic time'.[27] Budge was of the opinion that it existed before the time of the Pharaohs, but its head today certainly looks very dynastic.

The head of the Sphinx

Leading archaeologists established that the severe weathering of the Sphinx 'except for the head', was caused by water erosion. That could only have happened in distant times for the Sphinx was buried in sand for a recorded time of around 3000 years. In that time, documents showed the head was exposed above the sand for some 2000 years, yet today it showed less erosion than the sand-protected body.

Evidence of severe water erosion on the Giza Plateau: This extraordinary depiction was painstakingly reproduced from an original black and white photograph taken early during the 1920 sand-clearing years. The Pyramid in the background is Khephren's. One analyst of this picture claimed that the huge stone structure encompassing the front right of the picture is the south-east back corner of the Sphinx before modern refacing commenced (Boudier, from a photograph by Beats).

The premise being developed in this work contends that the erosion of the Sphinx was caused by the action of centuries of declining seawaters, and that the head seen today was the result of restructuring by a later Pharaoh. From the proportions of the current head relative to the size of the body, it appears that it was reduced by reshaping in later times. There are various ancient hieroglyphic stone inscriptions existing today that give clues to what the head of the Sphinx originally may have been.

The first of those thousands-of-years-old words recorded the reverence paid to the Ram, the sacred animal of Amun, god of the Air ('The Hidden One'). Today, two superb 'Avenues of Ram-headed Sphinxes' (criosphinx) line the grounds of the Great Temple of Amun, revealing the great respect for Amun. There is also circumstantial evidence accumulating in the understanding that the Sphinx was originally designed and intentionally built as a panther/leopard/lion.

In ancient times, the Sphinx was referred to as 'god', and in one old papyrus it was called the 'Great God Felis Leo who presided over the Divine Palace'.[28] Leo was the little-known Egyptian god mentioned earlier and it was probable that the Sphinx was originally named after him, or that he built it. A Roman inscription at Giza said the Sphinx was 'the work of the Immortal Gods', being an intrinsic part of 'a Message sent from Heaven by the Masters of Wisdom' and that directly connected Leo to the structure. Leo was also chosen as the emblem for an Egyptian city called Leo-polis and the word 'Leonine' was attached to anything pertaining to, or resembling, Leo. Because the original God Leo represented Mystery and divine leadership, thirteen popes subsequently called themselves 'Leo' and the first Christian Leo (d. 461) called his papal residence at Rome, Leonine. It was Leo I who wrote the *Tome of Leo,* a curious writing in which he tried to explain the two natures of Christ, a subject fully unravelled in *The Bible Fraud.*

Historical writings revealed that when the Sphinx was cleared of sand in 500 BC it sported 'pointed brass claws large enough for a workman to sit upon', and today the tufted tail of a lion can still be identified. It is not generally known that the Sphinx once had carved stone wings folded along its back and sides similar to the smaller lion sphinxes at Saqqara. When Norden was at Giza in the mid-1700s, they were still in place, and, for some reason, he extended the opinion that, 'the wings on the Sphinx were probably added later'.

The belief developed among Middle Kingdom Egyptians that the lion slept with its eyes open and for that reason the animal was chosen as a symbol of vigilance. That belief may have developed from the original lion Sphinx at Giza being carved with its eyes permanently open. The figure of a lion placed on either side of doors and gateways became an emblem of divine guardianship and maybe the lion sphinxes remaining today were smaller depictions of the Giza original.

To the temple priests, the cat-family was symbolic of the ancient teachings of the Panthers and they surrounded themselves with those animals in pious respect. Egyptians paid homage to all sorts of cats, especially when their fur was of three shades or their eyes of different colours. If a cat died a natural death in a house, all occupants of that house shaved their eyebrows. They embalmed their dead cats, and carried them to Budastis for interment in the sacred house of the famous goddess Bast, the cat-deity of the Ptolemies. Interestingly, mythology held that the cat was the only animal absent at the death of the great Buddha, because it had stopped on the way to his passing to chase a mouse.

© Archives Photo Library, Florence

The Horus Sphinx. This statue was found by Dr Heinrich Schliemann during excavations at the ancient city of Troy (1870-90). Its head has a remarkable likeness to stone depictions of Horus.

In later times, Pharaohs built an array of temples and tombs around the Sphinx and naked, uncoffined bodies of common people were buried in the sand about it, complete with provisions to nourish them during the period of their second existence. It was commonly believed that the Sphinx was hewn out of solid rock but that is not so. The Sphinx is hollow with three entrances and in the last decade or so, workmen internally strengthened its back with vertical trusses and criss-crossed steel supports to prevent the monument from collapsing.

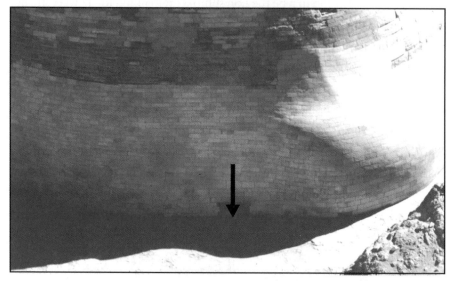

Rear entrance into Sphinx (arrowed).

The Sphinx mounted guard over the eastern extremity of the Plateau from the time of the Followers of Horus and the next chapter clarifies its direct association with the Great Pyramid. With the knowledge that the Temple of the Moon was on the western edge of the Plateau, the intriguing possibility arises of the existence of a second Sphinx-like structure yet to be found under the encroaching sands of Giza. There is significance in the fact that the jackal-headed god Anubis is constantly referred to by ancient Egyptian priests as 'he who is guide over Half the World' (evening), words of vital significance in this study. In the Tutankhamun tomb-discovery, the entrance was patiently watched over by a startling lifelike effigy of Anubis and it is not difficult to imagine the same black dog head, gilded collar, pointed ears erect, white eyes glaring, crouched, with its forepaws out-stretched, sitting in front of the Black Pyramid, 'waiting for his disc to appear in the night sky' (The Moon). The Greeks called the cult city of Anubis, Sinopolis (later Cynopolis) and this author contends that that complex still exists under the sand southwest of the location of the Black Pyramid.

The motif, however, of an animal, bird or serpent 'protecting' or looking over a god or secret place, was common in ancient Egypt and constantly depicted in two and three-dimensional sculpture. Anubis (canine), the lion (feline), and Horus (birds) were certainly guardians in that time...but what was the Sphinx at Giza protecting?

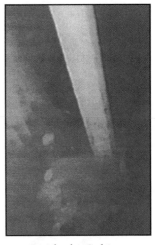

Inside the Sphinx.
Note steps leading down.

Two Babylons

When describing the city of Cairo, the opening words in a colour promotional brochure issued by the Egyptian Ministry of Tourism said: 'Founded on the site of Babylon, near the ruins of ancient Memphis, Cairo has been the largest city in Africa for centuries'. History books today, however, describe Babylon as 'a city of Babylonia, noted for its luxurious living, the most magnificent city in the ancient world of South West Asia'. That statement provides a confliction, for Egyptian records state that the original location of Babylon was at a suburb now called Old Cairo in Cairo city, and named after an ancient god called Babylon. Research at the spectacular Bibliotheca Alexandrina by the Mediterranean revealed that the Romans rebuilt an old fortress in now-called Old Cairo under Emperor Trajan (98-117) that was later enlarged by Emperor Diocletian (284-305). The old site the Romans redeveloped was originally called Per-hapi-en-on, and at that time, it overlooked the River Nile that has since shifted 600 metres to the west.

In the 19th century, European scholars said that there had never been a city named Troy as described in Greek legends. When Schliemann discovered the ruins of many Troys (1870-90), one built over another, historians were forced to admit their error. In light of that example, and accepting the veracity of Egyptian historical records, the ancient site of Per-hapi-en-on was the site of the original Babylon and it was an integral part of the Great Pyramid complex.

According to tradition, both the Tower of Babel and the Hanging Gardens were built at Babylon and the conclusion reached in this premise is that they were originally built at the 'first Babylon' in Cairo. Both Strabo (c. 24 BC) and St Epiphanius of Salamis (315-403) recorded that the original site of Babylon was in Egypt, and as recently as 250 years ago, Cairo was identified on maps as, 'formerly Babylon'.

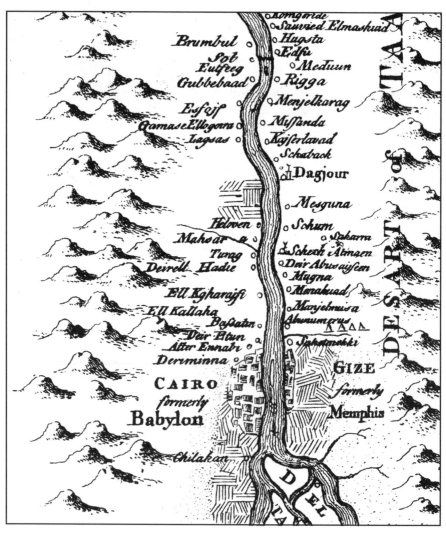

Nordan's map reproduced from 'Travels in Egypt and Nubia', 1757. Note the reference, 'Cairo, formerly Babylon'. Also relevant is the diagrammatic portrayal of four pyramids at 'Gize, formerly Memphis'.

The Mesopotamian Babylon was a much later development (the biblical 'daughter of Babylon?'), settled by emigrants who 'migrated from the east (east of the 'first' Babylon), and found a plain in the land of Shinar[29] and settled there. Come, let us build ourselves a city, and a tower with its top in the heavens. Come let us make bricks and burn them thoroughly'.[30]

There they re-established themselves, built a brick replica of the tower or ziggurat that stood within sight of the Nile at the 'first Babylon', and called their new 'sister city' after the original. An historical old writing titled *Expedition in Mesopotamia*[31] noted that a place called 'Borsippa (in Mesopotamia) became the name of the second Babylon', implying that it received its name from another and earlier Babylon. Borsippa was the home of the patron deity Nebo, one of Chaldea's great sovereign gods, who dwelt there in 'the eternal house' and was associated with the 'judgment on Babylon' in the Book of Isaiah.[32] Nebo was the inventor of the method of making clay tablets for keeping records and was the spouse of Nana, an aspect of Ishtar or even Ishtar herself.

Ziggurat was the Mesopotamian term for a step-pyramid, a pyramid-like tower consisting of a series of platforms decreasing in size as it climbed towards the sky. At the top stood platforms and tradition recorded that ziggurats were built as pedestals that enabled the gods to come down among their followers and bestow blessings on them. Like the Egyptian gods, they were described as heavenly beings, but not confined to the heavens and constantly involved in worldly affairs. They were shown with human features and had the same needs and passions as humans. The ruined state of ziggurats today makes them particularly difficult to study for they were built of clay bricks and constantly

An Assyrian alabaster statue of Nebo

menaced by erosion. The remains were often pilfered for house building, and leftovers were in constant danger of crumbling into dust. 'They had brick for stone'[33] and built inferior reproductions of Egyptian stone step-pyramids with the concept copied from the 'first' Babylon and used as the exemplar of later Mesopotamian ziggurats, including the main Babylonian tower.

That they were originally styled from Egyptian monuments was supported with the discovery of the remains of an Assyrian ziggurat at Khorsabad, near ancient Nineveh in Northern Iraq. It was built between 717 and 707 BC during the reign of Sargon II and showed seven successive painted levels of gold, silver, vermilion, blue, rose, black and white colours, inscribed with carvings and statues.

An inscription attributed to Nebuchadnezzar 11 (605–562 BC) declared that he personally built 'Etemenanki', now popularly identified as the Tower of Babel at Babylon, 'with baked brick enamelled in brilliant blue'. The step-pyramids Nebuchadnezzar II and others built around that time were some thousands of years after the time of this story.

Admitting to the confused history of ancient Mesopotamia, Professor Gaston Maspero, Director-General of Antiquities in Egypt, said:

> ...beyond the historic period the imagination was given a free reign, and the few facts which were known disappeared almost completely under the accumulation of mythical narratives and popular stories. While awaiting the means to restore a rigorously exact chronology, we must be content with the approximate information furnished by the tablets as to the succession of the Babylonian kings. For even comparatively recent periods of their history, the Chaldeans, like the Egyptians, had to depend upon a collection of certain abbreviated, incoherent, and often contradictory documents, from which they found it difficult to make a choice.[34]

The date of the foundation of the Babylonian empire is established by some historians at around 1750 BC and associated with the lifetime of Hammurabi. However, experts on Sumerian history could not agree between themselves on the date of Hammurabi's lifetime, for some argued that 2250 BC was his time. They drew their views mainly from Valmiki, the Hindu sage-historian, who said that they 'called the chief city Babylon and their settlement Babylonia'. His works were written maybe as early as circa 1300 BC, and provided ancient documentation revealing that the Babylon mentioned in today's history books was not the 'first Babylon' existing at Egypt at the beginning of the Old Kingdom. However, the building of the Great Pyramid preceded Hammurabi's time by centuries, for the Egyptian authorities claimed that it was built in the IVth dynasty, being 2720 BC to 2560 BC. The case being established in this book suggests that the Giza pyramids were built long before the IVth dynasty. However, adopting the extremities of the academic dating of 2720 BC and the founding of the Mesopotamian Empire at 2250 BC, the Great Pyramid and its adjoining city of Babylon were in existence 470 years previous.

The notice board indicates the extent of renovations at the Babylon Fort site in Old Cairo.

Two circular towers still survive in part and flank the original main gate into the 'first Babylon'. Egyptian archaeologists recorded the origin of the word 'Babylon', and that determined its precise and original location:

A water gate on the south side of Babylon is now known as the Bab al-Hadid (Iron Gate). The word Babylon is a corruption of Per-hapi-en-on which originally meant 'Estate of the god at ON', an ancient Egyptian name for this site. Hence Babylon meant 'Iron Gate to the god at ON'.[35]

ON was a city recorded in the Old Testament that is sometimes translated 'Onû', 'Anû' or 'Anû of the North', the capital. The first biblical mention of ON is in the history of Joseph, to whom Pharaoh gave wife Asenath, the daughter of Poti-pherah, priest of ON'. In Jeremiah[36] the city of ON was called Bethshemesh, the city of the Sun. ON was '…adorned by a gorgeous temple of the Sun, in which a numerous priesthood officiated. This city was in all ages the ecclesiastical metropolis of Lower Egypt, the prime seat of the sacred mysteries and higher science of the country'.[37] ON was later retitled Heliopolis when Greeks conquered Egypt, still meaning City of the Sun,[38] and Babylon (Old Cairo) was its entrance. ON was the home of the Sun-god RA and his family of gods, and was sometimes called 'the Residence of Life'. Hence, Babylon was the gateway to God residing at Egypt's holy ancient city Heliopolis and a Sacred Way called 'the Street on which may no Enemy ever tread' connected the two sites.

Accordingly, all biblical references to Babylon may have been references to the first Babylon within sight of the Great Pyramid. It was recorded that when Ezra led the exiled people from Babylon, he took with him not only the ancient Secret knowledge but also 'a great treasure for the Temple of Jerusalem'. If the Babylon of the Exile was in fact the 'original Babylon' at Cairo, then Ezra departed from the complex of the Great Pyramid, and that scenario provided an intriguing possibility.

Trusting the accounts given, it was possible to provide an opinion of what once stood on the summit of the Black Pyramid. Before the priesthood established the 'jealous god' of Exodus,[39] a metallic serpent and its wife were revered as great divinities in the Temple of Jerusalem: '…there was a brazen serpent worshipped in the very Temple of Jerusalem along with an image of his spouse, the mighty goddess who was known there as the Asherah (a 'she Ra')'.[40]

© AC Bushby 2002

© AC Bushby 2002

© AC Bushby 2002

The main gate to Babylon is flanked by two towers that still survive in part. Note the preservation of the original stones in the redevelopment of the 'gate to the god at ON' (arrowed). The 'Hanging Church' was later built on the top of the Gate. First mentioned in the ninth century, it was one of the oldest Christian churches known. It was rebuilt many times during the 14th to the 17th centuries.

The Talmud noted the miracle that no one was ever injured by the serpent in the Temple.[41] The Old Testament book of Jeremiah recorded a list of sacred bronze objects that were also on the altar in the Temple, circa 400 BC: 'As for the two pillars, the one bronze sea, the twelve bronze bulls which were under the sea, etc, etc'.[42] Several references to the 'sea' were recorded in the Bible, being obviously unrelated to the ocean, for it was described as a metallic object that was 'disassembled' and 'holy'.

The clue to its nature was in the phonetics of the word 'sea' and that simply derived from 'C' because of the object's shape. Thus, the Bible described the holy 'C' (Holy Sea; Holy See) as a religious item with horns and made of brass. It was a 'great treasure' that was held in high respect and worshipped as a god in the Temple of Jerusalem.[43]

From descriptions given, it was probable that Ezra and his group removed the depiction of Sin from the summit of the Black Pyramid before parting from Babylon at the end of the Exile. In ancient pictographs, Sin was represented in human form accompanied with a thin crescent with '…his horns breaking through to shine on the heaven…and on the seventh day, to a circle he begins to swell'.[44] They carried it to the Temple at Jerusalem, painted it red (the Red C), and reassembled it vertically on the altar amid great public fanfare. In later times, it was walked through in pious ceremonies and was subsequently destroyed in the year 68. The interpretation of the Holy C shown here was styled from the personal crest of Alexander the Great (c. 356-322 BC) who was called 'Ichthys' after his deification.[45] He was a dedicated worshipper of Sin, and the Ichthys logo was long associated with the worship of Amun (the moon). It was later used in Christian symbolism and revealed the importance of Moon worship in New Testament narratives, graphically illustrated when 'sin' is changed to read 'Sin'.

Artist's rendition of the Holy See

Other cities named in the Bible were also built within the precincts of the Great Pyramid. A notable example was Harran, recorded in the Book of Genesis as the home of Abraham.[46] During excavations at Giza in 1926, representatives of the University of Cairo discovered stelae inscriptions that recorded the existence of a body of star worshippers called Sabians who once lived at 'Harran near Giza' and paid homage to the Sphinx. Historians agreed that Harran was the ancient cult centre for lunar worship, and tradition revealed that Sin's primary Black Pyramid originally stood on the Giza Plateau. Biblical dictionaries today describe ancient Harran as a city of Northern Mesopotamia on the Balikh River, a branch of the Euphrates, but establishing which Harran was built first is outside the parameters of this book.

Amidst academic confusion surrounding the founding of the Mesopotamian Babylon, one thing is for sure...sometime in its ancient past, Old Cairo in downtown modern Cairo today, was called Babylon, 'the gate to the god at ON', and the eyes of the Sphinx looked directly at it.

© AC Bushby 2002

The Sphinx from the rear. The expanding city encroaches upon the Sphinx and high-rise development now obscures its original view of Babylon just 10 kilometres due East down the valley.

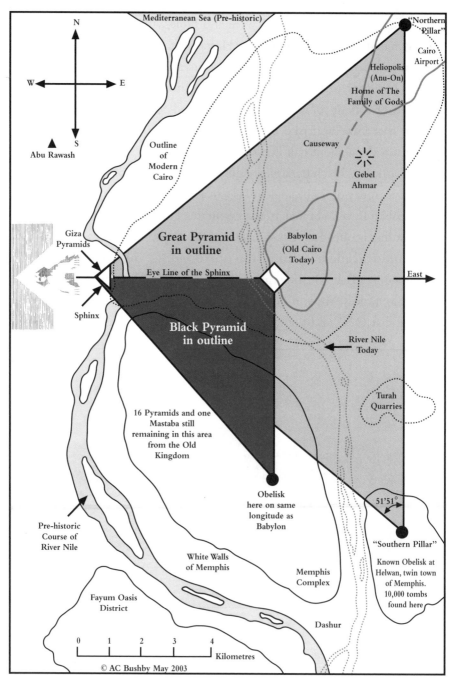

Designed from above?
Known physical markers reveal an aerial outline of both the Great Pyramid and the
Black Pyramid, complete with its capstone centred in Babylon.

CHAPTER EIGHT

UNDER THE SANDS OF GIZA

To fully comprehend the secret information in the Bible, it is important to understand the extent of the subterranean tunnel system and associated chamber facilities existing below the surface of the Pyramid Plateau, for it was there that major elements of Mystery School teachings developed. What happened under the sands thousands of years ago is not reflected in today's history books and discoveries made in the last eight decades or so verify that point.

The Fayum Oasis district just a few kilometres outside the boundary of the Memphis Nome presents a site of unusual interest. It was in that lush fertile valley that Pharaohs calling themselves the 'masters of the royal hunts' fished and hunted with the boomerang.[1] Lake Moeris once bordered the Fayum Oasis and on its shores was the famous Labyrinth, described by Herodotus 'as an endless wonder to me'. The Labyrinth contained 1500 rooms and an equal number of underground chambers that the Greek historian was not permitted to inspect. According to Labyrinth priests, 'the passages were baffling and intricate', designed to provide safety for the numerous scrolls they said were hidden in subterranean apartments. That massive complex particularly impressed Herodotus and he spoke in awe of the structure:

> There I saw twelve palaces regularly disposed, which had communication with each other interspersed with terraces and arranged around 12 halls. It is hard to believe they are the work of man. The walls are covered with carved

figures, and each court is exquisitely built of white marble and surrounded by a colonnade. Near the corner where the labyrinth ends, there is a pyramid, two hundred and forty feet in height, with great carved figures of animals on it and an underground passage by which it can be entered. I was told very credibly that underground chambers and passages connected this pyramid with the pyramids at Memphis.

The pyramids at Memphis were the pyramids at Giza, for Giza was originally called Memphis (See reference, 'Giza formerly Memphis' on Nordan's map from *Travels in Egypt and Nubia*, 1757, on page 152 in previous chapter).

The boomerang and the fighting bow. Drawn by Faucher-Gudin, from a painting in the tomb of the dwarf, Khnumhotpû, at Beni-Hasan (Champollion, Monuments de l'Egypte, pl. ccc).

At the time of Herodotus's visit, there were two large pyramids with 'colossal' seated figures on top in the centre of Lake Moeris. This is a pre-1851 engraving of one of those pyramids.

Many ancient writers supported Herodotus' record of underground passages connecting major pyramids and their evidence cast doubt on the reliability of traditionally presented Egyptian history. Crantor (300 BC) stated that there were certain underground pillars in Egypt that contained a written stone record of pre-history and they lined access ways connecting the pyramids. In his celebrated study, *On the Mysteries, particularly those of the Egyptians, Chaldeans and the Assyrians,* Iamblichus, a fourth century Syrian representative of the Alexandrian School of mystical and philosophical studies, recorded this information about an entranceway through the body of the Sphinx into the Great Pyramid:

> This entrance, obstructed in our day by sands and rubbish, may still be traced between the forelegs of the crouched colossus. It was formerly closed by a bronze gate whose secret spring could be operated only by the Magi. It was guarded by public respect and a sort of religious fear maintained its inviolability better than armed protection would have done. In the belly of the Sphinx were cut out galleries leading to the subterranean part of the Great Pyramid. These galleries were so artfully crisscrossed along their course to the Pyramid that in setting forth into the passage without a guide throughout this network, one ceasingly and inevitably returned to the starting point.[2]

It was recorded in ancient Sumerian cylinder seals that the secret abode of the Anunnaki was 'an underground place…entered through a tunnel, its entrance hidden by sand and by what they call Huwana…his teeth as the teeth of a dragon, his face the face of a lion'. That remarkable old text, unfortunately fragmented, added that, 'He (Huwana) is unable to move forward nor is he able to move back', but they crept up on him from behind and the way to 'the secret abode of the Anunnaki' was no longer blocked. The Sumerian record provided a probable description of the Lion-headed Sphinx at Giza, and if that great creature was built to guard or obliterate ancient stairways and lower passages leading to subterranean areas below and around it, then its symbolism was most appropriate.

Local nineteenth century Arab lore maintained that existing under the Sphinx are secret chambers holding treasures or magical objects. That belief was bolstered by the writings of first century Roman historian Pliny who wrote that deep below the Sphinx is concealed the 'tomb of a ruler named Harmakhis that contains great treasures', and, strangely enough, the Sphinx itself was once called 'The Great Sphinx Harmakhis who mounted guard since the time of the Followers of Horus'. Fourth century Roman historian Ammianus Marcellinus made additional disclosures about the existence of subterranean vaults that appeared to lead to the interior of the Great Pyramid:

> Inscriptions which the ancients asserted were engraved on the walls of certain underground galleries and passages were constructed deep in the dark interior to preserve ancient wisdom from being lost in the flood.[3]

A manuscript compiled by an Arab writer named Altelemsani is preserved in the British Museum and it records the existence of a long square underground passage between the Great Pyramid and the River Nile with a 'strange thing' blocking the Nile entrance. He related the following episode:

> In the days of Ahmed Ben Touloun a party entered the Great Pyramid through the tunnel and found in a side-chamber a goblet of glass of rare colour and texture. As they were leaving they missed one of the party and upon returning to seek him, he came out to them naked and laughing said; 'Do not follow or seek for me', and then rushed back into the Pyramid. His friends perceived that he was enchanted.

Upon learning about strange happenings under the Pyramid, Ahmed Ben Touloun expressed desire to see the goblet of glass. During the examination, it was filled with water and weighed, then emptied and re-weighed. The historian wrote that it was 'found to be of the same weight when empty as when full of water'. If the chronicle is accurate, that lack of additional weight provided indirect evidence of the existence of an extraordinary science at Giza.

According to Masoudi in the tenth century, mechanical statues with amazing capabilities guarded subterranean galleries under the Great Pyramid. Writing one thousand years ago, his description is comparable to the computerized robots shown today in space movies. Masoudi said that the automatons were programmed for intolerance, for they destroyed all 'except those who by their conduct were worthy of admission'. Masoudi contended that 'written accounts of Wisdom and acquirements in the different arts and sciences were hidden deep, that they might remain as records for the benefit of those who could afterwards comprehend them'. That is phenomenal information as it is possible that since the times of Masoudi 'worthy' persons have seen the mysterious underground chambers. Masoudi confessed that 'I have seen things that one does not describe for fear of making people doubt one's intelligence…but still I have seen them'. In the same century another writer, Muterdi, gave an account of a bizarre incident in a narrow passage under Giza where a group of people were horrified to see one of their party crushed to death by a stone door that, by itself, suddenly slid out from the face of the passageway and closed the corridor in front of them.

Herodotus said Egyptian priests recited him their long-held tradition of 'the formation of underground apartments' by the original developers of Memphis. The most ancient inscriptions, therefore, suggested that there existed some sort of extensive chamber system below the surface of the areas surrounding the Sphinx and pyramids. Those old records were confirmed when the presence of a large cavity was discovered in a seismic survey conducted at the site in 1993. That detection was publicly acknowledged in a documentary called 'The Mystery of the Sphinx' and screened to an audience of 30 million people on NBC-TV later that year. The existence of chambers under the Sphinx is well known and Egyptian authorities confirmed another discovery in 1994. Its unearthing was announced in a newspaper report that was carried under the headline, 'Mystery Tunnel in Sphinx':

> Workers repairing the ailing Sphinx have discovered an ancient passage leading deep into the body of the mysterious monument.

> The Giza Antiquities chief, Mr. Zahi Hawass, said there was no dispute the tunnel was very old. However, what is puzzling is who built the passage? Why? and where does it lead...? Mr. Hawass said he had no plans to remove the stones blocking the entrance. The secret tunnel burrows into the northern side of the Sphinx, about halfway between the Sphinx's outstretched paws and its tail.[4]

The popular supposition that the Sphinx is the true portal of the Great Pyramid has survived with surprising tenacity. That belief was substantiated by 100 year-old plans prepared by Masonic and Rosicrucian initiates showing the Sphinx was the ornament surmounting a hall that communicated with all Pyramids by radiating underground passages. Those plans were compiled from information originally discovered by the supposed founder of the Order of the Rosicrucians, Christian Rosenkreuz, who allegedly penetrated a 'secret chamber beneath the ground' and there found a library of books full of secret knowledge. The schematic drawings were produced from information possessed by Mystery School archivists before sand clearing commenced in 1925 and revealed hidden doors to long-forgotten reception halls, small temples and other enclosures. Those plans are included in The Master Plan section at the end of this book. The knowledge of the Mystery Schools was strengthened by a series of remarkable discoveries in 1935 that provided proof of additional passageways and chambers interlacing the area below the Pyramids. The Giza complex showed major elements of being a purposely built, uniting structure, with the Sphinx, the Great Pyramid and the Temple of the Solar-men directly related to each other, above and below the ground.

Chambers and passageways detected by sophisticated seismograph and Ground Penetrating Radar (GPR) equipment in the last few years established the accuracy of the plans. Egypt is also successfully using sophisticated satellites to identify sites buried beneath the surface at Giza and other locations. The novel tracking system was launched at the beginning of 1998 and the location of twenty-seven unexcavated sites in five areas was precisely determined. Nine of those sites are on Luxor's east bank and the others are in Giza, Abu Rawash, Saqqara and Dashur. The printouts of the Giza area show an almost incomprehensible mass of net-like tunnels and chambers crisscrossing the area, intersecting and entwining each other like latticework extending out across the entire plateau. With the space surveillance project, Egyptologists are able to determine the location of a major site, its probable entrance, and the size of chambers before starting excavations. Particular attention is being focused on three secret locations: an area in the desert a few hundred metres west/southwest of the original location of the Black Pyramid, around which is currently being built a massive system of concrete walls seven metres (22 feet) high covering eight square kilometres; the ancient highway that linked the Luxor temple with Karnak; and the 'Way of Horus' across northern Sinai.

Headline news

Among the mystics or members of Egyptian Mystery Schools, tradition explained that the Great Pyramid was great in many ways. Despite the fact that it was not entered until the year 820, the secret schools of pre-Christian Egypt insisted that the interior layout was well known to them. They constantly claimed that it was not a tomb, nor a burial chamber of any kind, except that it did have one chamber for symbolical burial as part of initiation ritual. According to mystical traditions, the interior was entered gradually and in various stages via underground passageways. Different chambers were said to have existed at the end of each phase of progress with the highest and ultimate initiatory stage represented by the now-called King's Chamber. Little by little, the traditions of the Mystery Schools were verified by archaeological discoveries for it was ascertained in 1935 that there was a subterranean connection between the Sphinx and the Great Pyramid, and a tunnel connected the Sphinx to the ancient temple located on its Southern side (Today called the Temple of the Sphinx).

As Emile Baraize' massive 11 year sand and seashell clearing project neared completion in 1935, remarkable stories started to emerge about discoveries made during the cleansing project. A magazine article written and published in 1935 by Hamilton M. Wright dealt with an extraordinary discovery under the sands of Giza that is today denied. The article was accompanied by original photographs provided by Dr Selim Hassan, the leader of the scientific investigative team from the University of Cairo who made the discovery. It said:

We have discovered a subway used by the ancient Egyptians of 5000 years ago. It passes beneath the causeway leading between the second Pyramid and the Sphinx. It provides a means of passing under the causeway from the Cheops Pyramid to the Pyramid of Chephren (Khephren). From this subway, we have unearthed a series of shafts leading down more than 125 feet, with roomy courts and side chambers.

Around the same time, the international news media released further details of the find.

The underground connector complex was originally built between the Great Pyramid and the Temple of the Solar-men, for the pyramid of Khephren was a later and superficial structure. The subway and its apartments were excavated out of solid 'living' bedrock, a truly extraordinary feat considering it was built thousands of years ago.

**THE DAILY TELEGRAPH,
MONDAY, MARCH 4, 1935**

SUBWAY FOUND BELOW THE PYRAMIDS

NEW DISCOVERIES IN EGYPT

COLONNADED HALL IN ROCK

2,500 YEARS' OLD CHAMBERS

FROM OUR OWN CORRESPONDENT
CAIRO, Sunday.

A subway connecting Khephren's Pyramid City to Cheops' Pyramid City has been discovered in the course of recent excavations. This had been cut through the living rock.

More remarkable still, a shaft, 11 yards long, was found to lead from the subway to the heart of the rock. When examined, it was found to end in a chamber some 6 yards by 11 yards.

From one side of it there was

This is how the British media reported the discovery of underground chambers at Giza in 1935 (passim).

There is more to the story of underground chambers at Giza for media reports described the unearthing of a subterranean passageway between the Temple of the Solar-men on the plateau, and the temple of the Sphinx in the valley. That passageway had been unearthed a few years before the release and publication of that particular newspaper article. The discoveries lead Dr. Selim Hassan and others to believe, and publicly state, that while the age of the Sphinx was always enigmatic in the past, it may have been part of the great architectural plan that was deliberately arranged and carried out in association with the erection of the Great Pyramid.

Archaeologists made another major discovery at that time. Around halfway between the Sphinx and Khephren's Pyramid were discovered four enormous vertical shafts each around eight feet square leading straight down through solid limestone. Called 'Campbell's Tomb' on the Masonic and Rosicrucian plans 'that shaft complex', said Dr Selim Hassan, 'ended in a spacious room, in the centre of which was another shaft that descended to a roomy court flanked with seven side chambers'. Some of the chambers contained huge sealed sarcophagi of basalt and granite 18 feet high. The discovery went further and found in one of the seven rooms there was yet a third vertical shaft dropping deeply down to a much lower chamber. At the time of its discovery, it was flooded with water that partly covered a solitary white sarcophagus. That chamber was named the 'Tomb of Osiris' and was shown being 'opened for the first time' on a television documentary in March 1999. While originally exploring in this area in 1935, Dr Selim Hassan said:

> We are hoping to find some monuments of importance after clearing out this water. The total depth of these series of shafts is more than 40 metres or more than 125 feet...In the course of clearing the southern part of the subway there was found a very fine head of a statue which is very expressive in every detail of the face.

According to a separate newspaper report of the time, the statue was a bust of Queen Nefertiti, an excellent sculpture described as 'a beautiful example of that rare type of art inaugurated in the Amenhotep regime'. The whereabouts of that statue today is unknown.

The report also described other chambers and rooms beneath the sands, all interconnected by secret and ornate passageways. Dr Selim Hassan revealed that not only were there inner and outer courts, they also found a room they named the 'Chapel of Offering' that had been cut into a huge rock outcrop between Campbell's Tomb and the Great Pyramid. In the centre of the chapel are three vertical ornate pillars standing in a triangular shaped layout. Those pillars are highly significant points in this study for their existence was recorded in the Bible. The conclusion drawn was that Ezra, the initiated Torah writer (c. 397 BC), knew the subterranean layout of passages and chambers at Giza before he wrote the Torah. That underground design was probably the origin of the triangular shaped layout around the central altar in a Masonic Lodge. In *Antiquities of the Jews*, Josephus, in the first century, wrote that Enoch of Old Testament fame constructed an underground temple consisting of nine chambers. In a deep vault inside one chamber with three vertical columns, he placed a triangular-shaped tablet of gold bearing upon it the absolute name of Deity (God). The description of Enoch's chambers was similar to the description of the 'Chapel of Offering' under the sand just east of the Great Pyramid.

An anteroom much like a burial chamber but 'undoubtedly a room of initiation and reception'[5] was found higher up the plateau closer to the Great Pyramid and at the upper end of a sloping passage, cut deep into rock on the north-west side of the Chamber of Offering (Between the Chamber of Offering and the Great Pyramid). In the centre of the chamber is a 12-foot long sarcophagus of white Turah limestone and a collection of fine alabaster vessels. The walls are beautifully carved with scenes, inscriptions and emblems of particularly the Lotus flower. The description of alabaster vessels and the emblematic Lotus flower have remarkable parallels with what was found in the temple-workshop on the summit of Mount Sinai/Horeb by Sir William Petrie in 1904.

Additional underground rooms, chambers, temples and hallways were discovered, some with vertical circular stone support columns, and others with wall carvings of delicate figures of goddesses clothed in beautiful apparel. Dr Selim Hassan's report described other magnificently carved figures and many beautifully coloured friezes. Photographs were taken and one author and researcher who saw them, Rosicrucian H Spencer Lewis PRD, recorded that he was 'deeply impressed' with the images. It is not known where the rare specimens of art and relics are today but some were rumoured to have been smuggled out of Egypt by private collectors.

The foregoing particulars are but a few contained in Dr Selim Hassan's extensive report that was published in 1944 by the Government Press, Cairo under the title *Excavations at Giza* (Ten volumes). However, that is just a mere fragment of the whole truth of what is under the area of the Pyramids. In the last year of sand clearing, workers uncovered the most amazing discovery that stunned the world and attracted international media coverage. This is how the unearthing of a lost city was reported in one of many papers, the Sunday Express of 7 July 1935.

Sunday Express

Founded by
LORD BEAVERBROOK

LONDON, JULY 7, 1935

CITY OF THE WORLD'S FIRST QUEEN

THE MYSTERY
OF THE
PYRAMIDS

MAY BE SOLVED BY NEW EXCAVATIONS

Mr. Edward Armytage, etymologist, and explorer of New Guinea and the South Seas, has just returned to England from Egypt, where he has been watching the excavating of a secret city which existed 4,000 years ago.

Below he describes what is happening.

By EDWARD ARMYTAGE, F.R.E.S.

A CITY, the existence of which had not even been suspected, has been discovered in Egypt. The discovery promises to throw new light on a highly organised civilisation that existed 4,000 years ago.

And it may provide the key to the mystery of how the Pyramids were built.

The city was discovered by accident.

For years Egyptian archaeologists have ignored an incompleted pyramid near the better-known Pyramids. They regarded it as nothing but a mound of débris. .

Then Professor Selim Hassan, the Egyptian excavator, declared that it was undoubtedly the tomb of a ruler. His opinion has been justified.

Not only has the mound proved to be the tomb of a queen who reigned 4,000 years ago, but close by has been unearthed the remains of a wonderful city. The city had a perfect drainage system and other amenities which were not introduced into Europe until 200 years ago!

The world hears of the discovery of a 'secret' Egyptian city (passim).

Archaeologists in charge of the discovery were 'bewildered' at what they had unearthed, and stated that the city was the most beautifully planned they had ever seen. It is replete with temples, pastel-painted peasant dwellings, workshops, stables and other buildings including a palace. Complete with hydraulic underground waterways it has a perfect drainage system along with other modern amenities. The intriguing question that arises out of the discovery is: where is that city today?

Its secret location was recently revealed to a select group of people who were given permission to explore and film the city. It exists in a huge natural cavern system below the Giza Plateau that extends out in an easterly direction under Cairo. Its main entry is from inside the Sphinx with stairs cut into rock that lead down to the cavern below the bedrock of the River Nile. The expedition carried down generators and inflatable rafts and travelled along an underground river that led to a lake one kilometre wide. On the shores of the lake nestled the city and permanent lighting is provided by large crystalline balls set into the cavern walls and ceiling. A second entry to the city is found in stairs leading up to the basement of the Coptic Church in Old Cairo (Babylon). Drawing from narratives of people 'living in the Earth' given in the books of Genesis, Jasher and Enoch, it is possible that the city was originally called Gigal.

Film footage of the expedition was shot and a documentary called 'Chambers of the Deep' was made and subsequently shown to private audiences. It was originally intended to release the footage to the general public but for some reason it was withheld. A multi-faceted spherical crystalline object the size of a baseball was brought up from the city and its supernatural nature was demonstrated at a recent conference in Australia. Deep within the solid object are various hieroglyphs that slowly turn over like pages of a book when mentally requested to do so by whoever holds the object. That remarkable item revealed an unknown form of technology and was recently sent to NASA in the USA for analysis.

Historical documents recorded that during the 20th century, staggering discoveries not spoken of today were made at Giza and Mount Sinai, and Egyptian rumours of the discovery of another underground city within a 28-mile radius of the Great Pyramid abound. In 1964, more than 30 enormous multi-levelled sub-surface cities were discovered in the old Turkish kingdom of Cappadocia. One city alone contained huge caverns, rooms and hallways that archaeologists estimated supported as many as 2000 households, providing living facilities for 8000 to 10,000 people. Their very existence constitutes evidence that many such subterranean worlds lie waiting to be found below the surface of the earth. Excavations at Giza revealed underground subways, temples, sarcophagi and one interconnected subterranean city, and validation that underground passageways connected the Sphinx to the Pyramids is another step towards proving that the whole complex is a carefully and specifically thought-out complex.

Official denials

Because of Dr Selim Hassan's excavations and modern space surveillance techniques, the records and traditions of the ancient Egyptian Mystery schools that claim to preserve secret knowledge of the Giza Plateau, all rose to the highest degree of acceptability. However, one of the most puzzling aspects of the discovery of underground facilities at Giza is the repeated denial of their existence by Egyptian authorities and academic institutions. So persistent are their refutations, the claims of MysteRY Schools were doubted by the public and suspected of being fabricated in order to mystify visitors to Egypt. The scholastic attitude is typified by the expression of the Harvard University that, in 1972, publicly stated:

> No one should pay any attention to the preposterous claims in regard to the interior of the Great Pyramid or the presumed passageways and unexcavated temples and halls beneath the sand in the Pyramid district made by those who are associated with the so-called secret cults or mystery societies of Egypt and the Orient. These things exist only in the minds of those who seek to attract the seekers for mystery and the more we deny the existence of these things, the more the public is led to suspect that we are deliberately trying to hide that which constitutes one of the great secrets of Egypt. It is better for us to ignore all of these claims than merely deny them. All of our excavations in the territory of the Pyramid have failed to reveal any underground passageways or halls, temples, grottos, or anything of the kind except the one temple adjoining the Sphinx.

It was well enough for scholarly opinion to make such a statement on the subject, but in preceding years, official claims were made stating that there was no temple adjoining the Sphinx. The assertion that every inch of the territory around the Sphinx and pyramids had been explored deeply and thoroughly was disproved when the temple adjoining the Sphinx was discovered in the sand and eventually opened to the public. On matters outside official policy, there appears to be a hidden level of censorship in operation, one designed to protect both Eastern and Western religions.

Ever-burning lamps

In spite of amazing discoveries, the stark truth is that the early history of Egypt remains largely unknown and therefore unmapped territory. It is not possible, then, to precisely say how miles of underground passageways and chambers beneath the Giza plateau were lit, but one thing is for sure, unless the Ancients could see in the dark, the vast subterranean areas were somehow illuminated. The same question is addressed of the interior of the Great Pyramid and Egyptologists agreed that flaming torches were not used, for ceilings had not been blackened with residual smoke. From what is currently known about sub-surface passageways under the Pyramid Plateau, it is possible to determine there are at least three miles of passageways 10 to 12 stories below ground level. Both the *Book of the Dead* and the Pyramid Texts make striking references to 'The Light-makers' and that extraordinary description may have referred to a body of people responsible for lighting the subterranean areas of their complexes.

Iamblichus recorded a fascinating account that was found on a very ancient Egyptian papyrus held in a Mosque in Cairo. It was part of a 100 BC story by an unknown author about a group of people who gained entry to underground chambers around Giza for exploratory purposes. They described their experience:

> We came to a chamber. When we entered, it became automatically illuminated by light from a tube being the height of one man's hand (6 inches) and thin, standing vertically in the corner. As we approached the tube, it shone brighter...the slaves were scared and ran away in the direction from which we had come! When I touched it, it went out. We made every effort to get the tube to glow again but it would no longer provide light. In some chambers the light tubes worked and in others they did not. We broke open one of the tubes and it bled beads of silver-coloured liquid that ran fastly around the floor until they disappeared between the cracks (Mercury ?).

As time went on the light tubes gradually began to fail and the priests removed them and stored them in an underground vault they specially built southeast of the plateau. It was their belief that the light tubes were created by their beloved Imhotep, who would some day return to make them work once again.

It was common practice among early Egyptians to seal lighted lamps in the sepulchres of their dead as offerings to their god or for the deceased to find their way to the 'other side'. Among the tombs near Memphis (and in the Brahmin temples of India), lights were found operating in sealed chambers and vessels, but sudden exposure to air extinguished them or caused their fuel to evaporate.[6] Greeks and Romans later followed the custom and the tradition became generally established, not only that of actual burning lamps, but miniature reproductions made in terracotta, were buried with the dead. Some lamps were enclosed in circular vessels for protection and instances are recorded where the original oil was found perfectly preserved in them after more than 2000 years. There is ample proof from eyewitnesses that lamps were burning when the sepulchres were sealed, and it was declared by later bystanders that they were still burning when the vaults were opened hundreds of years later.

The possibility of preparing a fuel that would renew itself as rapidly as it was consumed was a source of considerable controversy among mediaeval authors and numerous documents exist outlining their arguments. After due consideration of evidence at hand, it seemed well within the range of possibility that ancient Egyptian priest-chemists manufactured lamps that burned, if not indefinitely, at least for considerable periods of time. Numerous authorities have written on the subject of ever-burning lamps with W Wynn Westcott estimating that the number of writers who have given the subject consideration as more than 150 and HP Blavatsky as 173. While conclusions reached by different authors are at a variance, a majority admitted the existence of the phenomenal lamps. Only a few maintained that the lamps would burn forever, but many were willing to concede that they might remain alight for several centuries without replenishment of fuel.

It was generally believed that the wicks of those perpetual lamps were made of braided or woven asbestos, called by early alchemists 'salamder's wool'. The fuel appeared to have been one of the products of alchemical research, possibly produced in the temple on Mount Sinai. Several formulae for making fuel for the lamps were preserved, and in HP Blavatsky's profound work, *Isis*

Unveiled, the author reprinted two complicated formulae from earlier authors of a fuel, that 'when made and lighted, will burn with a perpetual flame and you may set this lamp in any place where you please'.

Some believe the fabled perpetual lamps of temples to be cunning mechanical contrivances and some quite humourous explanations were extended. In Egypt rich underground deposits of asphalt and petroleum exist and some would have it that priests connected asbestos wicks by a secret duct to an oil deposit, which in turn connected to one or more lamps. Others thought that the belief that lamps burned indefinitely in tombs was the result of the fact that in some cases fumes resembling smoke poured forth from the entrances of newly opened vaults. Parties going in later, and discovering lamps scattered about the floor, assumed that they were the source of the fumes. There were some well-documented stories concerning the discovery of ever-burning lamps, not only in Egypt, but also in other parts of the world.

De Montfaucon de Villars gave this fascinating account of the opening of the vault of Rosicrucian Christian Rosenkreuz. When the Brethren entered the tomb of their illustrious founder 120 years after his death, they found a brilliant perpetual lamp brightly shining in a suspended manner from the ceiling. 'There was a statue in armour (a robot) which destroyed the source of light when the chamber was opened'.[7] That was strangely similar to the accounts of Arab historians who claimed that automatons guarded galleries under the Great Pyramid.

A 17th century account recorded another story about a robot. In central England, a curious tomb was found containing an automaton that moved when an intruder stepped upon certain stones in the floor of the vault. At that time, the Rosicrucian controversy was at its height, so it was decided that the tomb was that of a Rosicrucian initiate. A countryman discovered the tomb, entered, and found the interior brilliantly lit by a lamp hanging from the ceiling. As he walked toward the light, his weight depressed the floor stones and, at once, a seated figure in heavy armour began to move. Mechanically it rose to its feet and struck the lamp with an iron baton, destroying it, and thus effectively preventing the discovery of the secret substance that maintained the flame. How long the lamp had burned was unknown, but the report said that it had been for a considerable number of years.

CHAPTER NINE

THE GOLDEN BOOK OF THOTH

Ancient Egyptians regarded Thoth as the personification of the mind of God, sent to earth to write for RA and the Goddess of Justice, Maat. He formed a feature of Egyptian religion that was as awe-inspiring as the belief in the resurrection of the dead in a spiritual body, and as the doctrine of everlasting life. The insight that the writings of Thoth provided humanity was far-reaching, and Egyptians today still believe the old words that he was 'Lord of the voice, master of words, possessor and inventor of those magic writings which nothing in heaven, on earth, or in Hades can withstand'.[1]

Thoth wrote a mysterious book of great secrecy for it seemed that he was the only god able to put into human words the divine knowledge of the 'gods collective'. In the *Book of Divinity*, Osiris instructed Thoth to 'place in man's hand the key to unlock the Mysteries of the firmament of heaven, and the power, and Wisdom, and riches, and glory of the Earth'. After the book was written, Osiris perused the work and observed, 'Here layeth the key to everlasting life'. During the earliest recorded times in Egyptian history, that document was known as the *Book of Thoth,* but was sometimes called the *Book of Truth* by initiated Egyptian priests. The general populace of the time called it the *Book of the Leaves of Gold* implying that it was written on gold foil, and in its original form, contained 22 separate sheets of symbolic drawings. Thoth personally recorded this extraordinary statement:

> I am the keeper of the Book of that which is, and of that which shall be, and that which makes its possessor the equal of the gods.

That narrative revealed probably the most profound and important statement in all ancient Egyptian writings. Thoth made it known that he was guardian of a prophetic book, and direct evidence of the Secret was in it.

An intriguing age-old Egyptian tradition maintained that the *Book of Thoth* contained a secret process by which the regeneration of humanity was to be accomplished and served as the key to other writings. Its pages were inscribed with strange hieroglyphic symbols that gave to those acquainted with them a particular power. The initiated priesthood maintained for centuries that those symbols contained the 'Key to Immortality' and when certain areas of the brain saw the symbols, the subconsciousness of that person was expanded, and he or she was permitted access to a superior level of knowledge. The *Book of Thoth* contains cryptograms whereby that stimulation was achieved and this premise maintains that the ancient records of large inscriptions on external faces of the

Thoth, the ibis-headed god, shown recording the years of the life of Rameses II.

Great Pyramid were identical to the pages of Thoth's original book.

In the oldest of Egyptian texts, Thoth, whom the Greeks called Hermes, was constantly styled 'Lord of the Divine Books' and the 'Scribe of the Company of Gods'. The *Book of the Dead* stated that he was:

> ...a god who was self-begotten and self-produced; that he was One; that he made the calculations concerning the establishing of the heavens, and the stars and the earth; that he was the heart of the great god, RA; that he was master of law, both in its physical and moral conceptions, and that he had special knowledge of the mysterious 'divine speech'.

That ancient reference to 'divine speech' sheds great light on the emergence of the Secret in the Bible. The *Book of the Dead* declared Thoth author of works by which, the ancients believed, the deceased gained everlasting life. In artwork, Thoth is often depicted with the head of an ibis, a bird to which the Egyptians paid divine honours for thousands of years. So precious was that bird, it was considered a cardinal crime to kill one, even by accident. The ibis was sacred to Thoth because when its head and neck were tucked under its wing, its body closely resembled a human heart.

A series of fascinating old stories about the *Book of Thoth* involved the mystery of 'a box made of iron'. In ancient records, the box of iron is mentioned on many occasions and always associated with mystery and intrigue. According to the Westcar papyrus, Cheops's son, Herutataf, told his father he was acquainted with a man 110 years old who knew 'the number of the secret chambers of Thoth'. Cheops subsequently questioned the old man: 'It is said that you know the numbers of the secret chambers of the sanctuary of Thoth'. To that, the old man answered:

> Please I do not know their number, O King my Lord, but I know the place where it is; there is a chest made of iron in the building called the 'inventory' in Heliopolis. It is in this chest.

Unfortunately, the Westcar Papyrus does not reveal whether Cheops gained access to the hidden chest, but it did reveal that the box of iron was still in existence around 2560 BC.

Another connection to a 'box of iron' was found some six centuries later. There is a text known to Egyptologists as 'The Admonition of an Egyptian sage, Ipuwer', who was a priest at Heliopolis during the reign of Amenemhet I (c. 1900 BC). Ipuwer referred to a missing box of iron that had once been hidden under the feet of RA/Khepra. He made the extraordinary statement that said, 'that which the Benben concealed has become empty'. He appeared to be voicing a strong warning to a large gathering of some sort about the loss for he feared that whatever was concealed in 'the box of iron under the feet of the god' was no longer there.

The oldest passages of the *Book of the Dead* also mentioned the box of iron and the 'Lord of the Hidden Chest' protected it. A copy of the Hieratic text recently found inscribed on the internal walls of the sarcophagus of Menthu-hetep, a queen of the Eleventh Dynasty (c. 2040 BC), recorded a particular chapter which was given the number LXIV (64) by Egyptologists. In 422 BC, that same chapter was again found in the tomb of Hesep-ti, the 6th king of the First Dynasty. Thus, Egyptologists established that particular chapter was at least as old as the time of the First Dynasty. Quoting from the records of a certain Chabas (c. 1400 BC), that chapter was regarded then as being 'very ancient, very mysterious and very difficult to understand', fourteen centuries before the commencement of the Christian era. The rubric on the coffin of Queen Menthu-hetep stated that, 'this chapter was found in the city of Heliopolis, in a box of iron, written in letters of lapis-lazuli, under the feet of the god in the writing of the god himself'.

Rameses the Great, Pharaoh of Egypt, had a son called Setna who was never so happy as when left alone to study. Not only could he read the most ancient hieroglyphic temple writings, but he was also a scribe who could quickly write the many hundreds of signs that made up the complicated Egyptian language. He had learned his art from the most secret of ancient writings that, it was said, even the priests of Amen-RA, Ptah and Thoth could not read. One day he came upon the story of an earlier Pharaoh's son who had also been a great scribe. His name was Nefrekeptak, son of Amenhotep (1448 BC), the first great Pharaoh of that name. Nefrekeptak claimed that he had found an old book that contained 'all the secrets of the gods themselves, and reveals all that is hidden in the stars'. That, he said, was the *Book of Thoth*, and he found it…

> … in a secret tomb in an iron box. In the iron box is a box of bronze; in the bronze box is a sycamore box; in the sycamore box is an ivory and ebony box; in the ivory and ebony box is a silver box; in that silver box is a golden box and in that lays the Book of Thoth. All around the iron box are carved twisted snakes and scorpions, and it is guarded by a serpent who cannot be slain.

Nefrekeptak removed the *Book of Thoth* from the 'iron box' and presented it to a meeting of prominent leaders, and 'they saw it as a marvelous thing.' They described it as a 'mystery, great, unseen and unbeheld', and gazed upon it with amazement. While Nefrekeptak was studying the curious symbols, he had a strange experience in which he saw 'the sun shining in the sky, the moon and the stars, and knew their secrets...and I saw the gods themselves who are hidden from mortal sight...and knew of things yet to come to pass'. Nefrekeptak was left in awe, and subsequently dedicated his life to carving the twenty-two symbols of Thoth's book into stone sarcophagi, temple walls, within tombs, and teaching its spiritual meaning to upcoming temple priests of Saqqara. Its preservation was thus assured, and later priests painstakingly copied the symbols FoR their own personal use.

It was probable that the old *Book of Thoth* that Nefrekeptak found was the very same book that priest Hilkiah found[2] around 400BC and later called the *Book of God*. It was also probable that the 'box of iron' was associated with the great god RA for that box was not the only one in Egyptian texts that was of special significance. Another striking tradition referred to a 'golden box' into which RA placed his 'rod' and a 'rearing cobra'. When Geb, the third Pharaoh, came to power, he ordered the 'box of RA' to be removed from its protective fortress and brought to him for inspection. It was opened in his presence and 'the breath of the divine serpent' issued from it, killing Geb's companions and badly burning Geb himself.[3] That ancient tradition may have been Ezra's source of the Ark of the Covenant story in the *Old Testament*. That Ark was also described as a box 'overlaid with gold', that held 'Aaron's rod', and occasionally killed people.

The Egyptian tradition of a book of symbols written on leaves of gold is not an isolated one and is found in later pyramidal records. The Arabic writer Idrisi, who wrote about 1226, stated that a person called Othman first opened Mycerinus' Pyramid in 1196, and the damage his team effected upon the north face of the monument is still evident today. Breaking into the pyramid took six months and was carried out by a huge number of people in search of riches and treasure. After passing through various passages, they reached a solitary chamber and found a long blue vessel of sorts. In it were decayed pieces of a human (not a mummy) and golden tablets inscribed with mysterious symbols. By pressing the leaves of the tablets into soft clay and then baking it, permanent terracotta reproductions were made. The original golden tablets were subsequently sold and the proceeds divided among workers involved in the discovery. Each man received one hundred dinars, being about US$100 in modern terms.[4] The fate of the golden tablets is not recorded, but the fact that they were found deep inside a sealed pyramid at Giza established their antiquity.

The house of the Alexandrian librarian

It is generally believed the *Book of Thoth* was lost to the ancient world with the burning of the library at Alexandria. Prior to the Christian era, 700,000 of the most valuable books, written upon parchment, papyrus, vellum and wax, tablets of stone, terracotta and wood, were gathered from all parts of the ancient world and housed in Alexandria in a series of buildings specially prepared for the purpose. 'The library was situated in the Alexandrian Museum, the apartments allotted for it were beautifully sculptured and crowded with the choicest statues and pictures; the walls were lined with marble'.[5] That magnificent repository of knowledge was destroyed by a series of three fires. The documents that escaped the original fire started by Caesar in 51 BC to destroy the fleet in the harbour were finally destroyed around 389 in obedience to the edict of Theodosius, and 'the appearance of empty shelves excited the regret and indignation of every spectator, whose mind was not totally darkened by religious prejudice'.[6] It was Theodosius who also ordered the destruction of the Serapeum in Alexandria, a building sacred to Serapis and his Serpents in which many ancient volumes were also kept. It was at that time, and during that event, that the library Mark Antony had given to Cleopatra was destroyed. That particular collection was presented to Cleopatra to compensate in part for that burned in the fire of the 51 BC. HP Blavatsky, in *Isis Unveiled*, wrote:

> They (the Rabbis of Palestine and the Muses) say that not all the rolls and manuscripts, reported in history to have been burned by Caesar, by the Christian mob, in 389 AD, and by the Arab General Amru (AMRU), perished, as it is commonly believed. At the time for the conquest for the throne, in 51 BC, between Cleopatra and her brother Dionysius Ptolomy, the Bruckion, which contained over 700,000 rolls all bound in wood and fireproof parchment, was undergoing repairs and a great portion of the original manuscripts, considered among the most precious, and which were not duplicated, were stored away

in the house of one of the librarians. Several hours passed between the burning of the fleet, set on fire by Caesar's orders, and the moment when the first building situated near the harbour caught fire in their turn, and the librarians, aided by several hundred slaves attached to the museum, succeeded in saving the most precious rolls.

Many volumes that escaped the fire were 'buried in the desert'[7] and their location was revealed only to a few high initiates of the Secret Schools, particularly the Rosicrucians.[8] A curious legend related that after the destruction of the Serapeum, the body of attendant priests banded themselves together to preserve the 'twenty two serpent secrets' of the rites of Serapis. Their descendants, carrying with them the most precious of the volumes saved from the burning library, became wanderers upon the face of the earth, remaining a people apart with an ancient language and a birthright of magic and mystery. They carried their books in a sealed, sacred casket and their faithful initiates eventually passed the valuable documents on to other lands.

The *Book of Thoth* universally exists today and carries within it the synthesis of all human knowledge as revealed by the Heliopolian 'Company of Gods'. It was said that those who 'are peculiarly fitted to serve the Immortals may discover this priceless document if they will search sincerely and tirelessly for it'. The next chapter attempts to unravel it.

CHAPTER TEN

THE BIBLE OF THE GYPSIES

A time arose in Egypt when control of the Mysteries began to fall into the hands of selfish men, ambitious to misuse the influence of that mighty Secret institution for their own personal ends. Sorcery replaced spirituality and the presumed ministers of the gods became devils in human form. Amid the spiritual gloom and chaos that fell upon the land, the Mysteries began to lose their true character and high purpose. Worthy candidates became hard to find and qualified hierophants all but ceased as a body to exist. The Magi could no longer struggle against materialist invaders and preparing for the end, they held an assembly to discuss how to save the *Book of Thoth* from oblivion. At first, they thought of confiding its secrets to virtuous, but uninitiated men, quietly recruited by initiates themselves, with the hope that the recipients of the knowledge would transmit it from generation to generation through their families. The high initiates however, observing that virtue was a most fragile flower and the most difficult to find, proposed to confide their most valuable secret to a simple game. 'Small plates were engraved with the mysterious figures which were in the Book of Thoth'.[1]

The small plates were 22 miniature reproductions of the original symbols from the *Book of Thoth*, drawn as simple sketches surrounded by inconspicuous aspects of ancient Egyptian pharonic life. The first master copy became the original pattern and, from that were produced numerous sets of identical copies. The initiates reasoned that the transmission from generation to generation of small packs of pictures would endure, and only the most virtuous upon Earth would know the true meaning of what was contained in them. The result was that the major aspect of the *Book of Thoth* was secreted into the background of simple line drawings and, to the uninitiated, the hidden information they contained was so subtly presented that 'it went over their heads'.[2]

The new form of the *Book of Thoth* still carried 'everything the gods wished to reveal'[3] and 'contain infinitely more than can be imagined' (Ibid). They became an elaborate allegory and subsequently evolved into sets of small coloured pictures, some exquisite in design. Many a person, even today, seeing the intricate pictures has found him or herself inexplicably drawn to the illustrations. After allowing their imagery to penetrate their consciousness, many experienced a veritable flooding of his or her mind with emotions or insights, feelings and concepts of an unusual and fascinating character. Those special pictures or symbols were imbued from the very beginning with a magical power and, in themselves, presented a complete picture of all possibilities in human life. The old adepts had preserved forever the symbolic drawings outlining universal knowledge and deeper truths of life. Hidden under glyph and symbol was also found the essential character of our own being and because of that profundity, ancient Egyptian priests called it the *Book of Truth*. Today it is called the *Book of Tarot* and it has the Secret in it.

The Book of Genesis recorded that the plural word for Torah was Torot.[4] Therefore, the Torah represents a singular body of instruction or guidance in book form, and the Torot signifies the plural version containing 22 individual picture cards of instruction or guidance. The word Torot became Tarot in the English language just as Ishtar became Easter. Some analysts suggested that the word 'Torah' was of French origin but Gustav Meyrink, in his book *The Golem*, established 'that the Taroh or Tarot has the same meaning as the Hebrew word, Torah'.

For centuries, the mystical art of Tarot has alerted humanity to a greater truth than the dogmatism of conventional thought. The Tarot is a symbolic storybook of timeless Wisdom in which lies an interpretation of every person's own unique life experiences. The complete deck of Tarot now consists of 78 individual cards divided into two groups: 56 cards of the so-called Minor Trumps and 22 cards of the Major Arcana, the latter being also known as the Great Trumps. The word 'Arcana' applied to Tarot cards means, 'something hidden, secret or mysterious'. The modern deck of Tarot is of profound symbolic performance, for its arrangement is in accord with the divisions of the year. Two colours, red and black, represented two grand divisions of the year: that during which the sun was north of the equator and that during which it was south of the equator. The 13 cards of each suit were the 13 lunar months in each year, and 4 separate sets of 13 cards represented the 52 weeks in the year. However, the 22 Major Arcana cards are the main interest in this study. There is evidence that the 56 Minor Trumps were added to the 22 Major cards at a much later date, the purpose being to conceal the importance of what the 22 Major cards really were.

During the second millennium before the Christian era, Egyptian colonists with their sacred Mysteries settled in various European countries. Significantly, it is believed the first migrants from Egypt travelled as far west as the British Isles; those people came to be known as Gypsies and they carried with them the precious *Book of Thoth*. Through the Gypsies, Thoth's book of symbols was traced back to the original gods of Egypt for the origin of the name Gypsy or Gypsies is a synonym for Egyptian, with the capital E dropped. In plural, they were called Egypties in medieval times and that became Gypsies by natural linguistic process. An initiated contributor to Lewis Spence's *Encyclopedia of Occultism*, Papus, in 1889 said:

> The Gypsies possess a Bible, yes this volume is called the Tarot which is the Bible of the Bibles. It is a marvellous book and immense antiquity is claimed for it. Under the names of Taro, Tora, Rota, this collection has formed successively the basis of secret teaching of all the ancient peoples.[5]

In modern research, the Tarot cards are traced back to the 13th century in Europe when the Christian church banned them. Through the Gypsies, the Tarot cards entered many European countries and were thereby established.

It is significant that the appearance of the Tarot in Europe between 1300 and 1322 coincided with the persecution of the Knights Templar by Philip the Fair of France and Pope Clement V, and the ultimate burning of their Grand Master De Molay in 1314.

The Tarot cards entered England with the Gypsies and they also carried with them the Book of Enoch. In his work 'The Gypsies', Samuel Roberts wrote:

> When Gypsies originally arrived in England is very uncertain. They are first mentioned in our laws by several statutes against them in the reign of Henry VIII (1491-1547) in which they are described as 'an outlandish people calling themselves Egyptians; who do not profess any craft or trade, but go about in great numbers with secret books'.

Remains of the original Tarot designs can be seen today in ruins of the temples of Thebes, capital of Egypt in 2000 BC, particularly on ancient ceilings in the halls of the palace of Medinet-Abou. Moreover, the 22 major cards are also found paralleled in the *Book of the Dead*, etched into stone crypts as vignettes or word sketches thousands of years ago. The great spiritual understanding concealed, yet revealed, in the Tarot, demanded admiration for the profound wisdom of the great sages who secretly preserved the cards for humanity, for they gave them in some form to every race and nation on Earth. Socrates once said that 'those who established the Mysteries were men of great genius'.

The oldest known collection of the Tarot in the world is being used in this work. They are imitative of the vignettes etched in the *Book of the Dead* and, as seen here by their reproduction, vary significantly from modern-day renditions. They are dated to the fourth century and are not unlike the set Ezra and his scribes had in their possession when they wrote the Torah.

Under the pseudonym of Jean Baptiste Pitois, initiate P Christian wrote one of the best works on the Tarot. In 'History of Magic', he described the ritual of initiation into the Egyptian Mysteries in which a leading role was played by the pictures of the 22 Major cards. He was the mouthpiece of a certain 19th century French Secret Society and this is what he said:

The neophyte enters a long gallery, supported by caryatides (columns) in the form of 24 sphinxes, 12 on each side. On each part of the wall between the sphinxes there were frescoed paintings, representing the mystical figures and symbols of the greater Arcana. These 22 pictures faced one another in pairs…As the neophyte was escorted past the 22 pictures of the gallery he received appropriate instruction from his conductor, consisting of an interpretation of the symbolism…Each arcanum, made visible and tangible by each of these 22 pictures, is a formula of the law of human activity in its relation to astral and physical forces, the combination of which produces the phenomena called 'Life'.

After each of the 22 pictures was explained to him, the initiate had completed Stage 1 of a particular secret ceremony. Edward Schure, whose source of information was similar to that of P Christian, hinted at an identical ceremony in his chapter on initiation into the Hermetic Mysteries.

The Tarot was a vital element in Rosicrucian symbolism, being the very book of universal knowledge that members of the order claimed to possess. The expression Rota Mundi is a secret term frequently occurring in the early manifestoes of the Fraternity of the Rose Cross. The word Rota, by rearrangement of its letters, becomes Taro and Tora, the ancient names (vocally sounding identical to Tarot and Torah) used for the plural and singular of those mysterious cards. A major researcher of Sir Francis Bacon's work, WFC Wigston, discovered evidence that Bacon employed the Tarot symbolism in many of his ciphers. The numbers 22, 56 and 78 are directly related to the division of the Tarot deck (22 Major cards; 56 minor cards, total 78) and are frequently found in Bacon's cryptograms. In the great Shakespearian Folio of 1623, the Christian name of Bacon appears 22 times on page 56 of 'Histories'.[6] Wigston's evidence pointed to the existence of a group of wise and illustrious 'Frates' who assumed the responsibility of publishing and preserving for future generations all clues necessary to link the Tarot cards with the Secret in the Bible.

The 22 Major Arcana cards are directly linked to vital physical aspects of the Giza complex and in an extraordinary manner, to the first five books of the Bible. Troward, the English metaphysician, knew that when he recorded; 'There are three gates to the Mysteries…the Bible, the Tarot and the Great

Pyramid'. The 22 Major Tarot cards must be considered firstly as separate and complete hieroglyphs each representing a distinct principle, law, power or element of nature. Secondly, they must be looked upon in relation to each other; that is, they must be viewed as the effect each one has upon the other. Both the *Book of Thoth/Tarot* and the *Book of the Dead* had a profound impact on the Torah and they, like the Great Pyramid, provided the reason for the Bible coming into existence.

The 22 picture cards of the Major Tarot possess an imagery of a unique psychological power that is strangely evocative of unexpected intuitions and glimpses of a world beyond the senses. The reason for that is they possess the same cosmic element that gave the Bible its reputation of being a divine book. The Major Arcana cards were purposely designed to outline the path of life of a human being from its beginning to its end, and altogether, they reveal a complete picture of all possibilities in human life. They also contain a summary of Initiation, and that formed the heart of every major Secret Society or Mystery School in the world. The extraordinary Wisdom contained in Tarot symbolism is two-fold and universal, and belongs to no one race, creed or culture, but constitutes a text book for every serious aspirant searching for truth or looking to solve the riddle of existence. In many respects, it is the Key to unlock the mythical doctrines and philosophies of the Old World and was at one time called the 'Arcana of the Clavicles of Solomon'.

The 22 letters of the Hebrew alphabet were formulated from the same source as the *Book of Thoth* and the secret to unlocking that mystery was ciphered into the Bible. The 22 picture cards directly represent the 22 letters of the Hebrew alphabet in which the Torah was originally written. For each of the letters there is a corresponding Major Tarot card, a number from 1 to 22 in a particular and direct sequence. The 22 Major Tarot Trumps and the 22 letters of the Hebrew alphabet cannot be synchronized without first fixing the correct position of the unnumbered, or zero card, usually given to the symbol now called the Fool, but in the original Egyptian pack it was called the Madman. Different opinions exist as to the position of that card in the pack, and why it was unnumbered is explained mathematically by the hidden code in the Tarot itself. If the zero card be considered extraneous to the Major Trumps, then the numerical analogy between the Tarot and the 22 letters of the Hebrew alphabet is destroyed by leaving one Hebrew letter without a Tarot correspondent and that conflicts with all ancient clues left behind to assist in unravelling the substance of those extraordinary mysteries.

The coded Psalm

The numerical sequence of the 22 Major Arcana cards is constantly in dispute and diverse opinions exist, all based on various personal lines of thought. Ezra knew the illustrious origin of the *Book of Thoth* and ciphered a code into the Book of Psalms to unlock its mystery. A detailed description of every Tarot card and its correct sequence was purposely recorded in the Psalms, a collection of 150 'songs sung to the accompaniment of stringed instruments', the longest and cruelest book in the Bible.

The popular church belief that David was the author of the whole Psalter is no longer accepted. Modern scholars now agree that the Psalms came from a variety of authors and are not as old as originally supposed. Uncertainty prevailed as to the actual date but it seems clear they were mostly, if not all, post-exilic, that is around the time of Ezra and Nehemiah (c. 397 BC). The parallels in the Psalms to Babylonian literature are quite extraordinary and that provided the reason why researchers agreed that the majority of the Psalms were written after the Babylonian captivity. Ezra himself said that he wrote some Psalms[7] and it is probable that he personally compiled the 'coded Psalm' to specifically leave clues for future generations to unlock the Ancient Mysteries. The Psalm of importance is number 119, and it directly identifies a major aspect of each Major Arcana card, but not in the order they are found in the *Book of Thoth*, for a particular reason soon explained.

The significance of number 22 becomes apparent, for Psalm 119 has 22 separate verses, each consisting of eight lines. Most important is the fact that all eight lines of each series of verse begin with a particular and identical alphabetical letter, proceeding successively through the 22 letters of the Hebrew alphabet. In simple terms, the same letter leads each line of each separate eight line-stanza. For example; the eight verses of the first section begin with the first letter of the alphabet, Aleph, and the eight verses of the second section begin with the second letter, Beth. The third letter, Gimel, leads the third verse, and that precision continues until all 22 letters of the alphabet are employed. The 22 stanzas are in a specific and particular alphabetical order and make up the correct 22 letter sequence of the Hebrew alphabet. The significance of that vital clue soon becomes apparent. Psalm 119 is a prime example of how Ezra left a series of biblical clues, a great many never being discovered by orthodox churchmen because they did not have the mystical key to their recovery and interpretation. Similar inklings of secret information were discovered in other areas of the Book of Psalms. There are no less than nine Psalms in which the first letters of each stanza (in Hebrew) are taken in alphabetical order. That is not immediately apparent in English translations, but in the Hebrew versions the clue is obvious. Psalm 119, therefore provides vital 'inside information' that identifies the 22 Major Tarot cards, and reveals their association with the Secret in the Bible.

An interesting series of coded verses also appears in the Book of Exodus.[8] Those narratives also have a direct link with the symbolism of the Mystery Schools and major elements of the Osiris saga. What was written is scarcely the result of coincidence for the letters of Verse 19 are separated from the words, and then written individually across the page. Verse 20 was then also taken as letters, and written in reverse order under Verse 19. Then, Verse 21, again in separated letters, was written under verse 20, but in direct order like Verse 19. When read from above, that peculiar series of letters yielded 72 separate words or names, all different and each having three letters. Those three consecutive verses all contain an identical number of individual letters, and, in the form they were written, conceal an ancient cipher or code related to number 72.

There are 72 divisions of the Hebrew astronomical system (6 x 12) and there are as many 'princes' or leaders of the twelve tribes, six to each tribe (6 x 12 again) who came together for the national council. In the Hebrew Cabala, there are 72 angels through whom the divine powers are approached, or invoked, by those knowing their names and numbers. In the Gospel of Luke (10:1 and 10:7), Jesus was attributed with 72 followers, and the Book of Exodus mentions 72 elders to whom Moses gave secret teachings. The Book of Jasher recorded that 72 elders were instructed into the 'Secret' in the Torah after Ezra and his scribes wrote it. The Book of Jasher (Jasher the Upright) is actually the original and condensed version of Genesis, and the church today has difficulty explaining why a title often in use for Genesis in old Bibles is the 'Book of the Upright' (Jasher). They also have problems explaining why the description of the establishment of the priesthood under one person (Ezra) appeared in Chapter 21 of the Book of Jasher, and that was perhaps the reason why the book was later suppressed.

Probably the fascination in the number 72 originated in Egypt when Seth led a group of conspirators to plot and kill his brother Osiris. The number of the schemers was 72 and they set the stage for the famous story of the death and resurrection of Osiris. Ezra subsequently structured the peculiar code of 72 separate words or names into the Book of Exodus and thereIN lies another mystery or secret in the Bible waiting to be unlocked.

Each of the 22 stanzas of Psalm 119 records within itself a subtle but distinct symbolical reference to each of the 22 major Arcana cards, but not in numerical order. That is because the 22 Arcanas work on a sequence of equidistant skips of two cards; they were not designed to run alphabetically with the Hebrew language but to a particular mathematical scheme or code explained shortly. The author of Psalm 119 revealed but concealed the direct connection. Each of the 22 stanzas (or Hymns) contains a distinctive clue that directly associates each stanza with a major aspect of the symbol on the face of each Tarot card. In-as-much as each verse of Psalm 119 represents a particular Hebrew letter they also provided a full description of the pictorial presentation on each Tarot card.

For example, Psalm 119:14 makes reference to 'a lamp to guide my feet', which is directly paralleled in the Tarot card called the Hermit, who carries a lamp to light his way. Likewise, the 'midnight watch' (Ps.119:19) relates to the card of the Moon, and 'fixed in the heavens' refers to the Tarot card of 'Stars'. A full description of the 22 clues in the 22 verses of Psalm 119, and their identify with each of the 22 Major Tarot cards, is provided in the following chart:-

22 Major Tarot Cards; The Ancient Egyptian Pack Originally Called "The Book of Thoth"	The Clue from Biblical Narratives from The Book of Psalms, 119, Consisting of 22 Verses	Psalm Numbers 1- 22
Magician	"... those who unlock the secret places..." "... thy hands formed me,...heart blameless"	119:10
Priestess (High)	"...wisdom is better than gold and silver..."	119:9
Queen	"...grant me life... give me life..."	119:5
Pharaoh	"...testimony before kings... the word of truth"	119:6
Priest (High)	"... just and right... justice and judgment..."	119:16
Decisions	"... teach me by decrees... a young man walks" (also) "... Learning..."	119:2
Lionpair (Chariot of Osiris)	"... wiser than the ancients... on the right path"	119:1
Truth & Justice	"... when you take the veil from my eyes..."	119:3
Pilgrim	"... a lamp to guide my feet...and light my path"	119:14
Wheel of Destiny	"... going around... holding a steady course..."	119:1
Courage	"Strengthen me... the chosen way to the truth..."	119:4
The Trial	"Set me free.. between heaven and earth...this affliction."	119:20
Reaper	"... my soul shall live... let my soul live..."	119:7
Incarnation	"... it is the course of life... turned my steps..."	119:8
Injustice	"Horror, the wicked... godless men."	119:15
Destruction	"trouble and anguish...down from the upright"	119:18
Union/Hope	"... fixed in the heavens..."	119:12
Moon	"... I set before dawn... the night-watch, of old"	119:19
Sun	"... gives light... all is light... to shine..."	119:17
Immortality	" lift me from the earth.. to salvation...Execute judgment..."	119:11
The Rhythm of World Life	"... created in seven days... seven days of time"	119:2
Madman	"... astray like a lost sheep..."	119:2

'Numbers begin at one and are made perfect at three'

There is another revelation concealed in Thoth's book of symbols and it takes the form of a purposely-designed secret mathematical code. The 22 major Tarot cards were designed as three separate sets of seven cards (3 x 7 = 21), plus the zero (0) card that defies classification. Multiplying 3 x 7, totals 21 cards, plus the addition of the unnumbered zero card makes 22 cards in total. The three sets of seven cards provide three distinct paths running through the original pages of the *Book of Thoth* and that relates to the ancient Egyptian belief in the existence of Three Companies of Gods.

The first group of seven cards start with the first symbol, the Magician; the second group of seven start at the second symbol, the Priestess, and the third group of seven start at the third symbol, the Queen. Every path of seven then continues on, leaving out two symbols (or cards) after each symbol on the way. The hidden code starts at the first symbol and continues in equidistant skips after every third card or symbol. The following chart clarifies the matter.

1st Series of 7 Cards All Connected		2nd Series of 7 Cards All Connected		3rd Series of 7 Cards All Connected		Added Across and Together
Magician	1	Priestess	2	Queen	3	1+2+3=6
Pharaoh	4	Priest	5	Decisions	6	4+5+6=6
Chariot	7	Justice	8	Pilgrim	9	7+8+9=6
Wheel	10	Courage	11	Trials	12	10+11+12=6
Reaper	13	Incarnation	14	Injustice	15	13+14+15=6
Destruction	16	Union/Hope	17	Moon	18	16+17+18=6
Sun	19	Immortality	20	Rythm	21	19+20+21=6

The code is confirmed mathematically. In each of the three groupings, not only the individual symbols relate to each other, insofar as they all constantly related back to the first three primary cards, but there is also a hidden mathematical relationship in the number of the symbols.

All cards or symbols in the first of the three groupings connect back to their lead card, No.1, supported by their numerical value. The same applies to the other two groupings. Every numbered card has a hidden value as well as its usual value, and the hidden value reveals its deeper significance. To discover that value, a special method of addition is used and it consists of adding together all the separate figures of a number. For example, the fourth card (Pharaoh) refers directly to the first card, the Magician (Magi), and is precisely coordinated to it mathematically. This is how it works.

Add up to the number of that card (4) like this: $1 + 2 + 3 + 4 = 10$. The two figures of 10 are then added together, $1 + 0 = 1$. The number 1 is the result, revealing that card No.4 is directly connected to card No.1. Thus, card four (Pharaoh) leads numerically to card No.1, the Magician, the ancient Egyptian priest. Now, skip three cards to card No.7 (Chariot of Osiris) and apply the same code. Again, add together all numbers up to 7, the number of the card. $1 + 2 + 3 + 4 + 5 + 6 + 7 = 28$; The two figures of 28 are then added together, $2 + 8$ and reduces to 10. 10 are $1 + 0$, adding to 1. Again, card No.7 numerically refers directly back to card No.1. The code is clarifying that this card belongs to the No. 1 set of three sets of seven.

Skip three more cards and take the fourth card (which is No.10 in a Tarot deck) of the first path. That card is called the Wheel of Destiny, and being Card No.10 again add up all numbers to 10, like this. $1 + 2 + 3 + 4 + 5 + 6 + 7 + 8 + 9 + 10 = 55$. However, 55 is $5 + 5$ which is 10; and 10 is $1 + 0$ that is again 1. Therefore, card No.10, the Wheel of Destiny, also refers back (directly connected) to the number one card of the pack. Take now the fifth card of that particular path, the Reaper being No. 13 in the Tarot pack. $1 + 2 + 3 + 4 + 5 + 6 + 7 + 8 + 9 + 10 + 11 + 12 + 13 = 91$. However, 91 is $9 + 1$ adding to 10 and 10 is again $1 + 0$ adding to 1. Thus the Reaper card also relates directly to the first card, the Magi. Card No.16 (Destruction), in the sixth position in the first sequence of seven cards, also totals to 'number one' and relates to the first card. It cannot be any other way, for every symbol in the three separate sets of seven, develops from another. The seventh and last card of the first path of seven cards is the Sun and No 19 in a Tarot pack. Again add up the numbers to 19 like this. $1 + 2 + 3 + 4 + 5 + 6 + 7 + 8 + 9 + 10 + 11 + 12 + 13 + 14 + 15 + 16 + 17 + 18 + 19 = 190$. Therefore 190 is $1 + 9 + 0$ which adds to 10; 10 is 1 + 0 which again equals 1. Again, a direct mathematical connection is established with card No.19 back to card No.1.

The numerical values of the Tarot cards on the second and third series of groupings of seven, which begin with Card No.2 (Priestess) and Card No.3, (Queen), express the same reciprocal relation as those on the first path or pattern. However, there is a small, but significant difference and that is left for other researchers to develop. The core of this work is to reveal the Secret, not fully analyze the code in the *Book of Tarot*, but the spirit of that code is provided here for those who wish to expand upon it. Any person who applies the hidden formula to the remaining two sets of seven cards (and combines the first set of seven) will see an extraordinary pattern of numbers emerge. When used with a cube like that on top of the Black Pyramid, and so often seen in Tarot and Masonic symbology, the numbers precisely relay the angle slopes of the surfaces of the Great Pyramid, being 51 degrees 51 minutes. The influence of the Number 3 is also important for it had a sacred significance for early Egyptians, and their principal gods were generally worshipped as a Triad, the third member proceeding from the other two. Thus, Horus was the child of Osiris and Isis and inferior to them in the Triad. That was the Egyptian Trinity.

The Gypsy Secret

The case for the study of Thoth's book needs to be restated and to fully understand its mystery, one should approach the original trustees, the Gypsies. That the author did, and after months of negotiations, a meeting was organized with a secretive Gypsy family near Cornwall in southwest England. The encounter was short and before leaving, an elderly lady passed me a handwritten list of 22 separate rhyming sentences saying, 'These are the secrets of the *Book of Thoth*. Take them and search'.

For the purposes of clarification, that document shall now be called *The Gypsy Secret* and each verse appears in the upcoming breakdown of the *Book of Thoth*. When the verses are analyzed, they show remarkable parallels to clues provided in the 22 stanzas of Psalm 119 and it is probable that Ezra also had *The Gypsy (Egyptian) Secret* before him when he compiled that Psalm.

The Divine Scale

There was yet another document vital in the development of this work. Titled *The Divine Scale*, it came into the author's possession by a curious course of events, as if a guiding hand was at work. The origin of *The Divine Scale* is not known, but it is Cabalistic in style and an internal reference to Vesper, the Goddess of Fire and Hearth, dates its compilation to around 400 BC. Vesper was renowned for wearing white and purple flowing costumes while holding a flaming torch. *The Divine Scale* may have originally been chanted or sung, which was an ancient way of memorizing traditions. It has profound depth of meaning and its verses are analogical with Psalm 119 and the Tarot symbols. Like the *Book of the Dead* and Psalm 119, it is possible to allocate a Tarot symbol to every passage of *The Divine Scale*.

Identifying secret locations at Giza

The following pages provide an individual summary of each of the 22 pages of Thoth's book, and show, by identifying hidden clues provided by initiates, the significance of those age-old symbols. Using *The Gypsy Secret, The Divine Scale*, the *Book of the Dead*, the Bible, plans of the Mystery Schools and modern-day archaeological results, it represents an opinion of which aspect of the Giza complex each of the 22 symbols of Thoth relates. An extrapolation is summarized in the Master Plans in the end section of this book.

SYMBOL No.1   The Magician (Magi) (Knowledge)

HEBREW LETTER   ALEPH

THE GYPSY SECRET   No.1
'Listen carefully to all my verses, I speak them without veil and without deception'.

REMARKS: This symbol reveals a man in the raiment of a 'Magician' (Magi), an Egyptian priest, one who knew and taught the Secret of the eternal cosmic laws of Nature. Shrouded in mystery and cloaked in secrecy, strange and unexplainable power puzzled and delighted those who observed him. Associated with the god Heka (or Hekau, meaning 'magical power'), son of Atum, he was a person of 'magic' responsible for passing on a 'cosmic awareness' called Heka by his candidates for initiation. Heka had some connection with the Benben, the Bennu bird and the 'vital essence' of the gods. The Magician was often associated with two serpents standing on their tails (the Caduceus in symbolism) and the 'Stele of Revealing'. The symbol represents ambitious people disliking restraint and who generally rise to the top in their profession or occupation.

THE BIBLICAL CLUE. '...those who unlock the secret places...thy hands formed they...heart blameless' (Psalm 119:10).

BOOK OF THE DEAD DESCRIPTION. The Magi are described as 'the Scribes of the House of Life' revealing the teaching called the 'Well of Life' ('If the beginning is unknown, the rest is unknown').

THE GIZA LOCATION. The Well of Life was Campbell's Tomb. (No.6 on The Master Plans)

THE DIVINE SCALE. KEY No.1 'A conscious active cause in all we see'.

SYMBOL No.2   The Priestess (Wisdom)

HEBREW LETTER   BET (BETH)

THE GYPSY SECRET   No.2
'The Book of Life and true Treasure of the World'.

REMARKS: Isis (Ast), the great Mother Goddess sits on a cube-throne between two vertical columns, one black, and one white. She holds two keys in her left hand and a half-covered papyrus Scroll in her right hand. That is the *Book of Thoth* …its pages are being unfolded in this chapter. Isis is indicating that the sacred Mysteries are there to be unveiled. These particular words have been attributed to Isis for thousands of years: 'He who possesses all, has no need of others. He will have the greatest treasure in the world' (The Secret). *The Gypsy Secret* also mentions 'The Treasure of the World' and that is of great interest, for ancient chronicles of Asia claimed that was the name given to a large mass of 'cosmic stone' that displayed a special 'inner heat'. It is relevant to this exposition.

THE BIBLICAL CLUE. 'Wisdom is better than gold and silver' (Psalm 119:9).

BOOK OF THE DEAD DESCRIPTION. Isis was the wife and sister of Osiris, mother of Horus. She was described as 'Blessed are thou among women'. What more needs to be said about the tradition of Isis?

THE GIZA LOCATION. Isis is directly associated with the Temple of Isis, discovered during eleven years of sand clearing at Giza (1925 to 1936). (No. 7 on The Master Plans)

THE DIVINE SCALE. KEY No.2 'And number (2) proves the living unity'. (No. 2 represented two vertical temple columns through which an initiate entered, i.e. I I).

SYMBOL No.3   The Queen (Intuition)

HEBREW LETTER   GIMEL

THE GYPSY SECRET   No. 3
'The Mother of the Sun, the sister of the Moon'.

REMARKS: This symbol is called the Queen ('she rules') because it represents the royal birth of Isis's son, Horus, shown here in his ancient guise as an eagle or falcon. The bird is not shown on modern versions of the card. It is symbolic, and said by initiates to show the original essence of God. Horus is sitting upon a stone perch in the shape of a concealed pyramid, for a series of lines drawn through connecting rock joints, create a perfect pyramid. In that form, the symbol represents the 8th - 12th divisions of the *duat* and reflects the Immortal Soul-body of Horus. The card represents ambitious people.

THE BIBLICAL CLUE. 'Grant me life...give me life' (Psalm 119:5).

BOOK OF THE DEAD DESCRIPTION. 'Horus is the thought, Isis is the word. Horus, open your eyes and see the wonders of earth'.

THE GIZA LOCATION. The Chamber of New Birth/Second Birth is associated with Isis. Later depictions of this symbol show the Queen without her offspring but always pregnant. (No.11 on The Master Plans)

THE DIVINE SCALE. KEY No. 3 'No bound hath he who doth the whole contain'.

SYMBOL No.4   Pharaoh   (Leadership)

HEBREW LETTER   DALET

THE GYPSY SECRET   No.4
'Three and One'.

REMARKS: The image represents the combined deity Osiris-Sokar sitting upon a solid cube with a triangular apron girdled around his waist and reveals him in the 4th –7th divisions of the *duat*. The cube is the symbol of an initiate who acted 'on the square' and the position of his arms in relation to his head forms a triangle. His crossed legs depict the form of a hypothetical square. The symbol reveals people with opposite views.

THE BIBLICAL CLUE. '...the testimony before kings...the word of truth...' (Psalm 119:6).

BOOK OF THE DEAD DESCRIPTION. Osiris is called 'A son of God', or sometimes simply 'God', and is often depicted crowned with a symbolic Sun and a Serpent. There are 21 pylons recorded in the ascent to the House of Osiris through which he passes (21 + 1). 'I cannot be crowned unless the three of us become ashes' ('Three and One'; Osiris, Isis and Horus were 'Three'; the Egyptian Trinity was the 'One').

THE GIZA LOCATION. 'The Hall of Ascent' under the sands below and behind what may be the true entrance into the Great Pyramid (Southern face). (No.9 on The Master Plans)

THE DIVINE SCALE.   KEY No.4
'But all preceding, fill life's vast domain'.

Part of a stone stele showing an inscription of Pharaoh sitting on a cube, circa 1350 BC

SYMBOL No.5   The Priest (Oral Instruction)

HEBREW LETTER   HE

THE GYPSY SECRET   No.5
'He has told the truth and it is not permissible to say more'.

REMARKS: His hand was raised up indicating an oral form of teaching. The two pupils in front of him are clothed in black and white, representing exoteric and esoteric knowledge. Again, black and white vertical columns feature (Jachin and Boaz; I Kings 7:21). Symbol number 5 represents people who are mentally highly strung. They are quick in thought and decisions, and impulsive in their actions. They have the most wonderful elasticity of character and rebound quickly from the heaviest blow. The setbacks of Fate leave no indentations on their character. A good card if drawn in a Tarot reading.

THE BIBLICAL CLUE. '...just and right...judgment and justice' (Psalm 119:16).

BOOK OF THE DEAD DESCRIPTION. It is best to attribute the Stone of God to the Priest symbol for it is there where he oversaw the initiatory process. 'The Symbol of the Secret Works', a human skull, is also associated with this card and according to the sacred tradition of Egypt, the head of Osiris was buried where the Great Pyramid stands. That was probably the origin of the use of a human skull in initiatory rites (the Place of the Skull).

THE GIZA LOCATION. The Stone of God is at the very top of the Grand Gallery in the Great Pyramid. It is a massive stone positioned to form a one-metre high step up into the antechamber leading to the King's Chamber. (No.13 on The Master Plans)

THE DIVINE SCALE. KEY No.5 'Sole worthy worship, he the only Lord'.

SYMBOL No.6   Decision (Decisiveness)

HEBREW LETTER   VAV

THE GYPSY SECRET   No.6
'Understand thoroughly what it is that man has on either hand if you wish to be enlightened'.

REMARKS: The symbol depicts a young man holding the hand of a naked woman (Vice) and another woman, clothed, representing Virtue. The arrow points towards Vice as a warning of punishment that awaits persons who prefer the easy road of Vice to the hard road of Virtue.

THE BIBLICAL CLUE. 'a young man walks...teach me by decrees...learning' (Psalm 119:2).

BOOK OF THE DEAD DESCRIPTION. The symbol is summarized in one specific passage, written, 'Are given to thee two sisters for thy delight...and cursed is the one shot by arrows'. The Egyptian goddess associated with a crossbow was Neith, mother of RA.

THE GIZA LOCATION. Because of its triple nature, this symbol is attributed to the Chamber of the Triple Veil. (No.14 on The Master Plans)

THE DIVINE SCALE. KEY No.6 'Does his true doctrine to clean hearts accord'.

The 1450 BC painted limestone statue shows a young man with two ladies, one sad, the other happy. The concept of Thoth's symbol No. 6 goes back at least 3500 years. Note the remarkable similarity to the presentation of the Scrolls of Knowledge in Chapter One.

SYMBOL No.7   Chariot of Osiris (Individuality)

HEBREW LETTER   ZAYIN

THE GYPSY SECRET   No. 7
'In my body I carry something the wise seek' (SA ?).

REMARKS: The Zohar identifies the symbol as the Chariot Throne and depicts a leader standing up driving a chariot with an iron throne and ornate sides. Two lions pull the chariot, one black and one white, believed to represent 'yesterday and tomorrow'. In Temple records, the symbol was sometimes called the Chariot of RA or the Lionpair, a reference to two Akka (sometimes Aker) lions of Egyptian texts. Preserved in the tombs of some kings was the 'Book of Akka' and that showed a double lion sphinx back to back. A vignette in the papyrus of Ani in the British Museum shows Shu and Tefnut as twin lions supporting the Sun. The symbol represents independent, original people with a strongly marked individuality.

THE BIBLICAL CLUE. '...wiser than the ancients ... on the right path...' (Psalm 119:13)

BOOK OF THE DEAD DESCRIPTION. The reference was to the Throne of Osiris being drawn across the sky above the Gate of the North (The references also continued in the Pyramid Texts.)

THE GIZA LOCATION. The Hidden Lintel or the False door described in the Book of the Dead is the Gate of the North in the Great Pyramid, now the modern-day tourist entry. It was once a hinged, concealed stone door, fitting flush in the white external casing stones. (No.22 on The Master Plans)

THE DIVINE SCALE. KEY No.7 'But since faith's works a single pontiff need'.

SYMBOL No.8   Justice (Truth)

HEBREW LETTER   CHET

THE GYPSY SECRET   No.8
'It is hidden'.

REMARKS: This is the 'scales of justice', one of the four cardinal virtues of the Mystery Schools. In Masonry, its practice is inculcated in the first degree and is 'the cornerstone' on which the Mason expects 'to erect a superstructure honorable to himself and to the Fraternity'. The blindfolded lady shows that true judgment takes place impartially, out of sight of the person concerned. Blindfolding was part of the initiatory process leading to Mysteries being revealed here. The symbol also relates to 'Weighing of words in the dwelling of the Old Man' (Wisdom) in ON (Heliopolis). In ancient Roman judicial trials, a white and black ball was used in the process of judgment. At the end of the presentation of evidence, one was cast into an urn, the white ball acquitting the accused, and the black ball condemning him. The symbol represents deep and intense natured people with great strength of individuality.

THE BIBLICAL CLUE. 'Take the veil from my eyes...' (Psalm 119:3).

BOOK OF THE DEAD DESCRIPTION. The scales and the balance in the Judgment scene revealed probably the most famous of all the ancient *Book of the Dead* depictions. The goddess of Justice and Truth was Maat, daughter of RA. 'The juice of the wise you should enjoy'.

THE GIZA LOCATION. The Hall of Judgment in the Great Pyramid was called the Grand Gallery. (No.12 on The Master Plans) It was called the Hall of Judgment in the Old Testament; 1 Kings 7:6-7.

THE DIVINE SCALE. KEY No.8 'One law have we, and at one altar plead'.

SYMBOL No.9   The Pilgrim (Illumination)

HEBREW LETTER   TET

THE GYPSY SECRET   No. 9
'The light of my eyes is a lantern to my feet'.

REMARKS: Showing a man upholding a lighted lantern on a pilgrimage through life, this card depicts an initiate into the Mysteries...one looking to learn the Secret and improve his knowledge of life. His decision to gain spiritual wisdom was governed by conscious choice and he forgave material possessions. The symbol shows an expansion of an enlightened person from 'the Line of the Immortal race' and called Akhîmû Sokû (the Indestructibles) in the *Book of the Dead*. Rabbi Jesus obtained immortality in his lifetime but was physically killed when he tried to reveal the Secret of the Mystery Schools. A vital clue to obtaining eternal life was provided by Jesus himself: 'Sell what you have, and give it to the poor' (Mark 10:21). The number 9 symbol represents people with a fighting nature, determined and strong willed, and, in the end, successful by their nature.

THE BIBLICAL CLUE. '...a lamp to guide my feet...and light my path' (Psalm 119:14).

BOOK OF THE DEAD DESCRIPTION. The symbol is associated with Khons, 'The Wanderer' who ambled the sky in the dark holding a star to light his way (Sometimes confused with Thoth). The *Book of the Dead* referenced the 'star' or the 'light' and reveals the process to obtain immortality.

THE GIZA LOCATION. The symbol is allocated to the Hall of Initiates, shown on the Mystery Schools plans under the Sphinx. In the Bible, there is also reference to the Hall of Pillars (1 Kings 7:6). (No.3 on The Master Plans)

THE DIVINE SCALE. KEY No.9 'Eternal God for age their light upholds'.

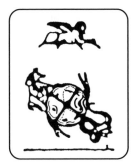

SYMBOL No.10   The Wheel of Destiny (Evolution)

HEBREW LETTER   YOD

THE GYPSY SECRET   No.10
'I am exalted above the circles of this world'.

REMARKS:The Wheel of Destiny turning on its axis represents the cyclical nature of things. Everything lives, turns, rises and falls. The symbol shows two figures sitting on the Wheel. On the left is the good god Hermanibus, and on the right is Typhon, the evil god, shown as a winged dragon. A Sphinx above called Akka, reveals the nature of those who guide the Wheel of Destiny. Good always moves up towards perfection...evil leads downwards towards both inner and outer dissolution, to end in downfall. Clement of Alexandria called the cycle, 'the mysterious wheel', and Plutarch, the 'world wheel'. It is a fortunate number in the sense that one's plans are likely to be carried out.

THE BIBLICAL CLUE. '...going around and around...holding a steady course' (Psalm 119:1).

BOOK OF THE DEAD DESCRIPTION. 'This is fortune with two wings' (good and/or bad). Knowledge and will, decision and advancement in silence are the ongoing and overall message of the Book of the Dead.

THE GIZA LOCATION. The Royal Arch of the Solstice is the name given to the arched entry into halls under the east-facing Sphinx. The Egyptian goddess of Destiny (or Fate) was called Meskhenet. (No.2 on The Master Plans)

THE DIVINE SCALE. KEY No.10 'Heaven and man's day alike, the rule unfolds'.

SYMBOL No.11   Courage (Mercy and Strength)

HEBREW LETTER   KAF

THE GYPSY SECRET   No.11
'The hands hold the symbols'.

REMARKS: The goddess Sekhemt is associated with a lioness, and the symbol shows the attainment of certain knowledge and strengths previously unknown, but with the ability to evolve in each person. The young woman with the garland of flowers whose hand is licked by the lioness is wearing a hat; its brim forms the figure eight on its side, the sign of balance and reminiscent of Eternity. It is known as the symbol of a 'lion muzzled' and that sign may have been the origin of the mode of recognition in Masonry called the 'lion's grip' or the 'lion's paw'. To occultists, the symbol warns of hidden dangers, trial and treachery from others.

THE BIBLICAL CLUE. 'Strengthen me...the chosen way to the truth' (Psalm 119:4).

BOOK OF THE DEAD DESCRIPTION. The lion-god called Reha, said:

Turn back Reha, shining of the mouth moveable of the head, turn back from his strength; otherwise said, turn back from him that keepth guard, and not seen is he. (Could also possibly be associated with the 'Opening of the Mouth' ceremony).

THE GIZA LOCATION. Passage of the Veil, the tunnel-way to the Queen's Chamber. (No.10 on The Master Plans)

THE DIVINE SCALE. KEY No.11 'In Mercy rich, in retribution strong'.

SYMBOL No.12   The Trial (Hanging Man; Balance)

HEBREW LETTER   LAMED

THE GYPSY SECRET   No.12
'God and Nature do nothing in vain'.

REMARKS: This symbol depicts a man hanging from a thick branch defenselessly tied up by one foot. Helpless and abandoned by everyone, he is suspended between heaven and earth. The symbol has a remarkable mythical parallel in the story of Shemyaza, one of the Fallen Angels and leader of the Watchers in the *Book of Enoch*. He was tied and bound before being hung upside-down forever between heaven and earth. It sometimes indicated 'the Victim', one being sacrificed for the plans or intrigues of others.

THE BIBLICAL CLUE. 'Set me free…between heaven and earth' (Psalm 119:20).

BOOK OF THE DEAD DESCRIPTION. The symbol related directly to the Chamber of Upside-downness. Also recorded were these words:

> I am the divine knot with the olive trees…doubly beautiful…(two trees)… I maintain an excellent balance…verily my form is inverted…Not shall I be seized by my arms, (because they are tied) not shall I be carried away by my hands. I maintain an exact balance…I am he who is without the power of walking.

THE GIZA LOCATION. The Chamber of Upside-downness under the base of the Pyramid. (No.19 on The Master Plans) In mythology, two vertical trees represented eternal life for those whose names were inscribed in the trunks.

THE DIVINE SCALE. KEY No.12 'His people's King he will upraise ere long'.

SYMBOL No.13   The Reaper (Transition)

HEBREW LETTER   MEM

THE GYPSY SECRET   No.13
'Thy death, my life, I shall not die'.

REMARKS: The symbol shows that death is not an end, but merely a transitional stage, both a beginning and an end – transformation. There was no death in the Osirian religion, only decay and change. Osiris rose after 3½ days, and a doctrine of resurrection on the 3rd day was bequeathed forever to Egyptian and other eschatology. One of the great objects of the Mystery Schools was to teach belief in a future life. Ancient Freemasonry taught that people disbelieving in a future state were already dead. Among the Ancients, sleep and death were fabled as twins, and in Mystery Schools, death was the symbol of a completed initiation. An ancient document said: 'He who understands the number 13 will be given power and dominion. It is a symbol of power that, if wrongly used, wreaks destruction upon itself'.

THE BIBLICAL CLUE. 'My soul shall live' (Psalm 119:7).

BOOK OF THE DEAD DESCRIPTION. A reaping skeleton said:

I have set them under thy feet; forever, twice…I have collected thy bones. I have come driving back for thee…Let me reap.

THE GIZA LOCATION. Attributed to The Gate of Death at the top of the Grand Gallery in the Great Pyramid. (No.15 on The Master Plans)

THE DIVINE SCALE. KEY No.13 'The tomb gives entrance to the promised land. Death only ends; life's vistas still expand'. Plato said: 'I have heard from the wise men (the initiates) that we are now dead, and that our body is our sepulchre' (*Gorgias*, Plato, Folio 493).

SYMBOL No.14   Incarnation (Equilibrium)

HEBREW LETTER   NUN

THE GYPSY SECRET   No.14
'If he thirst, give him a drink and he shall live'.

REMARKS: Ancient texts claimed that the gold urn filling the silver urn in this symbol represented the balance of life that was 'formed from death, and life is in turn followed by rebirth, just as sunset follows sunrise'. The tradition of water pouring from a gold urn was an emblem of plenty, because it indicated an abundance of water. The urn was used by the ancients to hold the ashes of the deceased after cremation and some believed that when the ashes were poured out, the soul of the deceased gained everlasting life. In Masonry, it is said that the heart of Hiram Abiff was enclosed in a golden urn to ensure him of eternal life.

THE BIBLICAL CLUE. 'It is the course of life...turned in my steps...' (Psalm 119:8). An additional clue is given in the Book of Ecclesiasts: '...or ever the silver cord be loosed, or the golden bowl be broken, or the pitcher broken at the fountain...then shall the dust return to the earth as it was, and the spirit shall return to God who gave it'.

BOOK OF THE DEAD DESCRIPTION. '...the gold and silver urns'. The goddess Anuket is associated with urns and the 'Waters of the Earth'. She was the daughter of Khnum.

THE GIZA LOCATION. The Instrument of Resurrection (or the Resurrection Machine) in the Book of the Dead. It is the lidless sarcophagus in the King's Chamber. (No. 17 on The Master Plans)

THE DIVINE SCALE. KEY No.14 'Good angels all things temper and assuage'.

SYMBOL No.15   Injustice (Demonic, the Lie)

HEBREW LETTER   SAMEK

THE GYPSY SECRET.   No.15
'Satan is almost dead'.

REMARKS: This symbol depicts the spirit of evil, shown as a repulsive creature, sometimes called 'The Great Terrifier' in Egyptian hieroglyphs. The winged figure is represented as a man with the head of a dog or jackal, a general and important pictogram among ancient Moon-worshippers. To them it was a symbol of Sin and the Lunar Mysteries taught that that figure had revealed to Isis the place where the body of Osiris lay concealed. Its left hand holds a spike that has pierced and removed a human heart, a sign of cannibalistic sacrificial rite. For some reason, this creature is connected to a royal family or a mysterious 'unlawful' (or *illicita*) Roman College associated with the Ides of March and the death of Julius Caesar. It is associated with 'good talkers' with strong personal magnetism.

THE BIBLICAL CLUE. 'Horror, the wicked...godless men' (Psalm 119:15).

BOOK OF THE DEAD DESCRIPTION. The creature is called 'the Eater of Millions, living in a lake of fire devouring bodies and swallowing hearts'. Apophis, the foe of RA, is the personification of the power of darkness and was not seen in daylight. His cavern in Hell is described as: 'His hall is Grief; his table Famine; Hunger, his knife; Delay, his servant; Faintness, his porch; Sickness and Pain is his bed'.

THE GIZA LOCATION. The Chamber of the Shadow is given as the home of that creature and it is assigned to the pit or grotto below the Great Pyramid. (No.20 on The Master Plans) It could also be the Black Pyramid.

THE DIVINE SCALE. KEY No.15 'While evil spirits burst with wrath and rage'.

SYMBOL No.16   Destruction (Forces of nature)

HEBREW LETTER   AYIN

THE GYPSY SECRET   No.16
'This is Nature'.

REMARKS: Sometimes called 'the Shattered Citadel', the tower is struck by lightning, splitting into two and burning. The builder, wearing a crown, is crashing down from the top window. In modern-day cards, two persons are shown falling. From a symbolic point of view, this symbol is highly suggestive. In the initiation ritual, the candidate was asked 'whence he comes and whither is he travelling' and was expected to answer, 'from the lofty tower of Babel, where language was confounded', meaning the end of an established understanding. In the Sacred Mysteries, a falling Temple or Tower meant that the profane had infiltrated the secret teachings and that effectively meant the end of that particular School. The Degree of the Tower is the name sometimes given to the second degree of the Masonic Royal Order of Scotland.

THE BIBLICAL CLUE. '...trouble and anguish...down from the upright'. (Psalm 119:18).

BOOK OF THE DEAD DESCRIPTION. Seth was the God of Storms and Violence and is associated with this symbol. He was responsible for the death of Osiris that ultimately caused his own destruction.

THE GIZA LOCATION. The Chamber of Ordeal, outside the Sphinx and to the South. (No.1 on The Master Plans)

THE DIVINE SCALE. KEY No.16 'God doth the lightning rule, the flame subdue'.

SYMBOL No.17   Union/Hope (Heavens)

HEBREW LETTER   PE

THE GYPSY SECRET   No.17
'Clear water made from the Sun and the Moon'.

REMARKS:The lady is pouring the contents of two jugs into the sea. To the right, a bird is flapping its wings in the Tree of Life, ready to depart, and represents the soul leaving earth. In the top left hand corner of the symbol are seven stars, one particularly large. In the Mystery Schools, seven lighted candles were called 'Seven Stars' and used in some ceremonies, especially when receiving distinguished visitors. Two special chalices of gilt metal and silver are used, their stem height being directly related to the diameter of the bowl and associated with sacred geometry.This is a highly spiritual symbol.

THE BIBLICAL CLUE. '…fixed in the heavens' (Psalm 119:12).

BOOK OF THE DEAD DESCRIPTION. 'Rains are made by seven stars', is one of two descriptions found.The other said that,'Out of the stars come rain'.Associated with Heket, wife of Khrum, Guardian of the Source of the Nile.

THE GIZA LOCATION. The Passage of the Polestar (also called the Gate to the Great God in the Pyramid Texts). That description is given to the top half of the now-called descending passage used by tourists today for entry into the Great Pyramid. It entered/exited on the northern face of the Great Pyramid. (No.21 on The Master Plans)

THE DIVINE SCALE. KEY No.17 'His word controls both Vesper and her drew'.

SYMBOL No.18   The Moon (Night/Darkness)

HEBREW LETTER   ZADI

THE GYPSY SECRET   No.18

'Without the light of the Moon the Sun does not heat the earth'.

REMARKS: A clear night-time scene shows the moon as both 'full' and 'new', with a crescent to the right depicting the 'new' aspect. The moon is positioned over a hilltop capped with two vertical parallel columns representing the symbol of initiation and enlightened knowledge. Wolves are 'howling at the moon' and symbolize unregenerate or lower minds that are excluded from entrance into higher esoteric knowledge. Under Mark Antony (c. 44 BC), a priesthood called 'Repellers of Wolves' was established to oppose followers of Sin (Sinisters) who 'operated in the shadow of the moon's reflected light'. That false illumination is guiding only the unenlightened and they 'faded into insignificance' in the light of spiritual knowledge. Their high priests practised Black Magic and were buried in black granite sarcophagi. Those priests suppressed the original '18 Laws of the Cosmos'.

THE BIBLICAL CLUE. 'I set before dawn...the night watch of old' (Ps. 119:19).

BOOK OF THE DEAD DESCRIPTION. The symbol relates to Thoth, patron of the Scribes and Inventor of Writing. At night, he sought and exposed those basking in the light of the moon and hiding from the sun.

THE GIZA LOCATION. It is the Hall of Truth in Darkness so often referenced in the Book of the Dead. The symbol is allocated to the dark subterranean passage shown on the plans leading from The Well of Life to the Great Pyramid. (No.8 on The Master Plans)

THE DIVINE SCALE. KEY No.18 'He makes the Moon our watchman throughout the night'.

SYMBOL No.19   The Sun (Day/Light)

HEBREW LETTER   KOPH (QOF)

THE GYPSY SECRET   No. 19
'Out of the Sun and the Moon make a thing of equal parts'.

REMARKS: This symbol is sometimes called the Sun of RA and shows the Giver of Life, the lord (or essence) of life on earth, the carrier of Wisdom. Hardly any Mystery School symbols are more important in their signification or more extensive in their application than the sun. As the source of material light, it reminded the initiate of that intellectual light for which he was constantly searching. The sun was originally presented as the symbol of light but then more emphatically as the sovereign authority, or the emblem of Divine Truth. Wealthy Sun-worshippers were buried in white marble sarcophagi. This symbol is fortunate and extremely favourable.

THE BIBLICAL CLUE. '...gives light...all is light...to shine' (Psalm 119:17).

BOOK OF THE DEAD DESCRIPTION. RA was the Sun-god, was directly linked to the divine and a deity of great Wisdom. He came to earth in the celestial Benben, 'The Throne of Radiance was that of RA'. RA had several aspects, those being Osiris, Khepra or Atum. In the Heliopolitan creation myth, Atum was said to have seeded the Universe with life. The Sphinx was sometimes called the 'Living Image of Atum'.

THE GIZA LOCATION. The very top pyramidion once on the Great Pyramid, the so-called 'missing capstone' today. (No.5 on The Master Plans)

THE DIVINE SCALE. KEY No.19 'His crown illuminates the mercy seat and glorifies the cherubs at his feet'.

SYMBOL No.20   Immortality (Spirit)

HEBREW LETTER   RESH

THE GYPSY SECRET   No.20
'The dead bodies remain, the spirits are freed by the death of the body'.

REMARKS: A father, mother and child rise from the grave, death behind them forever and are representative of the story of Osiris, Isis and Horus. This portrayal depicts in symbolic form the Egyptian belief in eternal life and is often associated with the ancient term: 'A dissolution of the body is the first step'. The symbol represents the awakening of new purpose, new plans, new ambitions, the call to action, but for some great purpose, cause or duty. It is not a material number and is a doubtful one as far as worldly success is concerned.

THE BIBLICAL CLUE. 'Lift me from the earth... to salvation'. Psalm 119:11 ('Its soul is all fair and sure, for it is the true him'; The Book of Jasher).

BOOK OF THE DEAD DESCRIPTION. The Book of the Dead, now thousands of years old, gives an impression of an ancient society not so much obsessed with death, but with one deeply involved in preparing for the afterlife. 'Whiteness forty days after ashes', and 'bodies built of lives' are the direct connections. In the Egyptian mummification process, some body parts were not removed from the corpse until 40 days after death. The Pyramid Texts described in detail an out-of-body experience or an after-life journey of the King.

THE GIZA LOCATION. That is the Chamber of Resurrection, sometimes translated, the Chamber of the Open Tomb. In modern terminology it is called the King's Chamber. (No.16 on The Master Plans)

THE DIVINE SCALE. KEY No.20 'When dust to dust returns his breath can call, Life from the tomb which is the fate of all'.

SYMBOL No.21 The Rhythm of Life (Balance/Time)

HEBREW LETTER   SHIN

THE GYPSY SECRET   No.21
'It is the end in which the beginning rests'.

REMARKS: This number is symbolized by a picture of the Universe and is sometimes called 'the Crown of the Magi'. In essence, it depicts that everything developed in space and time in accordance with the previous symbols, and then finally returns to its origin. The young girl dances with a veil revealing spirituality in the symbolism of her dance. Everything goes around...

THE BIBLICAL CLUE. '...created in seven days...' (Psalm 119:21)

BOOK OF THE DEAD DESCRIPTION. This symbol is associated with the Sky-goddess NUT. It was in the middle of her body that the Mysteries of life, death and resurrection took place. 'Await for me a month', she asked (In death). That statement has remarkable similarities with the previous symbol (No. 20; Immortality).

THE GIZA LOCATION. The Gypsy Secret provided a two-fold clue in this instance. This symbol is the Temple of the Grand Orbit, shown on the plans under the Sphinx, and connects by a stairway to the Gate of Coming Forth by Day between the paws of the Sphinx. The domed ceiling of the circular Temple represents the on-going movement of the Heavens. Its connection with the Gate of Coming Forth by Day is clarified in a later chapter. (See No.4 and No.18 on The Master Plans)

THE DIVINE SCALE. KEY No.21 'These doctrines sacred, pure and steadfast shine'.

SYMBOL No. 0   The Madman (Ignorance)

HEBREW LETTER   TAV

THE GYPSY SECRET   No.22
'He that cometh to know this figure will have no knowledge'.

REMARKS: This symbol represents a spiritually poor person 'awake but not aware', one who does not 'hear or see'. He is oblivious to the crocodile stalking him and the jackal eating him. He is setting out on the road of earthly attainment…that leads nowhere, means nothing and ends in nothing. The knapsack on his back is full of Errors and his hat depicts a new moon inverted, indicating his infernal or lower state of development. He operates mainly at instinct level and is of 'the Line of the Mortal race'. A passage in the Rig Veda corresponds with this symbol: 'Selfish desire was formed in his mind'. The fool/madman never read books or knocked on the doors of Institutes of Enlightenment…and has 'no part in the world to come'.[9] It is the symbol of illusion and false judgment, sometimes due to the influence of others.

THE BIBLICAL CLUE. '…astray like a lost sheep' (Psalm 119:22).

BOOK OF THE DEAD DESCRIPTION. 'But between the Alpha and the Omega there is the weary path, hedged in, that goes down to darkness, yes to the very end. This he has made in his own image'.

THE GIZA LOCATION. The passage or path of the descent of Man, the dark unused bottom half of the now-called Descending Passage. The Book of the Dead said it was 'reserved for souls who have failed their assignment to teach in the earth dimension.' (Lower portion of No. 21 on The Master Plans) That symbol is connected to the chief priests of Sin who were 'born of darkness'.

THE DIVINE SCALE. KEY No.22 '…and thus we close our number's scale divine'.

Revealed in this section were the direct correlations between:

1. The 22 letters of the Hebrew alphabet
2. The 22 verses of Psalm 119
3. The 22 *Book of the Dead* descriptions
4. The 22 Great Pyramid and Sphinx locations
5. The 22 stanzas of the Gypsy Secret
6. The 22 pages of Thoth's book (Tarot/Torah)
7. The 22 verses of The Divine Scale

THE DIVINE SCALE (As originally written)

1. A conscious, active cause in all we see.
2. And number proves the living unity.
3. No bound hath he who doth the whole contain.
4. But, all preceding, fills life's vast domain.
5. Sole worthy worship, He the only Lord.
6. Doth his true doctrine to clean hearts accord.
7. But since faith's works a single pontiff need.
8. One law have we, and at one altar plead.
9. Eternal God for aye their light upholds.
10. Heaven, and man's day alike, the rule unfolds.
11. In mercy rich, in retribution strong.
12. His people's King he will upraise ere long.
13. The tomb gives entrance to the promised land.
    Death only ends; life's vistas still expand.
14. Good angels all things temper and assuage.
15. While evil spirits burst with wrath and rage.
16. God doth the lightning rule, the flame subdue.
17. His word controls both Vesper and her drew.
18. He makes the moon our watchman throughout the night.
19. His crown illuminates the mercy seat
    And glorifies the cherubs at his feet.
20. When dust to dust returns his breath can call
    Life from the tomb which is the fate of all.
21. These doctrines sacred, sure and steadfast shine.
22. And thus we close our number's scale divine.

CHAPTER ELEVEN

THAT CELESTIAL OBJECT

In earlier chapters, brief mention was made of a sacred, strange and mysterious 'secret object' the Ancients called the Benben. The Pyramid Texts refer to it as the 'Celestial Chamber' and that truly enigmatic object holds within itself the primary element of all Mystery School teachings. A most telling passage in the Pyramid Texts reveals that the Benben was made of 'star' material and it 'came from the heavens'. According to ancient Egyptian and Sumerian depictions, the Benben was a pyramidal-shaped object maybe 15 feet high and credited with an inexplicable cosmic origin. Another intriguing description suggested that it was a 55-faceted sphere with one larger base facet upon which it sat and all facets pyramidal in shape. People of the time originally and consistently believed that RA, their Sun god, and Khepra, an attribute of RA, came to earth in the Benben from the 'Planet of Millions of Years'. In some old hieroglyphs, the Benben is called the 'Pyramidion Bird' and is usually associated with descriptions of beautiful colours.

Tradition maintained that the Benben was kept at Heliopolis in remote pre-dynastic times and was of extreme religious importance and value. It was enshrined in a special building called 'The Temple of the Benben', sometimes also called the 'Temple of the Obelisk', and devout Egyptians made long pilgrimages to Heliopolis to revere and pray to it. It was initially kept hidden in the Temple's inner sanctum and displayed to the public once every year. Pilgrimages to the shrine continued well into dynastic times and 'thousands of visitors'[1] paid their deep respects to it.

Hieroglyph showing reverence being paid in private to a scaled down version of a Benben on top of an obelisk.

Heliopolis was the great centre of learning, sacred and secular, with a huge population of thirteen thousand and a pre-eminent library that later helped form the famous Alexandrian complex. Ancient texts stated that the shrine was guarded and serviced twenty-four hours a day by two separate groups of dedicated priestly people. There were 'those who are outside' but were allowed into the shrine's most sacred areas, for it was their task to receive offerings from the pilgrims and respectfully place them at the base of the Benben; and the others, eight in number, who were called 'those who possess the Mystery', and were guardians, not only of the Benben but of 'the secret things of RA which are in the Benben'. Something being 'in' or, 'within' (in some translations) the Benben was widely reported, and a 'mystery' in itself existed around the interior of the object.

© Zecharia Sitchin 1993

Ancient Egyptian tradition held that a large pyramidal object like this came from the sky.

Some researchers call it the 'Benben Stone', but in its original form, it was not a stone as such, for in every recorded description, observers clearly stated that they could 'see into it'. Maybe it was the discovery of a Benben reproduction that was responsible for the object being considered something dense. This small stone carving, suffering some damage, was found in the tomb of an Egyptian priest and portrays the great god RA 'within' a pyramidal-shaped object.

That symbolic personification was the artist's method of showing that there was a god within the object, and he could be seen. It represents a stylistic approach, that being RA personally as a physical, actual god on Earth and inside the Benben.

It is not possible to offer a logical earthly solution as to where or how the Benben came to Earth, and many theories are posited about its origin. Some would have it as a meteorite, since the ancients believed meteorites were the physical representation of star gods arriving on Earth. The oldest written reference appeared in the *Book of the Dead* where it is called the 'Throne of Radiance' and Australian Aborigines preserved an ancient oral tradition that said 'the Benben rode the Milky Way call MU'. Tibetan belief maintained that it was 'from one of the solar systems in the constellation of Orion …a mineral from another world'[2] and in Lamaism, it is alluded to as the 'Treasure of the World'.

The truth of its origin and composition is not known, but words written in stone establish that it existed, and could be looked into. It is possible the object was clear-sided glass or crystalline in substance, or maybe a sealed, opaque chamber. It seems certain that it had some sort of supernatural origin and it is probable that the Benben was responsible for the creation of Heliopolis itself.

Egyptian history recorded that the shrine at Heliopolis was destroyed several times by enemy invaders. Nothing but a dismal solitary obelisk remains of Heliopolis today, but a large number of stones taken from the ruins were, at different periods, built into the walls of principal buildings at Cairo, particularly the mosque of Khaliph Haken. One large granite stone served as a doorsill to the mosque of Shâaban and can be seen today. The obelisk survived the destruction of the ruins, and its deeply cut hieroglyphs spoke of Pharaoh Usirtasen I who erected it. Even though a Cairo suburb in that area today is called Heliopolis, the ancient city has totally disappeared, along with the Benben itself.

The sparse plain and mounds of Heliopolis c. 1890, the original home of the Benben some thousands of years previous. In the distance, Cairo rises against the southwest. Note the solitary obelisk on the horizon. This portrayal was drawn on the spot by Faucher-Gudin, and produced as a watercolor (Published by Lepsius).

The sole marker of the great temple of RA. The granite obelisk of Usirtasen I, standing in the plain of Heliopolis, c. 1890. Pharaoh Usirtasen I originally raised two identical obelisks, one on either side of the principal gateway; the other either fell or was overturned in 1160. Drawn by Boudier, from a photograph by Insinger.

The obelisk at Heliopolis, 2003. It now stands between Terminal 1 and Terminal 2 at the Cairo International Airport and just 500 metres from the main runway. The scaffolding was erected for winter cleaning.

Ancient plan of the ruins of Heliopolis showing the gateway on the southern wall leading to Babylon. The location of the obelisk is shown and the 'irrigation canal' identified on the right of the drawing is today the location of the Cairo International Airport.

There are five excellent examples of the concept of the Benben in the main hall of the Egyptian Museum in Cairo today. The largest is the pyramidion of Amenemhet III (c. 1800 BC), a superbly crafted example in solid black granite and carved with exquisite hieroglyphs. It was found in 1902 by Professor Gaston Maspero, Director-General of the Antiquities Service, and is believed to have been intended for Amenemhet's pyramid at Dashur, some 40 kilometres south of Giza. One of the Museum's Benbens is of particular interest, being a slightly smaller version with a flat base on its top, reminiscent of a miniature version of the Great Pyramid itself. It provides further evidence that the very serious business of pyramid building was far more than the creation of elaborate tombs, and ancient texts reveal that many Benbens constructed during Egypt's 'Age of Gold' were sheathed with gold; as was the Sphinx according to one persistent theory.

Preserved in the angles of the Benben is the origin of the true pyramid shape, and the important pyramids known today are simply larger varieties of the original Benben. Egyptologists today agree that the original surge of pyramid building was directly related to the arrival of the Benben and that particular notion was further clarified in a British Museum publication, the *British Museum Dictionary of Ancient Egypt*. Authors Ian Shaw and Paul Nicholson extended the view that the Benben 'served as the earliest prototype for the obelisk and possibly even the Pyramid'.[3]

It is clear the original Benben was of immense spiritual importance, and all major pyramids in Egypt today appear to be gigantic recreations of it. The conclusion reached in this work is that the Great Pyramid was originally and specifically built to accommodate the Benben upon its platformed location at the highest point. When the object was in place, it somehow activated the Pyramid Effect, or invisible force, that subsequently 'switched the pyramid on'. It appears the Benben served as the catalyst to energize the specially designed interior chambers of the Pyramid, a point clarified later. When the Egyptian priests told Herodotus that the Great Pyramid was built from the top down, they meant that the Benben came first and provided the precise angles required to construct the Pyramid proper. When the main structure was completed, the smaller Benben was placed in its special position on top of the larger Benben. In other words, the top came first, apparently from some sort of supernatural or cosmic origin, and with it was the Company of Gods who subsequently instructed the locals in its purpose.

An ancient hieroglyphic symbol like this depicted a pyramidal shape with a smaller similar shape upon its apex, denoting the Benben. That symbol was secreted into Thoth's book and is discussed in a later chapter.

An interesting Pharaonic relief carving was recently found in a pyramid at Abu Sir, just 15 kilometres outside Cairo, and shows workers dragging the Benben depicted as illuminated. Under the carving is a hieroglyphic inscription variously translated as 'pure light', 'white light' or 'white gold'.[4] Permission to publish a photograph of that carving in this book was denied. An adjoining relief in the same pyramid shows people dancing and singing in an elaborate dedication ceremony that followed the placement of the Benben on the Pyramid, indicating the completion of a great national project. The event was announced to the people by a loud clanging of metal and from that ringing-out arose the call to prayer, thanksgiving and worship, as symbolized today in the church bell.

Home of the Benben. Flat top of the Great Pyramid looking south-west towards the pyramid of Khephren (From a pencil drawing by E. W. Lane, 1825, in the British Museum; Add. MS 34088, Folio 24).

A true pyramid is actually a Benben on top of a Benben and that was the ancient name given to their crowning pyramidions. The Great Pyramid is certainly a true pyramid and temple records confirm that it was void of its Benben for at least 4000 years. Roman historian, Diodorus Siculus, visited the Great Pyramid shortly before the beginning of the first century and wrote that the top of the structure 'appeared flat like a platform'. At the time of Senuseret (c. 1971 BC), stone records state that the Benben was sitting upon a large square stone pillar in its Temple at Heliopolis, a few kilometres away. There it became the first obelisk in mankind's recorded history and was the original concept of a square-base, pointed structure reaching high into the sky on a four-sided column. If the dating of the Pharaohs' lifetime is as Egyptologists calculated, then it is possible to determine that something unusual happened to the Benben just thirty years after the time of Senuseret. Pharaoh Sesostris I (c. 1940 BC), who restored the sacred city of Heliopolis, said the Benben was 'removed' and he personally ordered an inscription to be carved on a remembrance stele that said, 'My Beauty, Benben, shall be remembered in his House; (The Temple of the Benben) my name is the Benben'.

In researching *The Bible Fraud*, it was necessary to look well outside traditional church writings to discover the real story of New Testament origins and thus the story of Jesus Christ. The same process was required when researching early Egyptian history and a series of ancient Sumerian writings preserved an extraordinary tradition about the Great Pyramid and its Benben. Any ancient knowledge about the Great Pyramid related directly to the *Secret in the Bible* and what was recorded in Sumerian writings is of utmost importance in this work.

The Great Pyramid Robbery

The most important and valuable aspects of the Sumerian writings of interest here are the 'Inscriptions of Gudea', the 'Inscriptions on Statue B of Gudea' in the Louvre, and the poetically-rendered chronicles known by scholars as the Myths of Kur. Transcriptions vary with different scholars but taking the narratives as generally understood, they record an attempt to take possession of the temple on Mount Sinai, and steal the Benben from the summit of the Great Pyramid.

Gudea, son of Urbau, was a powerful king of Lagash and the sovereign of whom we possess the greatest number of monuments. He flourished around 2150 BC and, from religious texts and ancient inscriptions, he emerged as a ruler that strived for peace and piety. However, he also maintained a large fighting force to expand his empire and provide protection for his people from tribesmen in the north-eastern mountains. He captured the town of Anshan in Elam, and that was only one campaign in which he personally took part, for he spoke of similar successes in an incidental manner. That which was important to him in his reign was the vast number of temples he built or restored and enriched for divinities, distinguished as they were by beauty and splendour.

He claimed that the gods themselves inspired him in his devout undertakings, and they personally revealed to him the plans he was to carry out. King Gudea expended huge sums of money on temples in all cities over which his authority extended and each structure was dedicated to a god or goddess. Archaeologists are often puzzled to determine what those various divinities represented in the ancient culture for the number of great gods in heaven and earth was determined at 65,000, the figure mentioned in an inscription by Assurnazirpal, King of Assyria.[5]

King Gudea had several wives and was surrounded by a numerous progeny. Prince Ninagel was his eldest son and he later became the charismatic king. There is some confusion over the name archaeologists deciphered from monuments relating to Ninagel for it seems that he had a variety of names. King Gudea was piously devoted to the god Ningirsu and that was possibly a name also applied to Ninagel, for the application of names of divinities to leaders was their way of understanding the world. However, Prince Ninagel, 'of whose real name no one has an idea',[6] is used in this work.

King Gudea had a particular pre-conceived plan in mind for the construction of a special temple of exceptional beauty and Prince Ninagel was commissioned to build it. It was a major structural undertaking and its magnificence was recorded in detail upon two large clay cylinders compiled by King Gudea himself. The sections in the Gudea Inscriptions of greatest interest are those that deal with events preceding the construction of the new temple. Its orientation, its symbolism and its equipment, received an extraordinary amount of attention. It was said that 'a god' told King Gudea that the construction of the temple should begin 'on the day of the new moon' and at that time, 'the god's hand shall appear holding a flame, giving off light...that shall make the night as bright as day'. A young woman 'furnished with style and writing tablet was presented to him, Nisaba, the sister of Nina; she made a drawing in his presence, and put before him the complete model of the building'.[7] 'An old man of venerable aspect appeared to him in a vision' (Ibid) and assured Gudea of divine help in building the temple, but there was something else important recorded. An Egyptian god whose epithet was 'The Bright Serpent', was needed to complete the new temple and King Gudea's instructions were 'to build it to be like the House of the Serpent, and as strong as that place, it shall be built'. That ancient Sumerian documentation provided a direct link to the Great Pyramid for it was originally called by Mystery School initiates, 'The House of the Serpent'.[8]

There is a wealth of information in the Inscriptions of Gudea but its most striking aspect is a parallel description to the biblical account of the construction of Solomon's Temple. In King Gudea's writings LieS detail about the gold and silver decorations, the stelae and statues, all described in quite magnificent detail on King Gudea's two clay cylinders. The list of Prince Ninagel's building materials also included 'costly coloured stones in order to lay the foundation of the house with dressed stones', a narrative that is exactly paralleled in the First Book of Kings.[9]

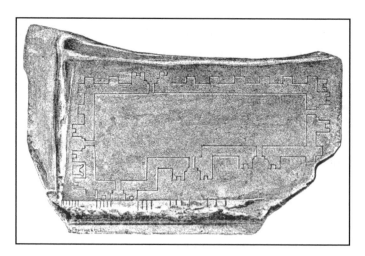

Plan of a temple built by King Gudea. The plan was traced upon the tablet held in the lap of a statue in the Louvre. Below the plan can be seen the ruler marked with the divisions used by the architect for drawing his designs to the desired scale.

King Gudea instructed Prince Ninagel to 'built the temple bright with metal and make it bright with jewels' and, 'on the temple's facade was two hand breadths of bright stone he faced over the brickwork'. The facing of the special temple was unique in Sumer, and identical with the Egyptian method of facing major pyramids with shiny stones. King Gudea's great temple was now nearing completion, but there was something important the builders needed to finish it. They wanted the sacred and enigmatic Benben, and that was in Egypt…on top of the Great Pyramid.

Prince Ninagel assembled an army and set off on the 800-kilometre journey to invade Egypt and steal the Benben. Sumerian clay texts described the Great Pyramid as 'The Formidable House Which Is Raised Up Like A Heap',[10] a description acknowledging the daunting nature of the structure that Prince Ninagel was to confront. The ensuing battle is described in several old texts, some found in original Sumerian, others, in Akkadian and Assyrian renderings. That remarkable story is also inscribed on the walls of an Egyptian temple in the ancient city of Edfu and is the mystical record of what was an attempt to steal the precious Benben. The Edfu hieroglyphs said:

> …and Horus, the Winged Measurer came to the boat of RA and said to his forefather; 'O Falcon of the Horizon, I have seen the enemy conspire against thy Lordship, to take the Luminous Crown unto themselves'. Then RA said unto Horus, 'go quickly and knock down the enemy who you have seen'.

Prince Ninagel and his army were coming for the 'Luminous Crown' capping the Great Pyramid, its 'Throne of Radiance' and RA's 'Celestial Chamber'. Prince Ninagel knew the object held some special power but it was probable he did not know what it really was.

Stories survived in various forms, and RA and Horus recorded in the Edfu texts were not the original gods, for the story was later in time. Old Sumerian tablets described the original Horus as the 'offspring who did not know his father', an epithet befitting Horus, who was born, according to Egyptian mythology, after his father, Osiris, died. The mythology of Horus is complicated, and as with other Egyptian deities, his stories are confusing and contradictory. For centuries, the kings of Egypt saw themselves as living personifications of RA, just as their sons were living Horuses. On penetrating into that peculiar world, over twenty individual Horuses covering centuries of time are found simply because later royalty adopted the name to indicate their relationship to a particular aspect of the god.

It is clear from Sumerian texts that Prince Ninagel's invading forces had their first battle encounters in the Sinai Peninsular area. Then, in its final phase, a battle of sorts was fought around the area of the Great Pyramid, the last and apparently impregnable stronghold of Prince Ninagel's priestly opponents. That battle is commemorated extensively in Sumerian records, both written chronicles and pictorial depictions. Prince Ninagel and his warriors arrived at the great structure of 'The Wise Craftsman' (Thoth?) and mounted an attack on the temples and structures around the Giza complex.

The defenders of the Great Pyramid hid in subterranean chambers attached to the Sphinx and the Pyramid itself. Horus, while trying to sneak out of an underground temple at night to replenish food stocks for his people, was attacked and lost the sight of his eyes. In Middle and Late Kingdom hieroglyphs, Horus is often shown without eyes, depicting blindness and reflecting the story. After Horus' capture, defenders of the Great Pyramid were starved into submission and eventually surrendered to their attackers. Having achieved the desired result, Prince Ninagel allowed the priests to leave the area unharmed and the great and impregnable structure stood unoccupied, silent. Prince Ninagel 'went in till I drew nigh to the temple…its ceiling was like the path of the stars'.

That is a significant statement for the premise presented in this book. From that description, Prince Ninagel had entered through chambers and described the starry ceiling of the Temple of the Grand Orbit under the Sphinx (No.4 on The Master Plans). Prince Ninagel spent three days exploring the interior of the Giza complex and provided an extraordinary description of the Grand Gallery, saying, 'its vault is like a rainbow, the darkness ends there'. The Sumerian Inscriptions alleged that Prince Ninagel carried off a quantity of 'stones' from inside the Great Pyramid, one being burgundy in colour and called 'the heart-stone'.

Sometime later Prince Ninagel made an announcement to his men. What he was about to instruct them to do was for the future benefit of his people and their later generations, 'Let the awesome of thee (The Benben) be removed; For my descendants, let their peace be ordained'. There was the Benben, 'high as the sky,' as recorded in Sumerian writings, its brilliance described 'as a diamond glows' in Eastern tradition, sitting proudly on top of the Great Pyramid, itself a magnificent sight, glistening white in the sun with colours of the rainbow running around its uppermost level. Those remarkable words preserved thousands of years ago on clay tablets described the theft of the Benben.

Prince Ninagel said, of the Egyptians: 'Let their mother's offspring see it no more'. He then ordered 'everyone to stand back and distance himself' and then his men 'sent the top (the Benben) sliding down to the west'. The Great Pyramid was now, in effect, 'switched off'. The loss of the energy cap over the crown chakra removed it of its power. The story proved not only the wide prevalence and mysteriousness of the Great Pyramid and its enigmatic Benben, but also the awe in which it was held. Prince Ninagel and his men hauled the Benben back to Mesopotamia to finalise his father's new temple now nearing completion and, whether they knew it or not, they had stolen the very nucleus of the 'religion' of the Egyptians.

With the placement of the Benben on the new temple, the project was finished. 'The dream', wrote King Gudea, 'was fulfilled...and so magnificent and marvelous was it, they were altogether seized with admiration'. It stood 'like a bright mass, a radiant brightness of its facing covering everything; like a mountain which glows, it joyfully rises'. They had built a showpiece, a reproduction of the Great Pyramid of Giza, complete with the original Benben. Whether the interior layout was similar to the Great Pyramid is unknown but there were two extraordinary parallels between the Mesopotamian temple and the Egyptian Pyramid.

The cylinder seals referred to King Gudea's temple as having an 'uppermost chamber' and a 'Chamber of Seven Zones'. That may have been a design aspect copied from the area of the secret chambers recorded on Masonic plans just below the pyramidion of the Great Pyramid. Those chambers were shown as being in the same location as the 'seven bands of colour' that were once painted around that area. Scholars were puzzled by the references to the word 'Shugalam' in Sumerian texts. That was the name Sumerians appeared to have given the top point, the 'highest place' of the new temple, 'the place of determining whose awesomeness is great, where the Brilliance is announced'. The substance of the Gudea inscriptions confirmed that the Benben from the Great Pyramid had now found a new home on top of King Gudea's latest Babylonian tower.

King Gudea was proud of his new possession and expended large wealth to special external adorning. Sculpted columns were erected, imported trees and shrubs were planted in landscaped grounds, and rare fish filled a large pool. Smaller temples were built along a causeway around its base as residences for priests, service buildings, courts and altars, including a special dwelling and sleeping quarters for Prince Ninagel and his spouse, Bau. Archaeologists believe that the sphinxes of Egypt inspired the 'mythical creatures' of the Mesopotamian stone sculptors, and the Gudea Inscriptions revealed that some 2100 years before the commencement of the Christian era, King Gudea positioned around his new temple a large array of sculpted Egyptian-styled stone sphinxes. They were variously shaped as 'a lion that instilled terror' and 'a wild ox, massively crouching like a lion'. Archaeologists found it difficult to believe that sphinxes could have been known in ancient Sumer, but it was confirmed when a statue of Prince Ninagel himself, depicted as a crouching Sphinx, was discovered among ruins in Lagash. The sanctuaries that he decorated, and of which he felt so proud, are today mere heaps of rubble, but many objects he placed in them, especially statues, traversed the centuries without serious damage before finding a resting place in the Louvre.

Pharaohs retrieved capstone

It appears the Sumerians were in possession of the Benben around 2100 BC, but Egyptian texts record that it was back in the original 'Temple of the Benben' at Heliopolis some 1350 years later. An inscription on a stele of Pharaoh Pi-Ankhi (c. 750BC) described in detail his personal visit to the shrine. The dedication made fascinating reading and furthered our knowledge about what the mysterious Benben might have been. Intent on seeing the celestial object for himself, Pharaoh Pi-Ankhi offered a series of elaborate sacrifices at daybreak in the Temple's forecourt. He then entered the Temple proper, purified himself in a type of baptism, and moved into a sacred area called, 'The Star Room':

> The king Pi-Ankhi mounted the stairs towards the large window, in order to view the god RA within the Benben. The king personally, standing up and being all alone, pushed apart the bolt and opened the two door-leaves. Then he viewed his father RA in the splendid sanctuary of Het-Benben.

He then stepped back in awe, closed the doors behind him 'and placed thereon a clay seal, impressing upon it his signet'.

An intriguing little mystery

Because the Benben was back in Heliopolis in 750 BC, the Egyptians had obviously retrieved it from 'new Babylon' but nothing was recorded that could be associated with the time or events of its recovery. However, it is probable that the Mesopotamian Babylon's loss of the Benben was the beginning of its demise. All that remains of the city today is a huge shapeless mass of brick rubble, mounds of mud-brick buildings and debris, rising in heaps above the surrounding flatlands. The ruins of a tower found there was identified as been built by Nebuchadnezzar II around 600 BC but was not the original Tower of Babel as supposed, for that was built some thousands of years earlier at Babylon in Cairo.

There is an interesting aspect to what happened on top of the Great Pyramid after the Benben was finally removed. Historian F Vansler observed in 1673:

> On top of the greatest pyramid there was anciently a statue or colosse. This appears because it is not sharp as the others, but plain; and there are yet to be seen great pits, which were to keep fast the colosse from falling.

The ancients built statues because they believed that the spirit of god dwelt within them, and for that reason, the colosse may have been of Osiris or Isis, a substitute for the god within the missing capstone. One old hieroglyph stated that 'a reptile had been fashioned in that place' (the Giza Plateau) and that reference provided the most probable option. The 'reptile' is recorded to have been a giant stone Serpent god and was associated with the words:

> If you do not tell me what I have not heard and what I do not know, I will cause you to pass out of existence like a flame which has been extinguished.

Exactly when and why the colosse was placed on top of the Great Pyramid is not known, but this old aerial photograph clearly shows two of four pits that Vansler said held the colosse in position. It seems as if some form of massive roping system was attached to the colosse, and then secured in the pits on the ground.

© Rudolf Lehnert

The two pits are shown arrowed. One was on the Northern side, directly north and below today's entrance into the Pyramid. The other was on the South side directly opposite to the northern pit. Today the southern area is a flat stand for vehicle parking.

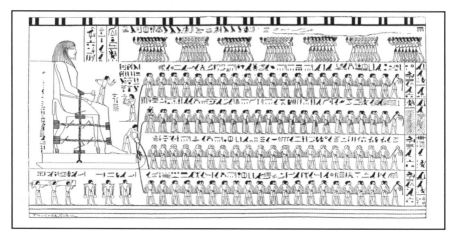

The colosse of Prince Thothotpu being dragged into position. This depiction shows the vast size of the statues and the huge number of people required to move them (Drawn by Faucher-Gudin, from Wilkinson, 'A Popular Account of the Manners and Customs of the Ancient Egyptians', vol. ii, frontispiece, c. 1890).

Where is the Benben today?

The Benben was too greatly revered to have been desecrated and some researchers found reason to suspect that it was hidden in secret chambers within or under the Great Pyramid. The occult tradition of Asia, however, alleged that many kings and leaders once possessed the magic object in former historical epochs. Akbar of India (c. 1600), and an unnamed emperor of China, were two mentioned in an old list of its temporary users in more modern times. Tibetan writings suggested that it was safely hidden in a monastery of the Olets, a Mongol tribe of Central Asia, but there is a more likely option as to its present location.

The holy Arabic city of M'akka (Mecca in English) in Saudi Arabia was at one time in its early history called 'Akka'. That came about in 487 BC after a Berber tribe of Northern Africa removed the Benben from Heliopolis and, after nearly 14 months of overland travel, relocated it in South-west Asia. They named their new settlement 'Akka' after the Benben's original name, and that evolved to M'akka (and Mecca) in later times. The settlement subsequently became the birthplace of Mohammed, the man who established the principles of Islam today found embodied in the Koran.

In Mecca stood the Ka'aba, a magnificent cube-shaped shrine to which millions of Muslims make annual pilgrimages to pray, believing it is the home of God. That large object derived its name from its cubical enclosure that was originally fifteen feet long, wide and high, with an aperture for light in the east end. Inside the cube was a stone called the 'Black stone of the Ka'aba', around which cluster many traditions, the most predominant being that it originally 'came down from Paradise illuminated and as white as milk, but the sins of mankind turned it black'. The original Ka'aba now sits inside a much larger ornate black and gold cube some six stories high and set in the centre of an elaborate open-air stadium around which believers circulate anti-clockwise inwards to touch the cube. Muslims themselves claim that within the Ka'aba is God's 'Celestial Chamber', the same term used in the Pyramid Texts to describe the Benben, and they recorded that it was some sort of cosmic stone.[11]

CHAPTER TWELVE

THE LETTERS OF LIGHT

Ancient Egyptian priests held a tradition maintaining that, 'A serpent lies coiled in the Great Pyramid', and serpents linked the three major components of this study. A 'serpent that could not be slain' safeguarded the *Book of Thoth,* ancient Rabbis regularly referred to the Torah as the 'Serpent Book of the Ages'[1] and Sumerians of 4000 years ago called the Great Pyramid 'The House of the Serpent'. The three major aspects of this work, the *Book of Thoth,* the Torah, and the Great Pyramid were all directly associated with a Serpent in ancient times. The age-old Pyramid Texts provide a fascinating description of a celestial Serpent 'who gives the food which confers eternal life' and that enthralling portrayal further strengthens the Serpent connection in this work for it directly involves the Secret in the Bible.

As long as humanity kept records of its existence, serpents were used as emblems of the intelligence of God. In ancient times and in places as widespread and diverse as Australia, China, Japan, Mexico, New Zealand, Babylonia, Sumeria, Egypt, India, and Central America, serpents were feared and worshipped as gods for thousands of years. If there is a common origin to the mythology of the serpent, it may have developed at the Great Pyramid of Giza. To this day, serpents or dragons signify divine heritage and royalty in many Asian countries, while in the West the serpent represents wisdom and knowledge.

'Serpents were everywhere connected with his worship', was said about Aesculapius, the Greek mythological god of medicine. He carried about a knotty wooden staff entwined with a single snake standing on its tail which he said represented certain powers. In 1910, the American Medical Association adopted the staff as its insignia, and the British and French armies, World Health Organization, US Air Force Medical Service and other groups the world over, also used the single-snaked staff to identify their medical professions. A staff with two vertical coiled snakes, the Caduceus, is the official symbol of the US Army Medical Corps Navy Pharmacy Division, and Public Health Service. The two-snake design dates back some thousands of years to Egypt and reappears in Greek mythology with a pair of wings added, as Hermes' wand or staff. In ancient Rome, the name for Hermes was Mercury and messengers carried his symbol as a sign of neutrality. Later medicos, searching battlefields for the wounded, carried the Caduceus to establish their non-combatant status.

The single snake represented life-giving powers and the two-snake design is a mirror reflection of the single snake.

The Cabalists beheld in their Mysteries the likeness of the sacred wand or staff of Hermes, with serpents twined around it. Mercury was the messenger of the gods and so it became that messengers from earthly kings customarily carried a staff wound with ribbons showing their official status. However, the 'ribbons' had a deeper purpose. Secret messages were written lengthwise upon a strip of leather, usually snakeskin, and wrapped vertically around the staff being unreadable when unwound. The recipient then wound the leather strip around a staff of the same dimension and read the hidden message.

Similarly, the ribbons on the Babylonian tree became the serpent on the Tree of the Cabala, its intricate paths clearly hinting of a secret message.

Offerings to the serpent. Redrawn from a photograph taken in the tomb of Khopirkerisonbu.

The serpent was chosen as the head of the reptilian family, and serpent worship in some form permeates nearly all parts of the world. The Orphites of the New Testament worshipped a mystic serpent, Orphite being Greek for 'Serpent'. The serpent mounds of the American Indians; the carved snakes of Central and South America; the hooded cobras of India; Python, the great snake of the Greeks (and the origin of Pythagoras' name); the sacred serpents of the Druids; the Midguard snake of Scandinavia; the half-human, half-snake Nagas of Burma, Siam and Cambodia; the brazen serpent of the Jews; the Sky Serpent of the Australian Aborigines; Zoroaster's serpent of the Universe; the snakes at the oracle of Delphi, twining themselves up and around the tripod upon which the Pythian priestess sat, the tripod itself constructed in the form of twisted serpents standing on their tales; the asp worshipped by Egyptians under the name of uraeus and the sacred serpents preserved in their temples…all bear witness to the universal veneration in which the snake was held. Among nearly all ancient peoples, the serpent was accepted as the ultimate symbol of wisdom or salvation.

The uraeus of Egypt. It occasionally obtained a length of two metres and when approached, erected its head and inflated its throat in readiness to dart forward (Drawn by Faucher-Gudin from pl. iii of the Reptiles-Supplement to the 'Description of Egypt').

An ancient legend maintained that in the beginning of the world winged serpents rained down upon the earth. Some researchers suggested that they were demigods that antedated the historical civilization of every nation. The symbolic relationship between the sun and the serpent found literal witness in the fact that life remained in the snake until after sunset, even though it was cut into a dozen parts. The Hopi Indians considered the serpent to be in close communication with the Earth Spirit, therefore, at the time of their annual snake dance they sent their prayers to the Earth Spirit by first specially sanctifying large numbers of reptiles and then liberating them to return to the earth with the prayers of the tribe.

Probably the most famous serpent is that seen graphically coiled on the royal crowns of Pharaohs and their regal spouses. The uraeus crown, a circlet of gold with a reared cobra in the middle of the forehead, is a mystical symbol indicating that the wearer has completed initiation and is an enlightened being with a secret purpose. When worn on the head of a Pharaoh or queen, the uraeus was superstitiously imbued with mysterious life and able to execute vengeance by spitting invisible fire at thE eyes of enemies. The supernatural virtues attributed to it made it an enchanted object and ordinary people believed that it vomited flames and destroyed those who dared to attack its master. It had its own protective god in Horus who was called the Lord of the Vulture and of the Uraeus.

Drawn from a tomb portrait of Pharaoh Seti I of the XIX dynasty (Faucher-Gudin). The intricacy of the necklace and headgear with uraeus is apparent but note also the eye makeup.

In ancient mythology, the serpent was variously used as the symbol of the Wisdom of God, and at other times of the subtlety of the evil one. As initiate De Chateaubriand wrote:

> Object of horror or of adoration, men have for the serpent an implacable hatred, or prostrate themselves before its genius. Lie calls it, Prudence claims it, Envy carries it in its heart, and Eloquence on its caduceus. In hell it arms the whip of the Furies; in heaven Eternity makes of it its symbol.

The serpent therefore had a good meaning and a bad one. It was an emblem of Wisdom, par excellence, and the symbol of Sin, the Moon-god. With a pair of wings, it became the Seraph, and curled up in a circle with its tail in its mouth, it stood for 'time without end', eternity. The Naasenes, a Gnostic sect described by St Hippolytus (170-236), believed that the serpent was 'the Moist Essence' of God,[2] just as did Thales the Milesian (c. 700 BC). Hippolytus reported another serpent sect known as Perates. He said that they worshipped a 'circling serpent, radiant in its own light'. In Indian tradition,

Amanta was actually a symbol of the Cycle of Life, which was inclusive of higher and lower forces, or realms, of existence:

> Narayama, with whom Vishu is identified, the oldest of all beings, who, carried up on the coils of Sesha or Amanta, the 'serpent without end', the symbol of Eternity, appeared at the beginning of things floating above the primeval waters.[3]

Indian tradition was identical to that of Egyptians in their early culture who called it the Primeval Serpent and directly associated it with the Sun-god RA and/or Atum.

An upraised serpent became the origin of a highly developed and sophisticated religion and was revered in ancient times as an emblem of extreme importance. From that region of unfathomable depth issued forth a powerful tradition of a vertical coiled Serpent, the ancient emblem of Wisdom and Eternity. The earliest initiates or 'The Wise Men' who were initiated into the Mysteries were called 'Serpents of Wisdom' and the curious reference to 'a serpent on two legs' in the *Book of the Dead* is not a description of an extra-terrestrial being from a spacecraft but simply means a high initiate. The serpent became the type and symbol of evil only later in time, and it subsequently developed into the Devil during the dark Middle Ages.

As an image, a serpent standing on its tail obtained a prominent place in ancient initiations and religions and so wide was serpent worship that it was sometimes regarded by ancient writers as the primitive religion of mankind. This author had the unnerving experience of meeting the Snake-worshippers of Grasshopper Valley in the USA, a sect that live in harmony with deadly snakes writhing through their houses. Biblical literature is replete with serpents, and when Rabbi Jesus instructed his disciples to be 'as wise as serpents', he meant to be as wise as an initiated person.

Respect for the 'fiery serpent set up on a pole' is mentioned in the Old Testament [4] and, in that representation, it was used in association with magic. The principle that Ezra called 'Moses' had a 'serpent of brass' named Nehush'tan that was worshipped by the Israelites as god.[5] It is not possible to reconcile those narratives with the Commandment demanding that no 'graven image' of God be made.[6] Their brass serpent was highly-revered, and before worship began, 'they would burn for incense, resin, thereby rectifying and purifying the air by its virtue, and blowing away the corrupted exhalation naturally given forth by the body, because this perfume possesses a strong and penetrating quality'.[7] They then formed a circle of sacred stones, knelt, and solemnly prayed to the serpent standing coiled upright on the sand before them. Not only did Moses and his associates pray to it, they studied intently the shadows it cast onto the sand. Subsequently, King Hezehiah ordered 'the brass serpent' to be destroyed,[8] and 'smashed the sacred stones'.[9]

The serpent god at Giza

There is an overwhelming reason why the serpent was held in such high respect, and looked upon in awe as God. Mentioned earlier was the Egyptian belief that 'a reptile had been fashioned in that place', the complex at Giza. But what was that 'reptile'?

Existing today is an ancient papyrus called 'The Book of Overthrowing Apepi'. Apepi, the Devil of Darkness, is the archfiend of RA, and is devoted to the protection of RA, the great Lord of the Temple. The present interest in that papyrus centres on the fact that it contains two copies of the Egyptian story of Creation and each story is entitled, 'The Book of Knowing the Evolution of RA and of Overthrowing Apepi'. The word rendered 'Evolution' is 'Khepra', derived from the root 'Kheper', which means 'to make, to fashion, to produce, to form, to become', so that the title of the writing might just as well have said, 'The Book of the Creations of RA'. The book outlines aspects that early Egyptians believed were made, created, or came into being through RA. However, the vital point is that RA said he took upon himself the form of a god called Khepra, a very early deity in Egyptian culture who was intimately connected with the creation of things of every kind. In some hieroglyphs, Khepra is described as 'Lord of Life and Death'. The temple priests believed that Khepra came into being as a direct form of RA who had specially 'worked a charm' upon his heart to create Khepra.

Khepra then, was a sacred essence that proceeded from a higher intelligence and formed the Secret in the Bible and other mystical matters. Khepra came to be symbolized by the famous beetle or scarab that belonged to the class of 'Coprophagi or 'dung-eaters'. After having laid its eggs in masses of ox-dung, the beetle rolled them along, east to west, until they built up into a large ball. Those balls, though made of dead, inert matter, contained the germs of life, which, under the influence of warmth and heat, grew, and in due course developed into living creatures that would move about and seek their food. At a very early period in their history, the Egyptians associated the sun's disc-shape with the dung-ball of the beetle, partly on account of its shape, and partly because it was the source of heat, and light, and life to man, even as the dung-ball was to young beetles.

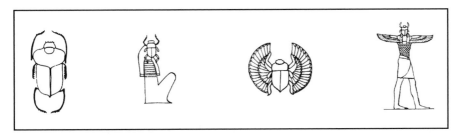

Some various pictorial forms used in ancient Egypt to represent Khepra.

The ancients believed that RA endowed Khepra with 'splendour and power in the form of a serpent' and that Khepra was another form of RA. Importantly, Khepra is identified as the god in the 'Temple of the Benben' at Heliopolis and that temple was dedicated to him. They believed all the attributes of RA were contained in Khepra and he was as great as RA. Like RA, Khepra was often described as 'the Sun-god of Heliopolis' and, importantly for the development of this premise, 'the Serpent god'. But what was Khepra? This hieroglyphic description provides part of the answer:

> ...the god Khepra who is unknown and who is more hidden than the other gods, whose vicar is the divine Disc...he is a flame which sends forward rays of light with mighty splendour but though he can be seen in form, observation can be made of him at his appearance yet he cannot be understood, and at dawn mankind make supplication unto him; his risings are in crystal among the Company of the Gods, and he is the beloved object of 'every god'.

In that extraordinary narrative Khepra is described as an 'object' in the form of a 'flame' that could not be 'understood' and rising in 'crystal'. He was in the 'Temple of the Benben' that was built to house the Benben while the Great Pyramid was under construction. In the interim, the Benben was placed high on a large square stone pillar creating the original concept of an obelisk, and that is why the enclosure was sometimes called the 'Temple of the Obelisk'. Combining the information recorded in ancient records, a precise description is given of an extraordinary luminous serpent-type coloured image rising vertically in the crystal Benben. It was called Khepra, the Serpent god, and the splendour of the phenomena was revered for centuries. But there is more to Khepra...

The invisible many-coloured bird

In the oldest Egyptian records, Khepra was directly associated with a brilliantly coloured bird that also lived in the 'Temple of the Benben'. That bird was beautiful, most holy, and entirely feminine. Because of its vibrant colours it was sometimes called the 'Sunbird'. More often, it was called the 'Pyramidion Bird', or the Bennu bird (Benu). In later times, the Bennu bird was called 'the Phoenix' in Greek, but it originated with the gods in Heliopolis. The earliest known reference was by Hesiod the Greek in the eighth century BC when he referred to it as the Arabian Bird. An extremely gentle and delicate creature, it was said to weep tears of incense, while its blood was balsam. Tradition recorded that the Bennu bird fed only on air, harming no other creature. It was extremely graceful, with brilliant plumage and a distinctive tuft of feathers at the back of its head. The length of the Bennu bird's life differed from ancient writer to writer but most believed that it lived for five hundred or a thousand years. In the *Book of the Dead,* it was called the 'Lord of Jubilees' and described as the free-flowing spirit of RA. It was the most celebrated of all symbolic creatures featured by ancient Mystery Schools and was used as an emblem for concealing the secret truths of esoteric philosophy.

The original sanctuary of the Bennu bird was called Het Benben, 'The Temple of the Benben' in Heliopolis where it lived in the Benben with the serpent-shaped god, Khepra. The Bennu bird subsequently introduced to mankind the belief of immortality of the human soul in a new birth, according to a particular cycle. The Bennu bird thus became the symbol of the flight of the soul and its resurrection. In the Late Period, it was considered a manifestation of the resurrected Osiris, and at one point in the *Book of the Dead*, the deceased stated, 'I have gone forth as the Bennu bird'.

The Bennu bird never died permanently. Legend held that it existed when the universe was created and that it knew the secrets of life and reincarnation that even particular Deities did not know. When the Bennu bird knew its time to die had come, it gathered a load of fragmented twigs and from them built a nest. At the next dawn, the great bird faced the rising sun and sang in a beautiful voice. The heat from the sun ignited the fragrant spices, and the Bennu bird died in its own funeral pyre. It then spent $3^{1}/_{2}$ days in a worm-like form before arising out of the ashes and recreating itself.

The *Book of the Dead* identifies the Bennu bird with Khepra, and the crystal Benben. In the 83rd chapter, which provides a curious formula for enabling the deceased to take the form of the Bennu, the bird was made to say: 'I came into being from unformed matter, I came into existence with the god Khepra; I am the germs of every god'.

In some ancient depictions, the Benben is shown with a ball nesting in its apex and that may have been the 55-faceted sphere mentioned earlier. In the Pyramid Texts, a hieroglyph shows a Bennu bird sitting on the top of the Benben, its claws wrapped around the ball. That bird is stylized as one of the heron species, known to ascend the air and 'fly to a great height while circling round and round in spiral wheels'.[10]

The Bennu Bird

Dazzling colours and their importance

Ancient descriptions of the mysterious Bennu bird portrayed its plumage as 'brilliant' and 'spectacular', which is not characteristic of the pale grey or white heron. The *Book of the Dead* provides a combination of descriptions of extraordinary colours associated with the Bennu bird, 'It had a red and golden neck and head…sea-blue was its body…azure, beautiful…around its feet…it had a scarlet to purple hue'. The picture that emerges is none other than a full and precise description of the seven colours of the spectrum, from red, orange, yellow, green, blue, indigo and violet, all in correct order from the top, 'red and golden neck and head', down through the range of greens and blues to the 'purple hue' around its feet.

Mentioned earlier were the seven colours of the rainbow running around the upper levels of the Great Pyramid, commencing at the base of the platform upon which the Benben once sat, then graduating down, one band merging into the next. The Benben and Bennu bird were both worshipped at sunrise because at that time the first rays of the sun hit the Benben and activated it, making it 'luminous' (The Luminous Crown). The refractory crystal reflections of vibrant rainbow colours were then seen lighted within, and reflecting about the 'Throne of Radiance', the shimmering and glistening Benben.

The ball or Divine Disc depicted on top of the Benben became associated with the Sun, the ball of the dung beetle and the god Khepra, and was probably depicted in later artistic representation as the silhouette of the sun rising behind the Benben's outline. To simple people, the seven swirling colours became the seven souls of RA spiraling up, around and away from the top of the Benben and represented God circling in the heavens. A female aspect called Aurora, the 'Goddess of the Morning', was applied to the phenomenon and was believed to be the daughter of the Sun (Ra). She was subsequently traditionalized as Dawn personified, and St Aurorius Augustine later adopted her name.

That radiating body of brilliant colours subsequently became the symbol of resurrection of mankind because the populace believed that the living sun of today had its origins in the dead sun of yesterday. Thus it was said the Bennu bird came into being out of fire, 'seven times seven times seven' (every day), and so it must be, in Egyptian religion, that again and again the spiritual nature of man rises triumphant from his dead physical body. In later times, that colour spectacular was called 'Phoenix rising' at sunrise and 'ashes of the Phoenix' at sunset.

Though modern scholars of natural history declare the existence of the Bennu/Phoenix purely mythical, the historian Pliny described the capture of one and its exhibition in the Roman Forum during the reign of the Emperor Claudius (d. 54). By his use of the word 'iridescent', it is probable that he was describing a peacock or pheasant. In days of old it was customary to refer to initiates of some orders as Phoenixes or men who had been born again, meaning after initiation they were born into a consciousness of the spiritual world. The Bennu bird was a fitting symbol of their spiritual rebirth.

Application of the pyramid colours

To understand the origins of religions, we must enter into the mind of primitive people and observe how the seven celestial colours later developed into various planes of human awareness. The colour cap on the Great Pyramid later became associated with the seven major world religions and depicted various levels of understanding in the psyche of the founders. The devil, for example, was portrayed as red in religious art, the lowest colour on the Pyramid spectrum, the furthest from God and therefore the lowest essence of life. The colours of the Christian priesthood today are misleading, for originally the cast-off purple togas of Roman emperors became the clothing of early bishops of Rome. The presbyters wore the 'toga-picta' bearing a wide red stripe and their followers opted for black or brown togas, colours below the spectrum.[11] Today, red is the primary colour of the garb of cardinals. That choice originated from the attire of St Jerome, who admitted that he wore red ladies clothing in transvestite activities.[12] In Buddhism, Yama, the King of Hell is portrayed in red and dark orange, and Buddhists monks opt for oranges and yellows in ceremonial clothing. Figures of the underworld in Greek understanding are also shown in dark orange. Religious representations of ancient Tibet, Mongolia, India and Japan show various shades of blue and the mythical founder of the Xia dynasty is depicted in mauve costumes.

Each colour is representative of seven plateaus of consciousness within the human makeup, or levels of internal personal development and understanding. A spiritual or evolved person is subconsciously drawn to mauves and violets, which represents a high level of inner understanding, the closest to the Source. In Egyptian art, RA, Osiris and Isis are usually shown in white, colours over and above the Benben and entering into it from a higher level. The pyramidal colours are also associated with the seven different coloured Egyptian flowers from which was extracted the seven sacred oils of Egypt, seen portrayed in the tomb-chambers of Har-hotpe. The seven levels of colours were later applied to the seven chakras of the human body, commencing with red at the base of the spine and spiraling up and out through the top or crown chakra.

Strange forces operating in the Great Pyramid

An earlier chapter mentioned the known existence of a strange force at work in the Great Pyramid. That force defies present scientific explanation and no one is able to adequately explain how it works. Special energy tests done with dowsing rods at the original location of the Benben detected a definite invisible force streaming down from the highest point of the Great Pyramid that pulled the tip of dowsing rods sharply down. One of the earliest researchers in that area was Verne Cameron, a well-known English dowser who developed a dowsing device called an 'aurameter'. In a series of tests under variant conditions, he was another that detected a positive downward flow of energy at the top of the pyramid, accompanied by a simultaneous upward flow. Others detected a similar force and described it as the feeling of a cool breeze flowing vertically against the fingers and palms when they held their hands above their heads. Once, while standing in the centre on top of the Great Pyramid with a companion and some Arab guides, British inventor, Sir W Siemens, noted that whenever his hand was raised with fingers outspread he could hear an acute ringing noise. Curious, he converted a bottle into a Leydon jar (one that accumulates static electricity), held it over his head, and sparks began to fly from the neck of the bottle. The guides became fearful and threatened him, and Siemens accidentally lowered the bottle towards one of them, giving the guide an electric shock that knocked him from his feet.

Planes and particularly helicopters are warned not to fly low over the tops of pyramids because of the force operating above the centre of the apex. Pilots reported that instruments go awry while flying over pyramidal structures and in one case, in 1968, at the Great Pyramid, a helicopter with crew photographing the platform at close range, was violently and inexplicably de-stabilized, causing a crash landing near the base of the Great Pyramid.

Inside the Benben

It can be confidently said that something of a non-ordinary nature is constantly happening within a Benben-type pyramidal space, and that claim is supportable with physical evidence. When a light is shone down into the apex of a glass or crystal pyramid of any size, but built to the same angles and ratio as the Great Pyramid, something remarkable occurs. Rising out of the area that would be the location of the Queen's Chamber and moving up through the King's Chamber area, a spectacular spiral or swirl of light resembling a serpent standing upright upon its tail is seen. That beautifully proportioned form is created in the seven rainbow colours, and its highest-most point disappears out of the top centre of the pyramid in an ever-decreasing spiral. Some have known for thousands of years of the existence of that marvelous occurrence and it holds untold ramifications for the spiritual development of mankind.

Because of its form and colour, the phenomenon shall now be called 'The Rainbow Serpent' because that is exactly what it looks like when viewed through any or all, four sides of a miniature clear model of the Great Pyramid. In its original form, it was visible in the larger Benben, and ancient Egyptian priests called the vertical spiral of light, Khepra. To them it was God.

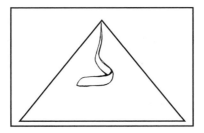

This is the shape of the spiral of light that is seen in a clear pyramid when a light is shone down upon it.

It is demonstrated with a transparent model of the Great Pyramid that there is a direct relationship between the shape of the space inside, and a particular process going on within that space. Whenever a light is shone down into a glass pyramid built in exact scale or proportion to the Great Pyramid, a Rainbow Serpent is created. The light provides a type of force or energy that in turn, creates the vertical spiral of light, a serpent upraised, invisible in rock, but visible in a clear substance. That is what the ancient Egyptian priesthood meant when they said that, 'a serpent lies coiled in the Great Pyramid'.

Priesthood knowledge appears to directly reference the known existence of an invisible spiral force operating within the confines of the Great Pyramid, precisely in the same manner as the spiral of visible light was seen in the Benben. That explains exactly what the Benben originally was, but much larger; it was a clear pyramidal structure acting as a focal point to gather in, convert and distribute light from the sun into energy, and project its force deep into the heart of the Pyramid. The conclusion reached in this premise determines that the cosmic Benben was a God-given perpetual generator, placed in a location where the sun shone 315 days every year.

Thus, the Benben served not only as a receiver of light but also as a self-feeding projector. The pyramid form itself sustained the constant charge of sunlight generated in the Benben gracing the peak of the Great White Rock. It appears that the Benben was primarily intended as a type of amplifying principle to activate power into the specially designed chambers and passageways in the structure below. With the Sun shining down upon it, a huge Rainbow Serpent was created and could be seen from miles away. Since the pyramid form was the only method to generate (or create) the Rainbow Serpent, the serpent became the symbolic form of initiates. The *Book of the Dead* said initiates into the Egyptian Mysteries entered 'a serpent', in which they 'shed their skin' and emerged 'in the form of a resurrected Ra, bright and shiny'. That is the fundamental nature of the initiatory process, explained fully in later chapters.

With the penetration of the sun's rays down into the Benben, the upraised serpent in the component colours of the spectrum was visible from all sides of the Great Pyramid and its crystalline cap glowed with the vertical spiral of light. The Bible said God's presence was seen on top of the mountain,[13] that being the 'mountain of stone' now called the Great Pyramid. God's presence was Khepra, the Rainbow Serpent spiralling in the Luminous Crown.

With the Benben in place, the Great Pyramid became a living ark of mysterious force. A fiery halo was often seen to glow around the apex and strange deep rumbling sounds arose around the structure.[14] That was one reason why the Great Pyramid was held in fear. With the sun shining down upon it, 'a serpent was seen lighted on top of the House of God',[15] and that Serpent could clearly be seen standing, as it were, upright in the middle of the Benben. That was what numerous ancient records documented, and Moses' 'bronze serpent' was a physical reconstruction of it.

A symbolic third century BC stone carving representing a large vertically standing serpent being revered.

The *Book of the Dead* provides a clear description of the Rainbow Serpent and its specially constructed location. Stone lasts forever and inscribed in it are these remarkable words: 'Hail, shining one, above the Temple of the Gods in visible form...swirling above the white Temple in the sand'. Moreover, what was being described in the Book of Enoch in this extraordinary collection of words?

> ...and he drew nigh to a large structure which was built of crystal...and containing tongues of flame...and the aslant walls of the structure were covered with a tessellated flow of crystal...and its base was of crystal.

Later in the Book of Enoch, that 'structure' is referred to as 'the holy radiating jewel', an exquisite description that supports Tibetan tradition of the Benben being 'surrounded by a radiance, and flowing with rivers of light'.[16]

Earlier chapters mentioned the 'old book' found by Hilkiah around 400 BC. Written on a peculiar fabric, that mysterious document was called the *Book of God* and carried within it coloured illustrations or depictions and precisely described the Rainbow Serpent. Look again, at what was said:

> One of its illustrations represents the Divine Essence...like a luminous serpent proceeding up to form a circle, and then having attained the highest point of its circumference, the ineffable Glory bends back down again.

That ancient description suggested the Rainbow Serpent was created from a force acting directly down and then shadowing up again (a twisted double helix format; like a DNA strand), creating an intertwined radiant spiral of vertical light with a mirror-type reflection (a twin, so to speak).

Australian Aborigines knew the Secret

A physical form of the Rainbow Serpent was used in sacred ceremonies by Australian Aborigines thousands of years before it found its way into the Bible and revealed direct parallels with the story of Moses' 'brass serpent'. It is a many-coloured wooden sculpture of two snakes entwined vertically from the base to the top where their heads protrude facing each other. They called it the 'Sky Serpent' and believed that 'it could never be slain'. The Elders claimed that ceremonial rites associated with its use were originally taught to them by 'blueberry-skinned sky gods' whom they called 'The Ancient Ones'.

The Elders allowed the 'Sky Serpent' to be drawn from a rare photograph and the following image is the first published in the world.

Artist's rendition of the highly revered Australian Aboriginal 'Sky Serpent'. It was used in rituals similar to those described in the Bible and was the physical representation of major elements of the Secret. Note its extraordinary resemblance to the ancient Caduceus shown earlier in this chapter. The object is around 30 inches high and its many colours have faded with time. The 'Sky Serpent' was of great spiritual significance to ancient Australian Aborigines; to them it was what the 'brass serpent' was to the biblical Moses.

The Aboriginal people believed the 'Sky Serpent' represented one's God-given spirit energy they called the Serpentine Life Force (Kundalini) and that knowledge is mostly lost to modern Aboriginal descendants. In their ancient culture, they directly associated the holy 'Serpent' with what they called 'The Spirit Bird', representing to them the flight of the soul, just as the Bennu bird was the symbol of resurrection to early Egyptians. The unprecedented parallels between those two bygone cultures raise thought-provoking questions, and the answers are not found in history books.

It was not only Australian Aborigines who maintained a sacred tradition about 'a serpent as large as a gum-tree'. The legend of Egypt's 'Luminous Serpent' was still fresh in people's mind dozens of centuries later and in one of numerous works called 'Confessions', a writer named Cyprinius, compiling his work in the year 252, recorded this extraordinary remark about the common knowledge of a famous 'serpent' in Egypt in years gone by:

The great serpent was placed to watch the Temple. How often have we repeated that it was no symbol, no personification, but really, a serpent occupied by a god. And we answer, that at Cairo in a Mussulman, not a heathen temple, we have seen, as thousands of other visitors have also seen, a huge serpent that lived there for centuries, we were told, and was held in great respect.

The ancients looked upon the spiral image in the Benben as 'a serpent occupied by a god' and they called it Khepra. The oldest writings known to mankind today make constant references to its existence and thousands of people over many centuries were recorded to have eye-witnessed the phenomena. However, there is more to that fascinating spiral of coloured light than is imagined and its visual presence on top of the Great Pyramid was only its earthly (exoteric) garment. There was also an esoteric nature to Khepra and that aspect raises the fundamental nature of the Bible to a stunning new level.

The only Holy Book

For thousands of years, spiritual teachers of Jewish traditions claimed that the five major Hebrew texts making up the Torah were 'holy', of special significance, and of supernatural origin – and they were right. By producing an exact physical copy of the spiral shape of the Rainbow Serpent from plastic, brass, a strip of metal or a similar solid substance, its significance becomes apparent, and that item could be best described as 'light descended into matter'. It is the primary element of both the *Book of Thoth* and the *Secret in the Bible* and the precise twisty shape of the Rainbow Serpent provides the necessary form to physically demonstrate a major part of the Secret. When the plastic or metal reproduction of the Rainbow Serpent is slowly revolved, 22 different shaped shadows are cast from that one element, and those shapes directly make up the 22 separate letters of the alphabet that the Torah was written in. Put in the simplest terms, the alphabet in which the Torah of the Bible was originally and secretly written was one composed of a series of 22 cosmic glyphs that emanated with 'splendour and power in the form of a serpent' from a vertical spiral of light in the Benben on top of the Great Pyramid in Egypt. Evidence of that knowledge points directly at the undeniable input of a higher intelligence, a superior mind source.

It does not matter, therefore, what the words of Ezra's Torah Scroll say or how inaccurate they are. It is irrelevant if they are fictitious; what matters is the knowledge that every word of the Torah Scroll was written in a Sacred Script - a Divine Language. The Torah is composed of a series of supernatural letters sourced from the shape and design of the Rainbow Serpent inside the Benben that 'came from the sky' thousands of years ago. Maybe the Great Pyramid was purposely built to such precise dimensions to preserve in stone for future generations, exact dimensions and angles of an object we now call a pyramid that holds within itself the prime element of a Sacred Secret known by initiated priests and Rabbis 2400 years ago, and by Egyptian priests thousands of years before that.

Ezra knew the Secret of the Sacred Script and instructed his scribes to write the Torah Scroll 'in characters they knew not', effectively secreting the extraordinary knowledge into the very text itself. The Sacred Script was never used by the Hebrew people but only by Jews of the Babylonian captivity onwards.[17] In other words, Ezra learnt the Panther Secret while at Babylon in sight of the Great Pyramid and the Panther Sphinx, subsequently taught five scribes the Sacred Language, and they wrote the Torah Scroll in that Script.

The sole individual element of the Divine Script is composed exclusively from the 22 different positions a shadow would cast from a reproduction of the Rainbow Serpent (or Serpent of Light). Initiated Rabbis knew the significance of the Sacred Script and jealously preserved the knowledge by writing and rewriting by hand every copy of the Torah using only that Script. It is not the words in the Bible that are inspired by God - it is the shape of the letters in which those words were originally written that is divine. This study, therefore, deals with a language that the Magi of Palestine claimed thousands of years ago was composed of 'Letters of Light'. They knew of its remarkable origin, and were aware that the Torah was purposely written in special letters. The shape of the 'Rainbow Serpent' is the very substance of every element of the 'Sacred Script' for it is the same spiral element in a different position in every word of the true Torah Scroll. The Torah, far from having to do with historical narration, is solely concerned with concentrations of Divine letters, in that the words were written from

22 individual elements woven out of one particular spiral form and developed into words that made up the narratives. Thus, the Torah is a structure, the whole of which was built on one fundamental principle, namely a Divine Language or Sacred Script.

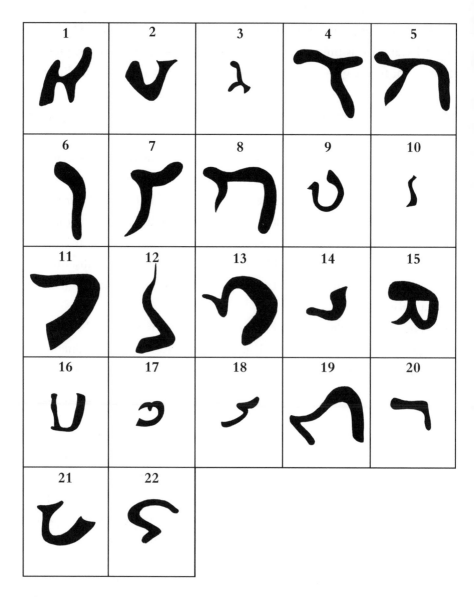

These are the 22 different views of the Rainbow Serpent. Each view is that of the sole element of the Rainbow Serpent being revolved within itself.

The weaving of the words of the Torah from the various positions of a single and solitary spiral element of light suggested an analogy that the Torah is a living texture, a fabric or live body of Sacred Letters, bound up in a single and special pattern. Down to the last seemingly insignificant detail of the body of myths, traditions, laws of life and commandments, the Torah was passed on with the understanding that it was an animate structure from which not one letter could be excised without harming the entire body, not even passages mythological or fictional in character. Ezra ensured that that knowledge was known to initiates, for he wrote, 'thou shalt not add thereto, nor diminish from it'.[18] That approach was well able to explain the contradictions, the stylist discrepancies and the serious chronological problems found in the Torah. It is made up of part narrative, part laws of life, commandments, part poetry, part raw statistic and major areas of unashamed fiction. The progression of stories it portrays are mainly exaggerated accounts of previous ancient traditions that may or may not have existed orally and woven together to form a new and captivating story. Behind the different problems and styles stands the mystic unity of the Divine Language, the Letters of God, not the words of God. Such outward appearances are simply the garments of the hidden inwardness that clothes itself in them, and, as the wise Rabbis 'who knew' the truth about the Torah said; 'Woe is he who looks only at the garments'.

A direct consequence of the Rabbis' belief was the principle that the Sacred Letters of the Torah possessed infinite meaning, which reveals itself differently at different levels and according to the capacity of its contemplator. The unfathomable profundity of the Sacred Text could not possibly be exhausted at any one level alone, an axiom that applied as well to traditions of the Torah. From the outset, the Torah possessed two aspects: a literal or surface reading or meaning which in most cases, particularly the supernatural narratives, are unhistorical and irrelevant; and a profound mystical understanding of immense depth, fully revealed in a later chapter. That is not all, for 'many lights shine forth from each word and letter', a view from ancient Rabbis that is summed up in the well-known statement saying that 'the Torah has seventy faces'. Those 'seventy faces' are associated with a prophecy in the Book of Daniel that speaks of 'Time, two times and half a time'.[19] The full revealment of that mystery may be recorded in the seventy missing books that 'Ezra delivered to the wise of the people' when he and his scribes wrote the original Torah and released only 24 of the 94 books they wrote. Those seventy writings are the original unpublished books of the Bible, the master hand-written texts; such was their importance.

The Benben and its Rainbow Serpent, however, had a much deeper meaning than just letters of the biblical alphabet. The symbols were preserved in the *Book of Thoth* and directly responsible for the coming into being of the *Book of the Dead*. That in turn led subsequently to the creation of the Torah. Ezra, in his wisdom, gave mankind the correct sequence for the use of the Divine Language in 22 consecutive verses of Psalm 119. The Rainbow Serpent was also directly responsible for the construction of the Great Pyramid that was built, in part, specifically to be a place of certain trials, temptations and difficulties that a person had to meet and overcome as he progressed from knowledge to knowledge before being given access to the greatest of all Secrets...and the Rainbow Serpent provided the mechanism.

CHAPTER THIRTEEN

THE ROAD TO HEAVEN

A tantalizing promise to reveal the secrets of the gods themselves is hidden in the *Book of the Dead*. It also provides a replica in literature for the interior layout of the Great Pyramid and associated underground facilities. Thus, the Pyramid and its environs, and the *Book of the Dead* reproduce the same original, one in initiated words written in stone, the other in physical structures built in stone. The ancient Egyptian name for the *Book of the Dead* was Per-am-rhid that is phonetically similar to the word, 'Pyramid'. When the ancients spoke of the *Book of the Dead* as Per-am-rhid, they were also speaking of the Great Pyramid, again showing the direct connection between the two. With that knowledge, and the principle of the Benben, it is possible to reconstruct the unique layout of the entire Giza plateau and show how Mysteries were divulged to those wishing to learn.

The pyramids of Giza could by no stretch of one's imagination, be an accident of construction or a coincidence in time, nor could the secret underground passageways and chambers be unrelated any more than their perfectly oriented structure. Hidden places in the Great Pyramid were the sites of the highest initiations into the Ancient Mysteries and secret priesthood doctrine was veiled in those rituals, and secreted into the *Book of the Dead*.

An original description of the system of gates, passageways, temples and chambers within and under the Sphinx and the Great Pyramid has been staring mankind in the face for thousands of years, for every key location is named in the *Book of the Dead*. Those localities are directly identified and relate to the most important areas of the Giza Plateau, both above and below ground. The Chamber of the Open Tomb, for example, mentioned on numerous occasions in the *Book of the Dead,* clearly refers to the now-called King's Chamber that contained only an open sarcophagus, lidless and empty, when the Pyramid was first unsealed.

The *Book of the Dead* outlines the path for the soul of the departed to follow 'in order that it might neither stray nor perish on the way' to Heaven and in doing so, directly and purposely allegorically records the layout of the Giza complex. Reading it with that understanding, the *Book of the Dead* describes the earthly pathways and trials an initiate took in the process of initiation and those rituals are found in the Pyramid Texts. The ceremonies originated from the famous story of Osiris and Isis, both universally worshipped in Egypt, and became the very essence of the Egyptian religion.

The three gods who preceded Osiris upon the throne had ceased to reign, but not to live. RA had taken refuge in heaven, disgusted with earth's creatures; Shu had disappeared in the midst of a tempest, and Sibu had quietly retired within his palace at the end of his sojourning upon earth. Osiris was the first among them struck down on Earth and hence to require funeral rites.

The Osiris account provided the original model of death and resurrection in major religions today. Resurrection to ancient Egyptians was the transformation of the soul into higher planes of God's creation, or the return of the soul to its original existence of that before its descent into the earthly body. The civilising mission of the original Egyptian Ennead was hindered by the actions of the 'red-haired, white-skinned' Seth,[1] a violent, gloomy and jealous character. Seth enticed Osiris to lie in a coffin 'of cunning workmanship'[2] that was then nailed, sealed with molten lead, and thrown into the river Nile. The casket slowly drifted into the Mediterranean and then on towards Byblos in Lebanon. In her sorrow, Isis instituted a search for Osiris' body, finally located the coffin and brought it back to Egypt. However, Seth, while hunting by moonlight, caught sight of the chest and recognized the corpse, cut it into fourteen parts and scattered them all over Egypt. Isis, lamenting 'Return to thy house, Osiris', then collected the pieces together, excluding the severed phallus, embalmed them, and made the first 'imperishable mummy, capable of sustaining forever the soul of a god'.[3]

It appears that the mummified body of Osiris was then placed in the Chamber of New Birth (called the Queen's Chamber today) after a long and elaborate ceremony. Illustrations in the *Book of the Dead* indicate that it was stood upright, possibly in the curious niche seen today recessed into the eastern wall. Pyramid Text 632 records that the last earthly duty of the dead king Osiris was to seed the womb of Isis and thus ensure a successor to the throne of Egypt. Dressed in striking white and purple garments, Isis and her assistants entered the Chamber and she miraculously conceived her son, Horus, 'after the spirit of Osiris came upon her'.

Upon completion of the ritual, Osiris' mummy was taken up to the Chamber of the Open Tomb and placed in the empty sarcophagus. The *Book of the Dead* calls that large stone structure the Resurrection Machine or, in some translations, the Instrument of Resurrection. The mummy was positioned facing south towards a small square opening in the chamber's wall that rose up through the body of the Pyramid to its outer surface. While in the Resurrection Machine, the Ancients believed that the mummy of Osiris was struck with a particular magical force that brought about an astral rebirth, and the 'star' of the god was reborn in the sky. Early Egyptian priests called that force the 'Secret Science' and today it is called the Pyramid Effect. The Benben on top of the Pyramid appears to have been the catalyst providing the force to achieve the 'Science' of the Pyramid Effect.

At that time it was believed that the soul of Osiris, now having completed its work on Earth, departed from the mummy and rose up and out through the inclined 'soul shaft'. The sight line of the shaft was thought to have been purposely designed to align directly with the stars in Orion's Belt, recorded in the Pyramid Texts to have contained the original home of Osiris. At sunrise, the mummy was removed from the Resurrection Machine and ceremoniously placed in a special white stone sarcophagus. It was then sealed and taken to a pre-prepared burial chamber deep in the Eastern sands around the Great Pyramid.

The death and resurrection of Osiris took 3½ days and the attending priests revered the ceremonial procedures that were involved. As the centuries rolled over, and with the power of the Great Pyramid lost with the removal of the Benben, later priests developed a re-enactment of the original rituals and effectively preserved the Osiris ritual. From what they had learned from 'the gods', they developed a special process through which they claimed they could, by a particular method of development, prepare individuals in readiness to receive the Seed of Immortality; then, after advancing them through other processes, move their soul out of the body and mingle it in the heavens with Osiris and other gods, then return it back to its earthly body to resume daily life. Through their initiation ceremony, a long period of training developed and subsequently became one of two ways in which the initiated could see 'God face to face',[4] the other being the use of the Secret in the Bible.

In reconstructing the Egyptian initiatory process, constant allegories found recorded in the *Book of the Dead* were shown to have always applied to chambers, temples and passageways in and around the Sphinx and the Great Pyramid. Drawing on that information, and what was gleaned from Masonic ritual procedures, an initiation reconstruction is possible, and it shows how the Giza complex was used after the era of the earliest Company of Gods.

It is also possible to show that Rabbi Jesus learned the 'magic' Secret at Giza, and New Testament narratives support that conclusion. In the Gospels, the ministry of Jesus terminated in a trial and sentence in which he was shown with the resolve to go through a particular $3^{1}/_{2}$ day period of suffering, after which 'I shall rise again'.[5] Before the candidate could learn the basis of the Mysteries, he needed to have reached the mystical 'age of thirty', which did not require a passage of thirty years. The first 12 years required an actual passing of 12 years of time, but the candidate could attain the mystical 'age of thirty' any time following that, depending upon the measure of effort the individual candidate wished to give, which is 22 years in modern Freemasonry. The mystical 'ages' of 12 and 30 are significant in this study, for they are precisely the two ages given of Rabbi Jesus in the Gospels. He was in the temple at 12 years of age 'with the teachers',[6] meaning that he had completed the compulsory 12 years of training. Then, in the very next chapter of the Luke Gospel, Rabbi Jesus was suddenly 'at about the age of thirty',[7] that being the mystical age of thirty, and ready to commence his initiation.

What went on inside the Great Pyramid?

The following chart lists the 22 major locations recorded in the *Book of the Dead* and their relative counterpart at the Giza complex. The current names of the chambers and passageways in the Great Pyramid were given only in the last 150 years or so, and this chart records what they were originally called:

Original Title of the Main Locations at Giza as Recorded in 'The Book of the Dead' (22 in Total)	Modern Day Title of the Same Locations Plus Location as Shown on the Master Plans
1. Chamber of Ordeal	Building south of the Sphinx, connected to Sphinx with underground passages.
2. The Royal Arch of the Solstice	Curved entranceway into the chambers under the Sphinx.
3. Hall of Initiates	Main passageway under Sphinx.
4. Temple of the Grand Orbit	Domed circular temple under the rear of the Sphinx.
5. The Well of Life	Vertical air and light shafts behind Sphinx.
6. The Hall of Truth in Light	First passageway leading from the domed temple under the Sphinx to the Well of Life.
7. The Temple of Isis	First discovered in 1935. Contains elaborate carvings and large white sarcophagus. Approximately 200 feet east of the Great Pyramid.
8. The Hall (or Door) of Ascent	Located under the ruins near the southeast corner of the Great Pyramid.
9. The Hall of Truth in Darkness	Passageway leading from the Hall of Ascent directly under the Great Pyramid.
10. The Passage of the Veil	Long low horizontal passage leading to the now-called Queen's Chamber.
11. The Chamber of the Second Birth	Known as the Queen's Chamber today. The gabled ceiling is on the centre-line of the Pyramid.
12. The Hall of Judgment	Known as the Grand Galley today. Slopes upwards at 27 degrees.
13. The Stone of God	Large fixed stone at the top-most level of the Grand Gallery.
14. Chamber of the Triple Veil	Three-tiered antechamber attached and leading to the King's Chamber.
15. The Gate of Death (Leads to the 'Fields of Peace')	Last gateway into the King's Chamber.
16. Chamber of the Open Tomb	Known as the King's Chamber today.
17. The Instrument of Resurrection	The lidless coffer in the King's Chamber.
18 The Gate of Coming Forth by Day	Exit door between the paws of the Sphinx.
19. The Chamber of Upside-Down-ness	The basement chamber of the Great Pyramid.
20. The Throne of Radiance	The Benben; the highest point of the Great Pyramid. Not in its location today.
21. The Passage of Descent (also called the Passage of the Polestar)	The narrow descending passage leading down from the northern face of the Great Pyramid. This is the entryway used by tourists today.
22. The False Door (Hidden Door, in some translations)	The swivel stone door that once hid the descending passage. Originally in place on northern face of Pyramid.

Each of the 22 aspects shall be individually approached, and the journey of the initiate into death and resurrection re-enacted.

1.   THE CHAMBER OF ORDEAL

Before journeying with his guide into the Great Pyramid, the candidate met in the Sphinx Temple, low in the valley and to the South of the Sphinx's right paw (See Number 1 on The Master Plans). The first initiatory step involved a procedure that took forty days and included purification, not only physically, but dissolving all tendencies to evil thoughts. He fasted, alternatively between vegetables, juices, and special herbal concoctions. The New Testament preserved the tradition, with Rabbi Jesus being 'led into the desert...and he fasted forty days and forty nights'.[8] Jesus 'was led' by the person or guide who was to see him through his initiation.

The number 'forty' used in relation to Jesus is found many times in the Bible and its use is of particular importance. Bishop Augustine of Hippo (354-430) expressed wonder about that number when he said: 'How then, is work perfected in the number forty?'[9] When analyzed, number forty is used in both Old and New Testaments as expressive of a particular period of probation or trial, and probably originated with the forty-year Venus Cycle revealed by astronomers of the Mystery Schools. The Israelites, for example, wandered forty years in the wilderness, and forty years of bondage they served under the hard yoke of the Philistines. Moses spent forty days on the Mount of Sinai and both David and Solomon were made to reign for forty years each.[10] Elijah was in hiding forty days, and for forty days the deluge fell, and for yet another forty days, Noah was shut within the ark. The men of Ninevah had a like period of probation under the preaching of Jonah. The punishment of scourging was limited to forty strokes,[11] so when Jesus entered into his probation period it was for forty days - it could be no other way in the mind of Gospel writers.

The trial period involved more than just fasting. The candidate was to avoid all contact with the world, all vacillation of mind, and all stimulation of emotions. During the forty days and nights of ordeal, he was required to study astronomical charts to supplement his skills in astronomy and to memorize charts of the heavens. He was also given a particular ritual from which to memorize certain passwords, secret signs and handclasps, skills still practised today in Freemasonry. In a daily sacred ceremony in the temple, he sipped Adibhuta, the juice of a sacred plant, and ate bread, and the *Book of the Dead* calls that ceremony Gyotishtoma Agnishtoma.

A 'private baptism' was conducted every day. The Edfu Texts recorded that there was once a low-lying Sacred Lake near the Chamber of Ordeal that filled from the waters of the River Nile. Even today, adjacent to every temple of initiation in India is a lake or reservoir of holy water in which the Brahmins, the Master Teachers, and their devotees perform daily ablutions. Beside the ruins of many Mystery Temples of ancient Egypt are also found Sacred Lakes and the water was consecrated for that purpose. The holy water of the present-day Christian church is symbolic and carried-over from the baptismal rites of Egyptian Mystery Schools. Baptism was anciently called 'illumination' and some versions of the New Testament still used that word.[12] The object of the ceremony was not to wash away material dust, but to symbolize the cleansing from ones sins, the purification of one's soul. Religious writings are replete with baptisms by immersion into certain sacred waters and such were the waters of ablutions near the Chamber of Ordeal – to purify the consciousness and prepare it for reception into the Mysteries. For the individuals 'chosen', much was required, for then imposed upon him was a severe test designed to prepare him for the grade of 'Neocoris'.[13]

The forty days having expired, he was then placed in an obscure chamber called 'Endymion', or Grotto of the Initiates, a room set aside for concentration and meditation, and was there 'tempted by the devil':

> Here he was served with a delicious repast to animate his failing strength, by beautiful women, who were either the espoused of the priests, or virgins dedicated to Isis. They invited him to love them by gestures. He must triumph over these difficult tests to prove the command which he has over his passions.[14]

Seven beautiful young women, each perfumed with a variant fragrance of the seven sacred oils of Egypt, were systematically sent alone into the room with the candidate to entice him into sexual intercourse. Had he succumbed to any of their advances, he was instantly dismissed and not permitted to proceed further into the initiatory process.

After a period of reflection came cross examination and he was interrogated as to the motives which lead him from worldliness to the sanctuary of the Hidden God. He was also examined on his fundamental knowledge of what he had learnt over the previous weeks and his fitness to progress was ascertained. If he answered satisfactorily, the 'Stolista' (or Sprinkler) purified him by throwing water over his head. He had then to categorically confirm in a loud voice that he had conducted himself with wisdom and chastity.

2.   THE ROYAL ARCH OF THE SOLSTICE

(Below 'The Guardian of the Secrets')

The ceremony started at sunset and was completed at sunrise $3^1/_2$ days later. The 84-hour duration period was determined from the *Book of the Dead* and is supported in the New Testament. The Gospels of John[15] and Mark[16] both state that Jesus was incarcerated on 'the preparation of the Passover' and Jewish calendars of the first century recorded that the Passover was celebrated on a Wednesday, hence, Good Wednesday. Therefore, it seems that Jesus began his initiation on Wednesday evening and completed it on Sunday morning. During that time he was permitted to sleep only on three brief occasions, called: the '3 Hours Sleep of Osiris', the '4 Hours Sleep of Sokar', and the '5 Hours Sleep of Horus'.

Wearing a plain white tunic, the candidate then left the Chamber of Ordeal in the company of his guide/initiator who was magnificently clad in the ceremonial Panther costume. At Hour Zero (7 pm) they approached the Royal Arch of the Solstice along pathways recently uncovered by archaeologists that led to the subterranean gateway located under, and in front, of the Sphinx (See Number 2 on The Master Plans). It was the TruE gateway to attaining initiation into that beyond the physical. The Masonic ground plans show 22 symbolic steps leading downwards at the front and the side of the Sphinx but the Rosicrucian plans revealed a greater amount. Large numbers of unenlightened but curious passers-by gathered at that point and gazed in wonder at the candidate heading towards the hallowed premises. Appropriately, his guide carried a scourge or whip of cords by which the profane were driven back from the steps of the sanctuary. That part of the pageantry is identical in concept to the Gospel episode applied to Jesus driving the worldly moneychangers from the holy temple of Jerusalem.

They approached the main entrance door inscribed with the following words, 'I will not let you enter through me unless you tell me my name'. That required the candidate to reveal the first password: 'The place of Light and Truth is your name'. An attendant called Keeper of the Gate stood at the South column bordering the main door and said, 'Unless you tell me your name, I will not let you past'.

The candidate then gave his name and the Keeper of the Gate at the North column bordering the main door said: 'I will not let you enter in by me unless you tell me my name'. The secret words for entry were 'Monarch Caron Mini', meaning, 'I count the days of anger'. If the candidate had remembered them, he was then blindfolded and allowed to proceed. Those two columns are called by Masons, Jachin (South) and Boaz (North) and are named and described in the Bible at the entrance to the symbolic Solomon's Temple.[17] Bible students would also be familiar with two columns of wind and fire that flanked the entrance of the Temple of the King of Tyre. The concept of two columns at the entrance to sacred temples had its origin in the rituals of the *Book of the Dead.*

Two vertical columns border the entrance to a chapel adjoining the pyramid of Medum, built for the first king of the IV Dynasty, Sneferu (c. 2600 BC). Note the Tablet of Offering on the floor at the base of the columns. They were generally inscribed with invocations to a Deity, such as Osiris or Isis, and venerated before entry into a chapel (Drawn by Faucher-Gudin, from a sketch by W. F. Petrie, 'Ten Years' Digging in Egypt'. p. 141).

The candidate and his guide entered through the two columns into the Hall of Initiates, well below the present level of the desert sands. The door was closed behind them and everything was dark save one beam of natural light that shone down from the vertical tunnel on the northern side of the Sphinx. That was the 'Mystery Tunnel in Sphinx' in the newspaper article mentioned earlier. There were 56 masked persons in the Hall of Initiates, all waiting to trial and judge the new candidate on his way to revealment of the Mystery.

3. HALL OF INITIATES

Upon entry into the subterranean Hall (Number 3 on The Master Plans), the candidate was brutally stopped to the sudden, violent and unexpected racket of abusive screams and shrieks, clapping hands, and stomping feet. It was designed to alarm him and he was verbally insulted until he yelled out the vital next password. In the initiation of an Apprentice in Masonry, it is called the Shock of Entrance and if he remained composed and knew the password, he was allowed to move forward where the 'Reader of the Laws' read to him the 'Constitution of the Establishment'. The officials demanded of him an answer if he had taken any part in the assassination of Osiris, their Master. After his reply in the negative, two black-habited persons who interred the dead violently manhandled him into their possession. A cable or rope was tied around his neck, firstly as a means of restraint should such be necessary, and symbolically to remind him that he was in a state of bondage. The cable-tow was also used in India as an emblem of Yama, the God of Death. The candidate's left breast was then made bare in token of his fidelity and to prove he was not an imposter as to sex, the rules being different for the entry of females into the Mysteries. To threaten him, a sharp implement like a dagger or a sword was pressed against his bare chest and the High Priest said:

> As this is a prick to your flesh, so may the recollection of it be to your conscience, should you ever contemplate the slightest revelation of the secrets about to be entrusted to you.

He was then divested of all monies and metallic substances to symbolize his poverty. That instruction revealed that a man was not esteemed because of his worldly possessions, for all were equal, meeting on the 'level' and parting on the 'square'. His right knee was then made bare and on it he 'knelt to the West', the direction of the Great Pyramid where he was heading.

Fortunately, three old engravings predating 1849 survive that show with extraordinary detail some of the later Masonic rituals, preserving within them all elements of the secret ceremonies. The first one features the initiation of an apprentice.

Initiation of an apprentice. The apprentice has his right trouser leg rolled up and his left breast bared. The number of persons at the ceremony represents the famous Masonic cipher number. There are seven globes making up the light and its sub-structure strongly resembles Sir Francis Bacon's cryptic illustrations used on his Title pages. The sash around the neck of the pipe-bearer is inscribed with the symbols of Thoth's book. Spear-shakers are present.

The candidate was now required to pass between two smaller columns before entering further into the depths of secret learning. The inner columns differed from the outer, being united by a crossbeam under which the candidate was required to walk. He gingerly moved forward between two rows of hooded personages and was asked to kneel again, this time to take the obligation from the Egyptian Magi (or High Priest). His right hand was then placed upon a sacred book with golden pages (*The Book of Thoth*). In Freemasonry today the candidate takes the obligation by placing his hand on the Volume of the Sacred Law, the Torah. During the procedure, two judges stood one either side of him with raised ceremonial rods crossed at the top above the candidate's head. The High Priest then read a prayer after which everybody chanted the words, 'so mote it be'. The sign portrayed by the judges was of a phallus nature and it became the secret sign in later centuries for entrance to an Egyptian tomb.

The candidate was removed of his blindfold, ordered to move slowly forward and stand perfectly still and erect before the vertical beam of light, 'squared' to it. An earlier chapter mentioned that a French Secret Society claimed that the candidate was required to stop before each of the 22 major pages of the *Book of Thoth* and receive instructions of the meaning of the cryptic hieroglyphs inscribed upon each plate. That was a secret ceremony and an extraordinary parallel is recorded in the *Book of the Dead*. It mentions 'bas-reliefs' that stood revealed for all who would 'see'. There were 21 columns standing in the Hall of Initiates, each described as 'lavishly carved with pictures' that revealed 'the inner message of the Mysteries'. The candidate was the 22nd aspect and he represented the unnumbered card of the Tarot pack (21 + 1). It seemed certain that the 21 (+1) major picture drawings from Thoth's book were not only etched onto the face of the Great Pyramid but were also etched on columns in the Hall below the Sphinx.

4.   TEMPLE OF THE GRAND ORBIT

The *Book of the Dead* description is applied to the circular temple behind and below the Sphinx (Number 4 on The Master Plans). The initiate-to-be again moved forward, was again asked for a password and entered into the circular temple with its domed ceiling. The floor was a chequer-board[18] of black and white stone tiles, symbolizing the principles of good and bad, day and night, life and death, and right and wrong. The ceiling was painted with a circular zodiac similar in concept to that found in the temple at Dendara, and represented the earthly depiction of what the *Book of the Dead* called the

Grand Wheel of Heaven. The candidate was required to explain the constellations, the solstices, the equinoxes, eclipses of the sun, and the zodiac proper, with its intricate but orderly mechanism of evolution.

Very few passed the seven tests making up the First Degree. Those that did received the coveted invitation to proceed further, and were given a pure white goatskin apron that was tied around their waist by the initiator. It symbolized the efforts of mental and physical purification over the previous 40 days and the retained knowledge required to pass the initial tests that actually made up the first three divisions of the Osiris *duat*.

Wearing his 'Apron of the First Degree', the candidate was then shown to the concealed door on the western side of the Temple of the Grand Orbit. The statue of a wolf-headed god guarded it, and had the candidate failed his First Degree, he would have been unaware of the door and of the process that followed, because initiation rituals did not allow for repetition of the test. That door was un-noticeable, being a stylized panel that, when activated, revealed itself to open into a long passage. He was now about to enter through that doorway and into the next four divisions of the *duat*.

The candidate was again blindfolded, led on, and the 'door to the West' closed soundlessly behind him. The initiation continued and the two oldest supervisors, Thesmothetes or Keepers of the Rites, then brusquely stopped the initiate in his tracks. They made him believe that he was standing on the edge of a wide and deep abyss and that if he stepped forward he would plunge to his death. One of the supervisors insistently intoned:

> This abyss surrounds the Temple of Mysteries and guards it against the brazen curiosity of the profane. However, we have come too early, for our brothers have not yet lowered the drawbridge, which the initiate must cross to reach hallowed ground. We must wait for them and therefore, if you love life, stand absolutely still. Cross your hands on your chest and keep the blindfold in place until the brothers arrive to lower the drawbridge.

The candidate knew that the hour of his trial had come. He will not only need great spiritual strength and self-control, but he will have to prove that he can obey upcoming instructions without hesitation. He therefore willingly obeyed the order given, surrendering his fate into the hands of his supervisors.

His burning desire to know the Secret made him strong and powerful; he knew that the key to the Mysteries would be his if he obeyed and persevered. He stood motionless on the edge of what he thought was, and may have been, a deep pit, waiting to progress. There may well have been a pit in front of him, for even today Giza tour guides tell of the initiatory tradition under the Sphinx involving a deep vertical shaft containing water at the bottom – and crocodiles. Eventually he heard a metallic clanging sound and was then told to step forward, but was again violently stopped and asked for the password into the Second Degree. The secret word was 'Zee-oo-kha-ee-zaza' that meant, 'do not discriminate'. His right arm was then uncovered in token of his sincerity and to show that he had no weapon of offence or defence about him.

5.   THE WELL OF LIFE

Providing he knew the password, he was allowed entry into a hall leading in a westerly direction. He was led blindly along by his initiator pulling the cable-tow until he came to natural light and fresh air from four vertical shafts cut down through rock and intersecting with the underground passageway. In that area, a series of passages juncture, with one leading away to the Great Pyramid. He was heading towards evolution, enlightenment and the Secret of the Mysteries. The vertical shafts or 'Well of Life' served as light and airshafts to the subterranean passageways.

6.   THE HALL OF TRUTH IN LIGHT

Leaving behind the fresh air of the shafts, they headed up the steep incline and entered, or passed through, the Chapel of Offering. The existence of that structure was known from the report of Dr Selim Hassan who assisted at the scene of excavations for the University of Cairo in 1935. Three ornate vertical pillars stood in a triangular layout in the centre of the Chapel and may be associated with 'the three pillars upon which the world rests' recorded in both the Psalms of Ezra and the Book of Enoch. The duty of the candidate was to wash the columns during which time he was to study an alphabet named 'Hiero-grammatical' inscribed upon them.

7.   THE TEMPLE OF ISIS

They then came to the Temple of Isis around 100 feet west of the Chapel of Offering. Dr Hassan described a beautiful goddess carved on one of the walls and a large white sarcophagus that he believed contained the mummy of Isis herself. Dr Hassan referred to the Temple as a 'place of initiation and reception' and maybe prayers of respect to Isis were extended here. That temple is close to the Great Pyramid and second-to-last to pass through before entering the sombre subterranean areas of the Pyramid proper. It is not possible to establish what happened in that Temple, only that tests for the Second Degree were carried out there and the secret password to gain entry was 'Chymia', meaning chemistry. It was probable that the candidate had his first sleep in that Temple.

8.   THE HALL (OR DOOR) OF ASCENT

In reconstructing the passageways and chambers under the Giza Plateau, it appeared that there was another entranceway into the Great Pyramid and that was confirmed in ancient records. In 24 BC, an historian called Strabo wrote a series of 47 books about Egypt after a long journey through the country. He mentioned a hidden southern entrance into the Great Pyramid and said that the northern door known today was concealed from view. There is the possibility of two subterranean entrances on the southern side of the Pyramid, one from the Temple of the Solar-men where the Initiators entered, and possibly one under the remains of a Temple today seen near the southeastern corner. It is probable that a stairway led down in that area and connected with the Hall of Ascent (Number 8 on The Master Plans).

For initiates and candidates to gain entry into the Great Pyramid, there is a subterranean entrance, and the Hall of Ascent is the name given in the *Book of the Dead*. It joined the Hall of Truth in Darkness that travelled up into the body of the Great Pyramid and connected with the King and Queen chambers by an arrangement of side-chambers. In that area, the *Crata Repoa* spoke of a dark vestibule filled with dead bodies and decorated coffins where blood-covered Heroi 'who open the corpses, occupied their time'. It is probable that the candidate was purposely conducted through that facility to witness the gory process of mummification and remind him of his physical inevitability.

9. THE HALL OF TRUTH IN DARKNESS

Passing deeper into the Second Degree, the candidate was given a secret pass grip and yet another password. He was then led along the dark Hall of Truth and, before ascending into the Pyramid itself, he was to handshake an instructor waiting at the end of the passage. The handgrip involved a particular pressure of the thumb between the first and second joints of the hand and the password he was to give was Shibboleth. That is a biblical word[19] and used with different pronunciation on either side of the Jordan. Depending upon how it was pronounced, the men of Gilead determined whether the speaker was of Ephrain or not. The candidate was then unveiled and shown the entrance to a long dark horizontal stone passage, so low that it could only be traversed on hands and knees. In the *Book of the Dead,* that area of the Great Pyramid is called 'The Passage of the Veil'.

10. THE PASSAGE OF THE VEIL

The guide instructed the candidate and he was then left alone: 'Take this lamp and go alone without fear. In the test of loneliness you have no one and nothing to fear but yourself. May this path be a foretaste of the grave for you…now conquer the terrors of the grave'. After he disappeared through the opening, he became aware of a thick timber door being wedged in with mallets behind him, blocking any exit. A piercing distant voice called out, 'Fools chasing knowledge and power die here'. Those seven chilling words, screamed out seven times, were echoed by the acoustics of the narrow passage and were designed to strike terror into the candidate, for he knew neither where the passage went nor how to exit from it.

On his hands and knees, he moved forward along the 127-foot seemingly endless tunnel, with his lamp purposely set to burn out before he reached its end. He was filled with panic in the pitch darkness but knew that he must go on. He arrived unknowingly at a sudden and mysterious drop that he was to think was a bottomless pit but it revealed a two-foot lower level in the passage floor-way.

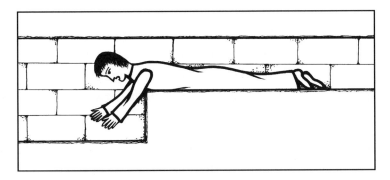

In the impenetrable darkness, the path seemed endless, but suddenly he saw a faint flicker of light before him and with a sigh of relief, crawled towards it. The light glowed stronger and gradually he could see where he was heading. Finally, he reached a room, entered through a low opening, and was able to stand up. He had arrived in a curious little chamber with a gabled ceiling, today called the Queen's Chamber. In the *Book of the Dead,* it is called The Chamber of the Second Birth.

11. THE CHAMBER OF THE SECOND BIRTH

Because of the custom among Arabs of placing women in tombs with gabled ceilings, as opposed to flat ones for men, that room was called in modern times, the Queen's Chamber. Egyptologists consider the name a misnomer, and claim that Egyptians did not place queens in major Pyramids but built adjoining small pyramids or mastabas for their final resting place. In the gabled chamber, however, the candidate met with twelve elders, and in the corner stood a table holding a seven-pointed rosette with seven triple lamps 'blazing with Eternal light' (*The Mysteries of Osiris and Isis*). The walls were covered with a mural tapestry embroidered with teachings left by the 'Great Revealer of Secrets', Thoth himself. Great secrets were structured into the tapestry and only the elders were capable of deciphering them. The candidate was introduced to those secrets, but only after he had taken an oath of secrecy in which he swore to keep everything he had seen and heard secret.

He was requested to repeat the following words:

> In the presence of the executors of the Will of the Almighty, Eternal and Unchanging One, I (name of candidate), son of (name of his father) born in, (country, place, date and time of birth), swear to keep secret all I have seen and heard as well as all I will hear and see in the Holy Place of the Magicians of Life and Death. If I should ever break this oath, I deserve to be put to death as a sick jackal, my tongue will be ripped from my mouth, my heart from my body, to be buried in the sand of the sea so that the waves can carry me away to eternal oblivion.

Any person involved in Freemason rituals will immediately see in that oath the origins of the obligations of the Entered Apprentice. The 1st Degree Masonic ritual referred to 'cutting of the throat and tearing out of the tongue' as penalty for anybody divulging secrets. The 2nd Degree threat promised 'the tearing open of the breast and the removal of the heart'. Punishment of the Master Mason's 3rd Degree was that of 'having the body severed in two and the bowels removed and burnt to ashes'.

The initiation in the Great Pyramid proceeded and the supervisor warned the candidate of the result if he broke the oath:

> We will all witness your oath, and if you ever break it, an unknown avenger will follow your footsteps and find you wherever you are, even if you are on the highest throne, in order to execute the punishment you pronounced upon yourself.

In that Chamber centuries earlier, Isis miraculously conceived Horus. The *Book of the Dead* referenced 'a prayer to the East' that was associated with the words, 'Kansa Aum Pakscha' translating to, 'worship the Deity alone in peace and quiet'. The candidate then knelt on the stone floor facing a tall statue of Isis herself, the Great Mother. In front of Isis was an altar upon which stood two large ornate chalices, side by side, one in silver and one in gold. Suddenly the twelve priests menacingly surrounded him, each pointing a sword at his heart and his head. Of the two goblets, the supervisor said: 'One contains a harmless drink, while the other contains a fast-acting Poison. I order you to drink one of them immediately'!

The candidate realized that he must decide without hesitating. He believed that he had no choice, since the twelve elders had their swords in their hands. He quickly drank one goblet and waited anxiously for what may come. If the initiate refused to take the drink, he was wrapped in a black cloth, taken away and imprisoned for seven months. During that time, he was given only bread and water once a day, served by a mute guard. After seven months of confinement, he was offered the goblets again. If he succeeded in quickly emptying one, he regained his freedom. However, he was never allowed to re-enter and resume his initiation. For anyone who hesitated to put his life in the balance for the belief he had just sworn allegiance to, was in danger of being forever unreliable because of the indecision in his spirit. He was exiled, and never allowed to return to his former life-style in case he revealed the secret processes he had experienced before his failure. Iamblichus recorded such an example in his book, *On the Mysteries, particularly those of the Egyptians, Chaldeans and the Assyrians*. He spoke in the first person and was obviously angry at his treatment:

> I wanted to be initiated into the Mysteries of the famous magicians before whom all Egypt bows down in the dust, as though they are demi-gods; but they have proved to be evil men, and no one can penetrate their Mysteries unless by some miracle he can escape the chance of being poisoned or killed. I was unable to pass one of their tests and they punished me with contempt; they are monsters and a disgrace to the entire nation.

As late as the fourth century, Egyptian priests were still called 'magicians', painstakingly guarding their Mysteries, now some thousands of years old.

Meanwhile, the initiate was told that he was not in any danger of poisoning, as both chalices contained only wine of different alcoholic strengths. After that reassurance, he was blindfolded again, the procession continued, and he now stood unknowingly at the bottom of the Grand Gallery. In the *Book of the Dead*, it was called the 'Hall of Judgment' and there he faced his greatest test.

CHAPTER FOURTEEN

THE MEETING WITH GOD

Extreme physical discomfort, sometimes pain and the use of 'the dramatic', were common ingredients in the initiation process. Proof of a candidate's courage and faith was required to be demonstrated, and in the final stages, the process worsened. This passage was preserved by Stobaeus from an ancient record, and confirmed the experience of initiates:

> The mind is affected and agitated on the way into the Grand Mysteries; the first stage is nothing but errors and uncertainties, labouring, wanderings and darkness. And now, arrived on the verge of death and initiation, everything wears a dreadful aspect; it is all horrors, trembling and affrightment.

In the Hall of Judgment (Number 12 on The Master Plans), the candidate was given a large wooden ankh cross. He now faced, but could not see, the steep incline up the Grand Gallery. The ceremony proceeded and the supervisor crossed his arms and called out: 'My sons, what time is it?' An answer echoed throughout the Hall: 'The hour of the law'.

The supervisor continued: 'When the hour of the law has come, I order that justice proceed'. From behind the blindfolded candidate came a sudden loud metallic crash, followed by a combination of eerie sounds. Firstly, the dragging of chains, followed by noises of a skirmish, then raging, and a human voice screaming for mercy in heart-rending death-throes; then nothing, the silence of the grave. After a short pause, the supervisor said: 'That is the death of those who have committed perjury. Justice has been done on those who deserve it. Go see, and be convinced'.

The candidate was now required to carry and/or drag the heavy cross up the 157 foot long, narrow and slippery slope to the highest level. A series of 27 oblong holes cut vertically along the walls and into the ramps to a depth of 8 to 11 inches appear to serve to hold benches or seats for 54 observers at regular intervals up each side of the Grand Gallery. The *Book of the Dead* recorded that there were 56 judges involved in the initiation of a candidate, twenty-seven on each side of the Hall of Judgment. The High Priest stood on the Stone of God at the top of the incline and, at the bottom or lower end, stood the most dreadful of judges, the one 'Whose mouth is twisted when he speaks because his face is behind him'. The 56 judges were therefore fully accounted. In Roman mythology, Janus, with two faces, front and rear, was the god of doorways and that myth may have originated in the Great Pyramid. As the candidate worked his way up the ascending passageway, he was 'struck with reeds and fists', symbolising the judges' pretended anger at his inferior wisdom, for he had not yet entirely departed from the lower levels of knowledge.

A counterpart of the pyramidal ceremony is carried in the New Testament when the procession of Jesus was hampered by bystanders who 'mocked and beat him' as he dragged his cross. He was scourged and abused and they said to him: 'Who is it that struck you?'.[1] The Gospel narratives said that Jesus 'carried his cross and came to the place of the skull' where he subsequently met his demise. Taking the Gospel account and combining it with initiatory processes, a new understanding of the 'place of the skull' emerges. In one Gospel the word 'skull' was translated 'Golgotha' which was simply the Greek word for 'skull' but it came to mean a barren craggy, oval-shaped hilltop outside Jerusalem. In the remaining three Gospels, 'skull' was not translated 'Golgotha', but simply 'the place of the skull', for that was what it was in the initiatory progression. Such a physical place as Golgotha, like Nazareth, is not documented in any historical records and is only found in the New Testament where it was mistakenly recorded as a location. The 'place of the skull' was a reference to the display of a human skull in the initiatory process and was used by Mystery Schools for thousands of years. For them it was symbolic, and connected the initiate with a higher awareness of his purpose that could not be reached with words. Associated with the chant, 'Remember you must die', later Egyptians adopted the concept and passed around a skull at feasts to highlight the reality of physical death. So important was the skull in mystical rites, it became the motto of the Order of the Death's Head and one modern Secret Society was called 'Skull and Bones'.

After enduring and accepting the abuse, the candidate reached the top and the High Priest asked for the next secret password, that was JO-AH-VA. That word has a remarkable vocal similarity to an Old Testament god, Jehovah, a word recorded in the *Book of the Dead* that preceded the writing of the Old Testament by thousands of years.

13. THE STONE OF GOD (No. 13 on The Master Plans)

Here was the beginning of the dreaded Third Degree. At the top of the Hall of Judgment is a massive stone, 3 feet high, 8 feet long and 6 feet wide, and covered with human skulls. The front edge of the stone is precisely positioned on the centre-line of the Pyramid, marking the transition between the northern and southern halves of the monument. Before standing on the Stone the candidate was told, 'put off thy shoes from thy feet, for the place whereupon thou standest is holy ground'.[2] Upon the Stone of God, the candidate was 'crucified'. He was firmly tied ankle, wrist and upper arm to the cross he had just carried up the long slope and it was secured in a vertical position. He then said three times: 'I raise myself to venerate God, the Master of the Great House'. Now with his blind-fold removed, he was able to look back down the long Hall of Judgment.

The act of 'crucifixion' was a symbol of the sacrifice of the individual self. It represented the whole of life being a surrender of the personage – a symbolic act of giving, rather than receiving. In that part of the initiation, the individual surrendered his own external will, with all its material desires and affections. It was designated the Passion because it represented the pain and stress that accompanied the process of initiation and his 'passion' to see it through; the pain of self-sacrifice, of resistance to temptation, the trouble connected with the maintenance of a constant life in the midst of a greedy and selfish world. That particular act was a surrender consummated and demonstrated by the candidate and witnessed by standers-by. He actually presented himself and symbolically gave up his life, representing a complete, unreserved surrender, to the physical death, if need be, without opposition. He was tied to a structure that positioned him in the form of a cross. Ancient Egyptians believed that the true posture of prayer was to stand with out-stretched arms that formed a cross. That belief was later carried into Jewish tradition and written in the 'Psalms and Odes of Solomon',[3] 'I stretched out my hands and approached God...for the stretching out of my hands is a sign; my expansion is the outspread cross'.

The symbol of the cross originated as part of an ancient Egyptian initiatory rite, and eventually found its way into Christianity. The church stated that in its history, 'there is no proof of the use of a cross until much later' than the sixth century.[4] It is recorded in Christian archives that the general use of the crucifix was ratified at the Sixth Ecumenical Council in 680 (Canon 82). The council decreed that 'the figure of a man fastened to a cross be now adopted' and the new church logo was later confirmed by Pope Hadrian 1 (772-95).[5] About a century later, the first pictures of Jesus Christ standing against a cross slowly started to appear, mainly in Syrian art. In those depictions, he was of ripe age, 'utterly divested of all circumstances of suffering'[6] and generally clothed in a long sleeveless tunic, called a 'colobium'. Earliest illustrations date from the end of the eighth century and probably the very first is called the Palatine Crucifixion, discovered in 1856 as a graffito on a wall in the page's chamber of the Imperial Palace on the Palatine Hill in Rome.

The 56 judges departed, leaving the candidate alone with his initiator. He remained tied in the position of a cross at the top of the Hall of Judgment 'until evening', approximately three hours. During that time, he was given a soporific drink. The hierophants of the Mystery Schools, the Brahmans of India in their sacred initiatory rites, the Druids in mystic ceremonies, and Greeks in their schools and academies of enlightenment all administered strong potions to their candidates to induce a supernormal experience. It was quite true that the sacred beverage, often the soma drink, was offered at certain stages of the initiatory process - and it seemed to possess the faculty of liberating consciousness from the bonds of matter.

The *Dead Sea Scrolls* bore testimony of the souls of Essene initiates loosed into another world with the use of powerful fumigants, who like Egyptians, followed such practices. John Allegro described in his work, *The Sacred Mushroom and the Cross*, how Essenes attained higher levels of consciousness by means of Amanita Muscaria. Initiates said that the divine potion of the Mystery Schools produced not hallucinatory brain visions, but the actual freeing of the soul to journey in full consciousness into the higher realms of light; to experience true rebirth. Egyptian priests discovered herb extracts by means of which temporary clairvoyance was induced and made use of them during the initiation rituals of their Mysteries. The drugs were sometimes mixed with food given to candidates, and at other times, were presented in the form of sacred potions. The effectiveness of the narcotics was a matter of historical record. That part of the initiatory process revealed where Gospel writers took their cue, for Jesus was offered 'wine to drink, mingled with myrrh', a soporific drink.[7] That august rite was a process which combined magical and *spiritual* forces to detach the candidate's soul from the heavy bondage of his fleshly body for a few hours, and sometimes for a few days, that he might ever live with the memory of that epoch-making experience and conduct himself accordingly.

The judges subsequently returned to the Hall of Judgment and took their seats in preparation for an extraordinary event. With the candidate still tied in the 'cross-position', they began to chant the three sacred syllables of the ancient mystic formula, being the word AUM. The 'science behind the science' of the Great Pyramid then came to the fore and not one aspect of the design of that structure should be underestimated. The vibrational tones of the chanting caused the Hall of Judgment to light up with a supernatural stream of vertical standing light. Evidence of that intriguing event was recorded in the Gospels during the crucifixion of Jesus: 'And behold, the curtain of the temple was torn in two from top to bottom'.[8]

That narrative had long puzzled biblical analysts but was explained in light of the initiatory process inside the Pyramid. The 'curtain' was the darkness in the great temple opening up into brightness with rays of light produced by chanting. That the Grand Gallery in the Great Pyramid can be made to light up by vibrational toning was demonstrated in recent times with amazing experiments witnessed and photographed by Egyptian authorities. In chanting specific ancient sounds, one particular scientific team produced visible standing waves of light that lit the Grand Gallery brighter than daylight.

During the chanting the candidate then called aloud a pre-memorized question: 'Do you deny me the entrance into heaven, I who have at last learned the mystery of myself?' In that ritualistic drama, a voice then answered, 'He who is aware, *is*, behold'. The candidate was told that the voice of the Serpent had spoken. Then the final words that concluded the performance were a thanksgiving prayer in which the candidate said: 'My God, My God, how thou dost glorify me'.

Attention is drawn to the 46th verse of the 27th chapter of the Gospel of Matthew that reads: 'Eli, Eli, Lama Sabachthani?' Translated, it said; 'My God, my God, why hast thou forsaken me?' words applied to Jesus, and further confirmation that he was an initiated man. To the unwary reader, that narrative also appeared in the opening verse of one of Ezra's Psalms (22:1), curiously carrying the important number 22. It read: 'My God, my God, why hast thou forsaken me?' However, the Hebrew version of that verse translated to: 'Eli, Eli, lamah azabutha-ni?' In English: 'My God, my God, how thou dost glorify me'. That sentence rendered in its original words classified Jesus directly with the initiates of the Egyptian Mysteries.

14. THE CHAMBER OF THE TRIPLE VEIL

The candidate remained in the 'cross position' (crucified) 'until evening' and was then removed, now being in a semi-conscious state. He was then carried into the Chamber of the Triple Veil through the first low passage behind the Stone of God into the antechamber constructed of three vertical stone panels. From the *Book of the Dead:* '…they found a passage… and entered into it… and put on the clothes which are there'. That area is a peculiar and complex part of the Great Pyramid and it appears that at one stage it had three raise-able and lower-able sliding stone doors to seal the entrance. In that antechamber, the candidate was wrapped mummy-like (like Osiris) to the mournful groans of the assistants before being taken through the Gate of Death and into the Chamber of the Open Tomb. At that point in the Gospels, Jesus was wrapped 'in linen',[9] again revealing that the Gospel writers were unknowingly recording major elements of Jesus' initiation.

15. THE GATE OF DEATH

The responsibility of those experiencing final initiation was so awesome many could not rise to the challenge. It was life threatening, and death could be, and often was, the result. The candidate was now carried from the anteroom through the second low passage and he was then at the Gate of Death - for that was what he was facing. He was looking at the highly polished, dark chocolate-coloured, lidless coffer sitting silently in the large and imposing Chamber of the Open Tomb. Many people have wondered that so incredibly awesome a structure as the Great Pyramid should be built around a single chamber with a single empty coffer.

16. THE CHAMBER OF THE OPEN TOMB

He was now in the final stages of initiation - the Third Degree. In his drowsy state he was asked to whisper the SecrET word, which was 'Mah-hu-ahboni', being Ma-ha-bone in Freemasonry today. The seven highest ranking judges then entered the Chamber wearing ritual headdresses in the form of animal masks representing the gods: Anubis, that of the Jackal; Horus, that of the hawk or eagle; Thoth, that of the ibis; Osiris, the lion; others wore their personal symbols. The headdresses of the Egyptians had great symbolic and emblematic importance for they represented the auric bodies of the superior intelligences of antiquity, the gods who gave them the Mysteries that they preserved for centuries. They were emblematic of ancient secret truths of the first revelations of the gods to mankind. The seven judges moved clockwise around the Chamber seven times and then sat on the floor in the lotus posture forming a circle around the coffer. They again began to chant the mystic formula, AUM. The candidate was now rendered unconscious by three sharp blows to his forehead with a wooden mallet - that was a symbolic death. Now in the Death Trance, the judges picked up his mummy-like body and lowered it into the stone coffer, the Resurrection Machine.

Initiation of the 33rd degree in Masonic rites. Note the use of the mallet to render the candidate unconscious. Ceremonial skulls are prominent.

That curious act symbolized a 'burial' in a 'coffin' and paralleled the Osiris ritual. An identical performance was endured by Jesus who was laid in the same 'rock-hewn tomb'[10] that encompassed Osiris some thousands of years earlier. At one point during the ritual, the sarcophagus was supposedly struck with a metal rod, producing an unusual tone that had no counterpart in any known musical scale. The sound resonance in the Chamber is exceptional, particularly in high notes that seemed to increase to even higher notes that in turn, seemed to again increase in volume and reverberate for what seems an unnatural period. The tonal value may have formed part of that combination of circumstances that rendered the Chamber of the Open Tomb an ideal setting for the conferment of the highest degree of the Mysteries. History recorded the existence of musical stones productive of the sweetest harmonies, which, when struck in caves or small confines, threw all who heard the sound into a state of ecstasy. The stones provided ongoing echoing images that 'whispered for hours' after the cave had become silent.

There is a profound mystery to the atmosphere of the Chamber of the Open Tomb. It is of a peculiar deathlike feeling that cut to the marrow of the bone. The *Book of the Dead* implied that the Chamber was the doorway between the material world and the transcendental spheres of Mother Nature. Thus in one sense the Great Pyramid was likened to a gate through which ancient priests permitted a select few to pass towards the attainment of individual completion.

This stylized drawing from a 14ᵗʰ century Latin manuscript shows seven attendants removing the previous candidate for initiation from the Instrument of Resurrection in the Great Pyramid before the placement of Jesus.

The candidate remained in the 'coffin' until he regained consciousness. The energy fields generated or enhanced by the pyramidal shape served to contribute to the elevation of consciousness. The aspirant had in fact been induced into a temporary 'death experience' with the departure from the physical body of the soul into the mysterious realms of the dead. There he learnt the 'Secret of the Dead', and the survival of the soul after death.

> They came, they unloosened the sealing stones, and he was awake from his trance, and remembered all he had seen in Heaven, which he related to the high priests who were with him.[11]

His removal from the 'stone tomb' to recover provided the reason why the Gospel writers expressed amazement that the disciples of Jesus 'did not find a body'.[12] The initiate had experienced the same ancient wisdom the Egyptian priests encoded into their writings ages before his time; the mystery of the human soul, of life and death; of initiation and liberation. He had learnt what the wise had sought to conceal from the masses. He knew well the penalties that awaited those who openly dared to reveal the Sacred Secret or any other associated teaching contrary to the theories of the reigning orthodox religious leaders.

In modern times, many people involuntarily, and often unexpectedly, experience something similar to the final part of the initiatory process. The phenomenon, now termed a Near Death Experience (NDE), has been experienced by eight million people in America alone (Gallup Poll), and so impressed George Gallup Jr that he published a book on his poll results called *Adventures in Immortality* (with William Proctor, 1983). The majority of those who experienced a near-death encounter underwent exactly the same type of transformation of an initiate, with a new and profound perspective on their lives. Early in the first century, Diodorus Siculus wrote: 'It is said that those who have participated in the Mysteries became more spiritual, more just and better in every way'. The same could be said of persons acquaintanced with a Near Death Experience, for its nature brought about extraordinary changes in their character, turning many from materialism into believers of the existence of the soul, and they henceforth lived life with new hope and purpose.

An initiate could justly say that he had died, ascended and resurrected, awakening to discover a higher understanding of the significance of death. The same rite of 'death' and spiritual 'resurrection' for the neophyte, or the suffering, trial and new birth, was later historicized by the Gospel writers who were not spiritually advanced enough to understand what really happened to Jesus. The nucleus of their story was built up from an outward interpretation of an inward initiation experience. They were 'simple creatures who understood nothing'[13] and an extensive chapter revealing the true nature of the early churchmen is recorded in *The Bible Fraud*. Their exoteric nature provided confusion and their understanding of what had happened became externalized as an earthly event, and not the esoteric personal experience that it was. The 'ascension' of Jesus subsequently carried a false, purely material connotation, and was added into the Mark Gospel in the fourth century.

The symbolism in the resurrection was that of a newness of life and the development of a higher consciousness, leaving behind the dead lower nature (the body) for it had in it, no true life. It would probably be best summarized as moving into the higher end of the cycle of life and resulted in a moral change of the initiate. The Chamber of the Open Tomb was the place where the drama of the spiritual rebirth was enacted; where a man became 'twice-born', the simple mystic fact that puzzled the uninitiated Rabbi Nicodemus.[14]

The ancient civilizations inherited the Mysteries from a remote antiquity and they constituted part of a primitive revelation from the gods to the human race. Almost every people of pre-Christian times possessed its institution and tradition of the Mysteries. The Romans, the Celts, the Cretans, the Syrians, the Hindus, the Maya and American Indians, among others, had corresponding temples and rites with a system of graduated illuminations for initiates. The modern world knew little of those ancient rites yet they were conducted not only in the Great Pyramid, but also in a variety of structures the world over. In Persian Mysteries were seven spacious caverns through which the aspirant needed to pass. Still existing today in India is the magnificent cavern of Elephanta, supported with four massive pillars, and walls covered with statues and carved symbolic decorations. The caverns of Salsette greatly exceeded in magnitude that of Elephanta, being three hundred in number, all adorned with symbolic figures that were placed in the most secret caverns, accessible only by hidden entrances.

Dozens of hypotheses are resorted to regarding the 'Round Towers' of Ireland. The 'Towers', also found throughout the East in Asia, were directly connected with Mystery-initiations. The candidates for initiation were placed within them for $3^1/_2$ days whenever there was no temple with a subterranean crypt nearby. The round towers were built for no other purposes; they were sacred places of initiation. Discredited, as were many such monuments of Pagan origin by the Christian clergy, they are still the living and indestructible relics of the Wisdom of old.

The scientist and the theologian alike gazed upon the sacred Great

Pyramid of Giza wondering what fundamental urge inspired the Herculean labour. There was only one urge in the soul of humans capable of supplying the required incentive - namely, the desire to know, to understand and to exchange the narrowness of human mortality for the greater breadth of scope of divine enlightenment. Some said the Great Pyramid was the most perfect structure in the world, the source of weights and measures, the origin of languages, alphabets, and scale of temperature and humidity. That it probably was, but few realized that the Great Pyramid, when fully operational with the Benben in place and under-ground temples clear and functional, was the gateway to the Eternal.

17. THE INSTRUMENT OF RESURRECTION

The candidate had learnt that initiation itself involved 'dying', not a real physical death, but a symbolic one in which the soul was temporarily released or freed from the body and 'resurrected'. A journey into the realms of Beyond had been experienced by the successful initiate - he had met with God, and now knew the highest hidden mystery - the continued existence of life after physical death. The precise north/south setting for the Resurrection Machine placed it right in line for the so-called Pyramid Effect that somehow, it seemed, helped in the process. Those who emerged from the portals of the Pyramid belonged ever after to a secret order of exclusive Panther initiates who had glimpsed the eternal life that was lived in the heavens. That was the 'Final Revealing', and every initiate thus obtained personal proof of the immortality of his spirit and the survival of his Soul. His last 'epopteia' was alluded to by Plato in *Phaedrus*:

> Being initiated in those Mysteries, which it is lawful to call the most blessed of all Mysteries, we were freed from the molestation of evils which otherwise await us in a future period of time. Likewise, in consequence of this divine initiation, we became spectators of blessed visions resident in a pure light. There can be little doubt, then, that during a period of the initiatory ceremony, the candidate experienced visions of gods and spirits. Indeed, the most sublime part of the ceremony occurred when the initiate beheld the gods themselves, invested in a resplendent light.

That extraordinary veiled confession of one who had experienced initiation shows that the candidates enjoyed Theophany - that is, they saw visions of gods and immortal spirits. The most sublime part of the 'Final Revealing' consisted of beholding the gods themselves, always it seemed, invested with 'resplendent light'. This statement of Proclus, another successful initiate, is unequivocal:

> In all the initiations and Mysteries, the gods exhibit many forms of themselves and appear in a variety of shapes. Sometimes, indeed, a formless light of themselves is held forth to the view. Sometimes the light is according to a human form and sometimes it proceeds into a different shape. Some of the figures are not gods and excite alarm. These highest visions are seen only after the neophyte, through a regular discipline of gradual initiations, has developed psychical powers of clairvoyance, clairaudience and clairsentience.

When Proclus said that 'Some of the figures are not gods and excite alarm', he was referring to degraded invisible beings the initiated called, 'Inter-Dimensionals' (IDs). Those 'infernal deities' were described as grotesque creatures operating in the nocturnal shadows of the inferior sphere. It seemed that their purpose was to negatively affect the life of every human being on Earth and guide unenlightened souls to their undoing.

The conclusion drawn is that the Great Pyramid was designed as a place of initiation; not only as the major site of initiation but as an Instrument of Initiation - its shape having something special to do with a kind of power or energy conduit concentrated in the Chamber of the Open Tomb. The subject of the Pyramid Effect is a serious matter and scientists admit that it provides for mankind a vast new principle. That principle can be demonstrated in a twelve inch high glass or crystal mini-Benben built to the same proportions as the Great Pyramid. To that end, the Great Pyramid, when operating, was understood as a purposely-built apparatus for the exodus of consciousness from the three-dimensional plane of existence into realms of Higher Intelligence. Thus, the experience of going into other worlds through the initiatory process in the Great Pyramid is revealed.

The Pyramid Texts speak of the builders of the Great Pyramid as 'the Nine' and they knew a great deal more than they were later credited. Those ever-so-old Egyptian scriptures show a direct relationship between the Great Pyramid and Orion through the body of death and resurrection of Osiris. The Great Pyramid provided mankind with the shape and design of a structure to move human consciousness into other worlds. The 'soul shafts' from the Chamber of the Open Tomb were intended for the souls of those who had been placed in the Resurrection Machine that they might ascend to join Osiris in Orion.[15] In the structure of the Great Pyramid was designed a principle to reveal to mankind that his destiny was to be able to indwell in a higher evolutionary body. An educational vehicle, it revealed that individuals could be synthesized into new forms and go beyond his immediate system. It provided a stepping-stone to another consciousness that showed mankind that when he completed the earthly phase of life, he moved onto the next evolution. The populace is ever craving for a 'beyond' and cannot live without an ideal of some kind, as a beacon and a consolation. The Company of Gods left behind a structure today called the Great Pyramid that proves there is a 'beyond'.

18. THE GATE OF COMING FORTH BY DAY

The *Book of the Dead* records that when the new Third Degree Initiate departed from the Great Pyramid, he 'travelled East on the third day' and exited by a different way to that which he entered. One old tradition stated that the stone sarcophagus in the Chamber of the Open Tomb tilted to one side, revealing a series of steps leading down to presently unopened chambers. When Frederick Norden was in the Chamber in the mid-1750s, he observed that:

> To the north of the sarcophagus, you perceive a very deep hole, made since the building of the pyramid was finished. The reason of it is not known. It is however to be presumed, with a great deal of probability, that there was underneath, some cavity, for it looks as if the pavement has fallen of itself, after the foundation of the chamber had sunk in.

Both the Chamber of the Open Tomb and the Chamber of New Birth have side or service chambers, with a stairway spiraling down to lower levels. They were recently opened and found to be filled with sand. Wherever was the exit from the Chamber of the Open Tomb, the graduate subsequently descended through various levels, then down a passage-way, back through the Temple of the Grand Orbit and finally climbed the stairs under the Sphinx. There he received his gold-trimmed 'Robe of Office', the Panther attire, and 'his name was inscribed in a book amongst the Judges of the land'.[16]

He then walked out through the stele doorway between the paws of the Sphinx, 'The Gate of Coming Forth by Day', into the morning sun and was met by his family and friends. His 3½ day ordeal of initiation in the great Egyptian temple had ended and death held no more power over him. He had physically 'resurrected from death' and then walked among the living on Earth. The last words he heard from his guide were: 'Farewell, thou who has experienced what thou hadst never yet experienced, from a man thou hast become a god'.

A completed Masonic initiation. There are 21 persons in attendance PLUS the symbolical skeleton (21+1=22 symbolizing the 21 numbered Tarot Cards plus one unnumbered card). With its left hand, the skeleton draws back the curtain to reveal the 'Pyramid of Light' in its prime position. The Torah is open on the table. The initiate now knows the 'Secret'.

It is probable that Jesus himself originally propounded as allegories the events of his initiation in Egypt. First century Roman historian, Suetonius (70-140), referred to the famous old Roman adage of tradition that said: 'It is better to copy than envy', and copy they did. So intrigued were the populace with Mystery Teachings that a body of people now called 'the early church fathers' mimed Panther concepts from their portable pulpits, and from that public reenactment developed the word 'Pantomime' (Panther-mime). Imitating the initiatory drama became widespread on street corners and town squares throughout the Roman Empire as presbyters orated the 'good news' to the 'rabble' in eking out their miserable living. Celsus, himself an initiate, was moved to ridicule their nature and orations, describing them as:

> ...weavers, tailors, fullers and the most illiterate and rustic fellows, preaching strange paradoxes. They openly declared that none but the ignorant were fit to hear their discourses and that one of their rules was 'let no man that is learned come among us'. They never appeared in the circles of the wiser and better sort, but always took care to intrude themselves among the ignorant and uncultured, rambling around to play tricks at fairs and markets.[17]

To appease the 'rabble', the church fathers embellished their discourses with 'splendid exaggerations' and created curious spectacles to entertain the 'grovelling flock'.[18] Jesus' symbolic journey into death and back was presented as the story of a supernatural being and became the essence of Christianity. The writings presbyters compiled subsequently evolved into the New Testament and the essence of original Panther truths are still embodied in them today.

The sacred initiatory experience was the true secret origin of the world's major religious systems and provided answers to some of the most enigmatic mysteries of their development. It was not just Jesus who 'suffered, died, ascended and returned' in that ritualistic manner but others connected to mystical initiation were Indria, Buddha, Krishna, Quetzalcoatl, Pythagoras, Hercules and Apollonius. Those great characters were Panther initiates of the same line of teaching by degrees that arose originally in ancient Egypt at the Great Pyramid. The chief feature of their lives is found to be in common, and the unmistakable sameness of the means of construction of their respective biographies is apparent - every one had passed through the trials of initiation

– they knew the Secret. It was not in the course of their everyday life then, that the great similarity was to be sought, but in their inner state and in the most important events of their career as teachers of an esoteric (spiritual) principle.

The next four *Book of the Dead* references are not directly related to the physical initiatory process but are associated with various aspects of spiritual teaching involved in initiation and vital in this study.

19. THE CHAMBER OF UPSIDE-DOWN-NESS

In that strange chamber, the ceiling is dressed smooth and completed but the floor is uneven, jagged, unfinished and resembles a quarry. That chamber was built upside-down, with unfinished passages leading to dead ends and a strange rough shaft descending vertically to nowhere. That curious part of the Pyramid's sub-structure appears to have been purposely left uncompleted and may have once been filled with water. Its purpose in the function of the Pyramid is difficult to ascertain, but the *Book of the Dead* claimed the pit was 'reserved for souls who have failed their assignment to teach in the earth dimension'.

20. THE THRONE OF RADIANCE

That is the *Book of the Dead's* name for the Benben, once glittering on top of the Great White Pyramid.

21. THE PASSAGE OF DESCENT
(or PASSAGE OF THE POLESTAR)

The Mysteries always used inscrutable language to safeguard secret knowledge. However, two references in the *Book of the Dead*, 'The north door opens up from the Chamber of the Polestar' and 'The Gate of the North is the gate of the great god', refer directly to Sothis/Sirius, the Polestar, with its sight-line looking straight down the descending passage used today to enter the Great Pyramid. The Egyptian calendar was based on movements of the star Sothis or Sirius, which was sometimes called the Dog Star. Its annual appearance shortly before sunrise between July 19 and July 21 marked the beginning of the 'dog day' in the Mediterranean region. Sothis was dedicated to Isis and occasionally identified with Hathor. There is a hieroglyph inscribed in the limestone above the (now) entrance that best may be translated as 'Horizon of Heaven'.

22. THE FALSE (HIDDEN) DOOR

Strabo mentioned a hinged stone door on the Pyramid's north face made of 'one piece of marble' that could be raised with no great effort. He said the innovative hinged door was so beautifully built that it was indistinguishable from the white casing-stones when closed and could only be opened from inside. Strabo reported that it 'easily opened up and out' to allow uninhibited access into a 'tortuous passage' which descended directly down a long straight inclined slope to 'the depths' below the centre of the Pyramid.

Such a perfectly balanced rock door adds to the Pyramid's inner mysteries that touch on the intelligence of technologies of the 21st century. It was called the 'False or Hidden Door' in the *Book of the Dead* and the description given probably provided the clues for its discovery. A similar swivel door was found at the south pyramid at Dashur, constructed to hinge on two large stone-ball-bearings. No remains of the swivel door were found at the Great Pyramid probably because it was removed with the 22 surface acres of casing stones.

The False Door on the North Face is used today by thousands of tourists and is the only acknowledged entrance into the Great Pyramid. With a touch of irony, the *Book of the Dead's* description of the once-secret entrance (or exit) evolved at number 22 on The Master Plans, the most influential number of all mystical associations.

CHAPTER FIFTEEN

THE MYSTERY BOOK OF THE NEW TESTAMENT

With the 1925 discovery of a mystical old writing in the Vatican called *The Mysteries of Osiris and Isis*, the hidden message in biblical writings took on a new and uncanny significance. There is nothing unreasonable about the conclusion that any religious text developed around the cipher number 22, whether in pages, verses or letters, contains secret information. A term used by ancient Egyptian priests for documents associated with number 22 was 'a writing from the god himself', referring originally to Thoth's 22-page book of exotic symbols. However, it is not only Egyptian writings that conceal extraordinary information coded around number 22, but also later Christian texts. Recorded church history revealed that secret ciphers were used in the New Testament as early as the first Christian Council at Nicaea in 325 and early churchmen themselves believed that one of their canonical texts held secret information. Eusebius Pamphilius, Bishop of Caesarea (260-339), wrote that there were particular words 'which hid themselves in Scripture to the end they may be found' (*Ecclesiastical History*), but he failed to elaborate on what those words were and where they were to be found.

Looking at the New Testament, it is apparent there is one specific canonical book showing Secret signs of being directly associated with the number 22. It is also connected to Psalm 119, the *Book of Thoth*, the Gypsy secret, the Divine Scale, and King James' Bible editor, Sir Francis Bacon. That writing is Revelation, the last book of the New Testament, and in its original pre-Christian form, it was the aforementioned document called, *The Mysteries of Osiris and Isis*.

That text was the second of a small collection of writings compiled by a woman named Herophile (circa 500 BC) who lived in a cave near the ancient town of Cumae, in Campania, Italy. She was known as the Cumaean Sibyl, and the general populace spoke of her as 'a slowly ageing but immortal priestess'.[1] Her writings subsequently became known as the Sibylline Books and were highly prized in the Roman Empire for more than 1000 years. They were kept in a specially sculpted purple-lined marble chest commissioned by an early king of ancient Rome, Tarquin the Proud ('traditionally 510 BC') and, in later times, priests were appointed to interpret the manuscripts and scribes assigned to reproduce exact copies. In times of peril and disaster, the original copies were entrusted to curators who were assisted by two Greek interpreters to read the oracles aloud to the Roman Senate.

The Sibyl's works were regarded as 'the mouthpiece of God' (Irenaeus) because they were believed to contain all directions needed to worship any Egyptian god. Later Roman kings and emperors saw Apollo Palatinus as the equal of Osiris and overlaid his name as the source of the Sibyl's enlightened words. Her writings were recognized at Rome as one of the most efficacious instruments in Roman religion and were observed and accepted by all Romans. It was believed the Sibylline Books were 'possessed with the spirit of divination' and they subsequently became the 'Bible' of the Romans.[2]

Church records stated that an Egyptian presbyter 'wrote over' the original Sibyl's document to create the fabricated version now in the New Testament.[3] The forged document was renamed 'Apocalypse', and to imply an apostolic origin from 'divine revelation' it was re-titled 'Revelation' by Emperor Justinian at the second church council of Constantinople in 553, the same council that officially removed all references to reincarnation from the New Testament.

It is no coincidence that the Book of Revelation has 22 chapters. Somebody knew what it really was and restructured the singular rhyming sonnet into 22 separate segments to purposely leave an editorial clue to the book's nature. Francis Bacon was suspected of reshaping the book, and other initiates after his time revealed that they also knew the secret of the Book of Revelation. Author and Masonic initiate, Ian Browne, wrote that Revelation was 'scarcely a revelation, since the cipher in which it is printed renders it a sealed book to all who do not possess the key'.[4] Masons clearly accepted the

Book of Revelation as something special, for they developed a rite called 'Masonry of the Apocalypse' and adopted St John as a patron of their Craft. That curious move gave rise to a number of theories as to why only St John was connected to the Institution and not Matthew, Mark or Luke.

Tradition revealed that some Masonic Lodges were dedicated 'to the memory of the Holy St John', particularly in America. It seemed that St John was selected as a Patron of Masonry in consequence oF the mysterious and emblematic nature of the Apocalypse. The early Masons believed that he wrote it and assumed 'there is something special in the life of St John which closely connects him with our mystic Institution'.[5] However, St John did not write it, and a true understanding of what the Book of Revelation originally was nullifies everything the church ever said about the origin of its entire New Testament. Anyone investigating the ceremonies performed in the Ancient Mysteries and comparing them with the mystical machinery used in particular passages in Revelation will find that the author was intimately acquainted with the whole process of the Egyptian Mystery School initiations and knew the Secret of Eternity.

Due to the amount of space needed to divulge the true nature and origin of Revelation, it is not possible to fully reveal its mysteries in this work and it therefore became the essence of this author's next book, *The Crucifixion of Truth*. However it is possible to disclose that the imagery of Revelation, from Alpha to Omega, was extracted from the superstructure of Ancient Mystery Schools and completed with the strictest attention to poetical decorum. The whole work bears the appearance in outward form of an intimate connection of the result of a ritual of initiation of the Ancients. It speaks of a 'realm of light', a rainbow around the throne, a secret book with golden pages, fourteen particular 'fruits', the shape of a serpent, the mountain of the Lord's house, the seven stars of Thoth's book (the Tracing Board of Masonry), and the key to unlock the 'seven seals' and thus the mystery of the Mysteries. The 'seven things' said to have existed before the beginning of the modern world that the author was obligated not to divulge are recorded in Revelation and reference to 'the bridge of light between heaven and earth' revealed that its author was fully acquainted with the phenomena of the Rainbow Serpent.

CHAPTER SIXTEEN

AN ECSTATIC DEATH

Warning

Whoever seeks to perform the Experience discussed in this chapter
without necessary training, does so at his or her own
physical and spiritual peril.

Early Christian churchmen knew that the first five books of Hebrew scripture were special and 'came from a time when gods ruled on Earth'.[1] They persisted in keeping the Torah 'attached with binding'[2] to the growing body of Christian literature and thus the 'divinity' belief carried over to the Gospels and Epistles. However, they did not know that the Torah reflected the Divine Mind and was the earthly storehouse for the revelation of esoteric knowledge. The original version was written 'continuous, without break of letters or words' and only later was it broken into five separate books. An ancient rabbinic tradition held that the last book of the Torah, Deuteronomy, folded around and connected back to the opening words of Genesis, making the original scroll one continuous work, 'without beginning and without end'.[3] The Torah scroll, if wrapped around a drum or cylinder, was reminiscent of the continually spinning Buddhist prayer wheel, and may have been used in that manner at some early stage.

Was the future predicted in the Bible?

An unusual scribal trait is found in the Torah – time is reversed. The future is written in past tense, and the past written in future tense. The concept is confirmed by 'gods' in the Book of Isaiah[4] who said: 'To see the future you must look backwards'. Therefore, anything written in the Bible that appears to be prophecy is something, in biblical terminology, that has already happened. That raises interesting prospects because the reverse also applies. Events that appear to be talking about the past would therefore be talking about the future and the intriguing prospect arises that the books of the Torah are visionary.

One could argue, for example, that the Exodus story is a model of that yet to come; a journey in which enlightened people will travel towards a greater universe. The same could be said of Jacob's ladder[5] for maybe it reveals a coming step up to the next realm or dimension which cannot be seen at this time, a symbol of progress between earth and heaven, so to speak. The ladder and its seven steps finds its analogue in all ancient initiations, and is represented as the symbol of moral and intellectual progress in personal development. And what about the flood and survival of a few persons depicted in the story of Noah's Ark? Of such great cataclysms, there appears to already have been at least one and humanities seemed to have all but disappeared. Perhaps the Noah's Ark story is a warning to expect another cataclysm in due course of time, a great catastrophe in which only few will survive. Viewed in that light, the story of Noah could be seen as a cosmic allegory concerning the re-population of the planet at the beginning of each world period. It is intriguing to think that the first section of the Bible may have recorded the new story of creation emerging from calamitous changes that may one day spin Earth into a new program of existence and thus fulfill the cycle prophesied by so many.

The hidden under-meaning of the Torah is directly connected with the experience of initiation and that raises another fascinating aspect. It could be considered that the Torah is a duplicate of the whole experience that is destined to become that of the human race, through the process of initiatory evolution – the psychic and spiritual growth of mankind developing upwards through seven particular levels of consciousness. Thus, the ordeals and enlightenment of the initiate may have been a miniature representation of the entire drama of human evolution, the ineluctable fate of mankind over vast eons of time, from totally irreligious, like the sub-species existing when the gods came, to a fully enlightened world of initiated peoples.

Therefore, the message of the Torah may be twofold. Not only did it connect a spiritual universe with a physical universe through the Rainbow Serpent, but it may also be suggesting that mankind should work towards a higher spiritual evolution by understanding that the Torah was revealed by a higher or supreme intelligence. Knowing the profundity of the Sacred Language, it is possible that future prediction is another aspect of that remarkable old book. Everything that is encompassed in this world of creation, the life that now is, the life that is yet to come and the life that has already been, may well be coded, allegorically, in the Torah and predicting in advance a sequence of subsequent Divine unfoldment. That way of viewing the Torah stories makes it certain that none of the major characters were historical personages.

If the Torah contains predictions of the future then that is one way to view them. However, is it coded in another way? In 1994, three Israeli mathematicians, Professor Eliyaha Rips, from the Hebrew University, Dorn Witzum and Yoav Rosenburg, published a paper in a scholarly journal called, 'Statistical Science'. Their study was extensive and revealed an extraordinary skip pattern of letters found in the Book of Genesis that they called, 'Equidistant Letter Sequences' (ELS). That skip pattern is similar in concept to what was found in the *Book of Thoth* and analysed in an earlier chapter. A computer was programmed to search Genesis by 'skip code' in an effort to find the names of 32 particular sages who had lived in earlier Old Testament times. It checked every 9th letter, where the value for N can take any value. Amazingly, the program produced most names in the search with the odds against that occurring by chance being more than 60,000 to one. The word 'Torah' was found in both the Books of Genesis and Exodus at the same ELS of 50 letters, starting with the first occurrence of the letter TAU. The odds of that happening by random chance are 3 million to one. How then, could this be explained?

The Sacred Language of the Torah is a computer program in itself and therefore a complete code from beginning to end by just being what it was.

In its original form, its existence was entirely an inner code structure of Divine Letters and capable of saying anything, for each letter generated itself from one primary component - the Rainbow Serpent. Put in another way, the shadow-graphs that the Rainbow Serpent fashion when reproduced in solid earthly form, are all identical but in a different position. The first, or any letter of Genesis, for example, contains the whole, because it is the same as every other letter of the Torah. Thus, the Rainbow Serpent displays all symbols of the Sacred Language when it is viewed from 22 various directions. Within itself, the mathematical keys are revealed in every letter because they circle endlessly in their own image.

The Secret and Sacred Language was subsequently given a unique form in a book, small in size, but enormous in influence. The book's great success, especially in Hebrew, showed how much it answered the religious needs of the time. The obvious connection with oral Hebrew traditions that served as the departure for explanations of a remarkable hidden spiritual intent is the distinguishing feature in the work of Ezra and his scribes. It was Ezra's specific intention to produce an instructional manual of Jewish pietism secretly written in 'holy' letters that were sourced from celestial, sacred and coloured geometry. Since that unique book was composed of letters that were nothing more marvelous than reproductions of elements of light, the question arose as to what happened when the Torah's earthly garments were cast off and the spiritual aspect revealed. That unlocks one of the Torah's deepest secrets.

The secret of the Secret

The original Torah Scroll provided a practical way of life for semi-savage peoples of early times and simultaneously provided a spiritual guide for candidates struggling to commune with God. However, to those 'in the know' it provided something more, and that is a matter of truly staggering proportions. Those wishing to reach the highest spiritual level need to understand the Torah in four levels called Pshat, Ramaz, Darash and Sud. The Secret in the Bible is hidden in those four words - the initials yield the word PRDS, which, when vocalized reveal Pardes or Paradise. Those initials, and the knowledge they represent, originated with the Leo-prds (Leo-PRDS) at the Great Pyramid and it seemed that those gods introduced the Wisdom to Earth. Deep within the Book of the Zohar, a reference is made clarifying the four ways of understanding the Torah. That information discloses exactly what the first five books of the Old Testament really are and unlocks the hidden system of knowledge.

The Pshat (or Psht) is the plain or simple literal surface reading. That rendering provides superficial knowledge and is presented by orthodox Jews and the Christian ministry as the words of God. Where, in the Book of Exodus, it states, for example, that men are not to shave, then particularly orthodox Jews accept those words as being a direct command from God and refuse to shave or even trim their beards.

The second method is called Ramaz, or Rmz, literally meaning 'a hint', and is intended for persons who are developing their intellect and who do not wish to be taught by those who understand only the surface meaning.

The third, Darash or Dsh, is the inferential method of reading, in which the eye of intuition is opened. The student transcends far above the lower mind and far beyond the intellectual reasoning of brain-consciousness, and is well known to Occult students. At that level, they learn that there is an esoteric side to scripture.

Finally, there is the fourth and most important method, called Sud or Sod, literally 'secret'. That method is taught by initiates to their disciples only and they were very careful to whom they divulged that knowledge, the deepest of the Mysteries, for a very good reason, now explained.

The Rabbis laid down particular conditions for entry of those seeking initiation into the doctrines and activities bound up with those fields. The basic teaching was, like Masonic tradition, communicated in a whisper. The earliest conditions governing the choice of those suitable were of two types. In the Gemera,[6] basic intellectual conditions were formulated as well as age limits ('at life's half-way stage') and certain ethical qualities required of the initiate were enumerated. Some of those conditions described the physical and psychological conditions needed in a candidate before the commencement of training. However, very little of their inner teaching was set down in writing despite the volumes of documents produced by the people involved at the time. That made it difficult to research but there is some information available to analyze.

Death had forgotten them

When the candidate reached a particular point of development he knew there was more to the Torah than what was generally known. The mystique drew him further into its study (Sud) because he knew that somehow he could learn to participate in the work of higher worlds. He had learnt that by discipline he would be able to experience some inner journey, some sort of remarkable event that would change the course of his life. That occasion was called the 'Pardes Experience', or 'Paradise Experience', emanating from the letters, PRDS. The first chapter referenced Paul's claim of knowing a person 'caught up into Paradise',[7] meaning one who had actually experienced the extraordinary mystical encounter. With the correct use of the Secret he knew he would be taken through some mystery or miracle of rapture into another dimension, where he would be spared a physical cycle of destruction. To arrive at that stage required great patience and mental stability. One reason for that tempo was that everyone had to mature his potential gradually and thoroughly at his own natural pace. In that way, the dramatic experience unfolded at the right moment in his good time. To rush into the experience was known to have caused insanity to the Rabbi involved, so powerful is the Secret information in the Bible. The timing appears to have been of vital importance and for that reason the more experienced rabbinic priesthood constantly advised their more inexperienced members to go slowly.

To access the Secret, a deep inner connection needed to be developed in order that there was personal contact with what was called, the 'Academy on High'. Some called that level of reality the Isle of Saints or the Great Brotherhood of Initiates. They said that it has no location in this world – its place, according to the Rabbis 'who know', was in the upper part of the psyche (Yezirah) and, in some respect, in the lower part, the spirit (Beriah). They said it was outside time and space, hence the difficulty of explaining it, because of the inability of the human mind to grasp that which is not contained in a frame of recognition. Corresponding to levels within the individual, that was the place where it was possible to come into the presence of the abode of God. Some people explained that experience in profound awe in which they said they were filled and surrounded by golden light and a sense of love, unity and peace. The depth of their penetrating experience was beyond the scope of intellectual perception to conceive, except to those lucky enough to have experienced it.

The Rainbow Serpent, the absolute essence of the Torah, was a unique product of divine revelation and a conscious creation from beyond our existence. Regarded from that point of view in its quality as being composed of Sacred Letters of Light, the Torah becomes a book unparalleled by any other in the world. For the Rabbis its fundamental nature was the object of an original mystical way of a particular meditation, whereby, with its correct use, they personally came 'face to face with God', just as Ezra recorded when he wrote it.[8] Some of them, it was said, were so advanced in the use of the Secret that 'death had forgotten them'. That was not to say that the Rabbis sought to deny the traditions and commandments that the Torah carried on the surface level, but what interested them mainly was something quite different, namely the personal use of the special knowledge they had. Far from being merely a literary device, the Torah was, and still is, a specific spiritual experience. For the Rabbis, its secret, or mystical character, became its most powerful means of expression for it allowed them to turn away from the attractions of the outer world and all that was meant by 'money and metals'. They learnt how to use it for inducing states of mystical or ecstatic experience, not just once, but repeatedly at will. Their ancient writings recorded a beautiful passage that spoke of the 'healing which comes to the tongue' of persons who knew how to successfully achieve the spiritual experience by contemplation and meditation using the hidden information in the Torah. Here, by way of illustration, is an especially vivid description from the philosopher, Plotinas:

> Many times I have plunged into myself leaving the body behind, having passed beyond all else, and deep within myself. Then I see such an extraordinary beauty and am convinced that I belong to a mighty order of things. I live life at its peak and become one with the divine. Once firmly fixed in this state, I come into that sphere of activity above all that is intelligible and am transfixed within myself.[9]

To souls achieving that extraordinary vision were revealed the Secrets of Creation, reached by a technique of meditation, turning the letters of the

Rainbow Serpent repeatedly over in their mind's eye. Sometimes, and unexpectedly, just writing the letters of the Sacred Language quickly induced the experience. Chanting the Torah was another way to enter into the 'Experience'. The divine letter patterns of the Language were far more than a priesthood tool for everyday communication of ancient texts – the letterforms themselves allowed a qualified individual to attain a special state of ecstatic vision. The letters provided for a mystical experience of spiritual awakening, through which something like a Near-Death Experience was revealed and the Torah became the human storehouse of the secret components needed for that communication. The power of the Sacred Language allowed them to have a direct interior experience, one of leaving the old order of consciousness and learning God's higher Mysteries. They came to see the existence of a Creator, usually manifested in an indescribable white light. The Gospel of Thomas,[10] recorded a description:

> When you see one that was not born of a woman, prostrate yourself on your faces and worship him. That one is your Father.

Such was the instruction received in the Mysteries, an institution so celebrated in antiquity, yet so disregarded in modernity.

According to ancient Rabbis, the elements of the Rainbow Serpent, when properly used in meditation (or viewing ancient Tarot Card Designs) activated a conscious return to higher planes of awareness. The individual literally stepped into the next order of evolution that is described in the Zohar as 'the ether, which cannot be grasped'. His experience emanated from what was called the 'mastering of light' in a language that came, manifested, was brought or sent to Earth in the crystalline Benben, waiting to be unpacked as it were, sourced originally from a higher level of consciousness. When Jesus and other initiates said that the 'kingdom of heaven is within you' that was exactly what they meant, because they knew that the meditative use of the Sacred and Secret Language provided the evidence of God's presence within each and every person. Jesus also said that he knew the Secret of the kingdom of heaven and that he did, for he was a full initiate into the Mysteries.

In ancient times the rabbinic process of going deep into oneself during meditation or contemplation was called 'going down in the Chariot'. That action simultaneously precipitated the rising up out of the physical world and through what was called the seven lower or lesser Halls of the psyche. The seven halls in rabbinic mysticism have a remarkable parallel in the *Book of the Dead*, where the soul of the deceased passed through seven halls, making offerings and being purified as it proceeded towards its ultimate goal. The similarities are extraordinary and are again paralleled in the seven distinct initiatory processes conducted in the Great Pyramid complex.

Those properly trained in the meditative use of the Secret could enter and experience another world while still in the flesh and see the panorama of the Heavens and its habitants. Such an inner journey, however, was fraught with hazard for the immature, the unbalanced and the wrongly motivated. An ancient account of four Rabbis who meditated using the Rainbow Serpent and entered the world of pure spirit is often given as a warning against unprepared excursion into the realm of what has become called Heaven. It makes fascinating reading and reveals the supreme power of the Secret in the Torah, that being the Sacred Language is an interior tool for communicating directly with God. Its correct use provides a journey through physical death itself – a journey into the realms of beyond – and, usually, but not always, back.

Ben Azzai, first of the aforementioned Rabbis died while out of body. Ben Zoma, the second, returned to his body but in an insane state of mind. Elisha Ben Abyah also returned but became a disbeliever in his faith and went and lived in a cave for the remainder of his life. It was said he yearned for physical death to 'come upon him' so he could return permanently to where he had been during his 'Pardes Experience', a place he called the 'Celestial Empire'. Only the fourth, Rabbi Akiba, came back in a state stable enough to tell of what he saw. It was believed that Rabbi Akiba then wrote the celebrated Sepher Yetzireh (Book of Creation) that was first printed at Paris in 1552.

The dialogues of those men are intended to illustrate the principal theme of this book – the existence of a superior knowledge of cosmic origin concealed in the Bible. What follows is a rare précis of Rabbi Akiba's extraordinary experience. It is one of only three documented accounts of the 'Paradise Experience' that the author was able to find. The others are carried in the Books of Enoch and Revelation, but firstly to Rabbi Akiba's description of his journey through seven different levels into 'the company of the highest created beings':

In the first Hall, which corresponds to the Kingdom of Creation or the spiritual aspect of the Self, Akiba says that he was in a state of Hassid devotion. Here where what is called Vilon, the Veil of Heaven, is rolled away, he entered the world of pure spirit. From this place where angels and humans may converse he rose in Tahor, a state of purity, to the second Heavenly Hall, called Rakinyah or the Firmament, where the great archangel Gabriel is said to reside. Here in the Yesod of Beriah, the Foundations of Creation, in the level where the signs of Heaven are revealed to the prophets. It is also the place of the Holy Spirit in man and corresponds to Daat, the non-Sefirah of Knowledge in his psyche. The third level is called Shehakim, the Skies, and here in a condition of Yasher, sincerity, Akiba was in the third Heaven, where the millstones of the Universe slowly turn to grind out Time. He then rose to the fourth Heaven, where he came into direct contact with the Divine in a situation of Tamim or wholeness; this is the place where the three upper Worlds meet, as the Tiferet of Beriah and the Malkhut of Azilut, the Kingdom of the Divine, touch the Keter of Yezirah, the Crown of the psyche. At this level, occupied by the great archangel Michael, is the Heavenly Jerusalem and its Temple. Passing beyond the normal limits of the human psyche, because he had developed a stable spiritual vehicle, Akiba entered the fifth Heaven, called Maon, or dwelling, where he encountered the great archangelic guardians Samuel and Zadkiel, in front of whom he had to speak the Kedushah Prayer of sanctification Holy! Holy! Holy! To demonstrate his holiness before he could pass on to the sixth Heaven of Makom, or the Omni-present, where he came into the company of the highest created beings before the celestial Throne. Here he sang the heavenly choir the praise of God, into whose Presence he came when he ascended into the seventh Heaven, the Great Hall of the Arabot. Here he stood...'erect holding his balance with all his might as he trembled before his Creator'.

Amidst that complex mystical terminology, a description is given of something known to millions of people who have never been involved in initiation or years of specialized religious training. He is describing a Near Death Experience, one which the meditative use of the one single element of the Rainbow Serpent allowed him access to that Divine state at any time. It was controlled and inducible at will and used by 'those who know' for centuries. It enabled them to come 'face to face with God' and then return to their body as Akiba did:

> Akiba then descended safely out of the Presence of the Divine, down through the seven states of the spirit into the seven lesser Halls or levels of the psyche, and back into the body, because he was well-grounded in ordinary life. In Cabala, this stability is an absolute pre-requisite because any major flaw or imbalance in body or psyche is magnified during such an experience. Thus the Cabalist does not withdraw from the Lower Worlds and seek special conditions or isolation in which to develop, but uses the daily situation and ordinary events about him both as a working method and as an anchor for the moments when he enters the highly charged and rarified levels of the upper worlds. Existence emanates from God, and therefore, while there are degrees of increasing separation, not a fraction of existence exists for a second without Divine Will...not even evil, which has its own cosmic task to perform.

Rabbi Akiba had, while using the Secret in a meditative trance, gained access to a higher state of consciousness in an out-of-body situation and then returned to his body and everyday life. He had ascended through seven prescribed degrees to a full participation in the spiritual world. By turning over the spiral element of the Rainbow Serpent in meditation, he induced a transcendental experience, one that understandably left him and his associates emotional. This interesting passage from the 'The Great Holy Assembly' in the Zohar showed how earnest were the feelings of the ancient Rabbis:

> Rabbi Simeon sat and wept, and he said, woe if I reveal these secrets and woe if I do not reveal them. The companies who were there remained silent until Rabbi Abba stood up and said to him; 'If our Master wants His most valued Secret revealed, than it will be so, for is it not written in biblical prophecy?' The Secret of the Lord belongs to those who fear him, and do not these companions tremble before the Holy One blessed be he?

The Rabbis in possession of the celestial knowledge were faced with the same problem that Rabbi Jesus had – they wanted to tell people 'there was no death', but were restricted by secrecy vows. They moved among people with absolute certitude of immortality, and although they kept the sources of that conviction to themselves, they could not help, even unconsciously, communicating some elements of their sureness to fellow beings. Pythagoras provided an example: 'Where we are, death is not; where death is, we are not. It is the latest, best boon of nature, for it frees man from all his cares. It is, at the worst, the close of a banquet we have enjoyed'.

The Book of Genesis[11] relays the story of Enoch's translation to heaven where he 'walked with God', but it was an incomplete description of Enoch's personal 'Pardes Experience'. The Book of Enoch records the full story and when stripped of its figurative language, it describes in extraordinary detail Enoch's journey through the seven heavens and his return to the physical world. Not only was the Book of Enoch written in the Sacred and Secret Script, it was written to fully reveal, yet conceal, the journey to 'Paradise'. An initiate who knew the Secret in the Bible wrote the Book of Enoch and recorded his perception of what was revealed to him when he activated it. When Rabbi Akiba's 'Experience' was compared with Enoch's 'Experience', two identical descriptions of a controlled journey into heaven and back were relayed. Both men were left overwhelmed by what had happened to them.

The original version of the Book of Revelation[12] also records the Pardes Experience into 'the realm of Light'. The entire substance of the canonical Book of Revelation was in existence five centuries before the commencement of the Christian era and the version official to Christianity today is a later forgery of the earlier work. The genuine version is reproduced in its pristine simplicity in *The Crucifixion of Truth,* thus allowing direct comparison with the fabricated account in the New Testament.

The meditative use of the Secret could only be imparted to minds prepared to receive it for in the wrong hands it was destructive. The Zohar recorded several descriptions of the bizarre fate of Rabbis who were not mentally prepared for the overwhelming effect of the 'Experience' and 'fashioned their own destruction'. In its current literary form, the Zohar (the word itself meaning 'brightness') is a collection of several books or sections that include discussions on many topics including the 'Pardes Experience'. The Zohar is more of a library than a single book, being the main textbook of Cabala and, it too, was originally written in the Sacred Script. Those writings were not originally published as manuscripts to the uninitiated but were secret rabbinic instructions. Presuming it to be of great antiquity, tradition maintained that it was discovered in a cavern where it had lain for many centuries. One section is called, 'Book of Concealment', a kind of commentary delivered in short obscure sentences. In that section, an assembly of ten Rabbis gathered to discuss 'the most profound mystery' in which three of the participants, while trying to speak 'face to face with God as a man speaks to his friend',[13] meet with ecstatic deaths. That was most probably what happened to the thirteen skeletons found in the cave at Sacro Monte (Chapter One).

The Torah is a sublime book of material beyond the range of ordinary knowledge and not a mere haphazard collection of primitive and obscure old texts. The Torah's higher understanding comes from reading letter sequences, not narrative descriptions. In most cases, the surface meaning is totally irrelevant, but the Secret of the 'superscript' in which it was written was handed down to pious and worthy men as the secret of secrets and came eventually to be known as 'the Sacred Mysteries of the Hebrew Alphabet', for that was exactly what it was. In the opening chapter of this book, reference was made to St Jerome's complaint about the difficulty he had in translating the original Gospel of Matthew because it was 'sealed up in curious Hebrew characters'. It was written in the Sacred Script, and he did not know what it was. Other early Christian and Essene texts were also written in the Divine Letters, the Gospels of Mark and Thomas, and the books of Enoch and Jasher, being examples. The author of Isaiah actually referred to 'a language I did not know, I kept hearing', an extraordinary statement supported in the 81st Psalm.

The Torah is a three-dimensional language that brings together the spoken word and the earlier written words and combines them together in a new script of extraterrestrial origin. The secret of scripture is in the meaning of the now-called Hebrew letters themselves. Because they lead to a transcendental experience, the book that they were written in became a sacred text. Therefore, the Torah of the Bible is a holy book, just as Rabbis claimed for centuries. When an initiate mentally wove the patterns of the Rainbow Serpent onto his mind, he had a near-death or out-of-body experience; he 'entered Paradise' and came to behold the Deity.

The Secret in the Tarot Cards

The divine significance of the 22 letters of Thoth's book provides yet another surprise. Each letter of the Sacred Script is secretly drawn into the background of every page of Thoth's book or the Book of Tarot. When psychically-advanced souls looked at the cards they were unknowingly seeing the Divine Language in their mind's eye, or subconscious. That is the reason why a so-called clairvoyant can foresee the future. He or she is receiving messages or pictures from the subtly concealed Divine Language drawn secretly into the background of the symbols displayed on the face of the cards. That sensational knowledge was preserved thousands of years ago by ciphering the 22 Divine letters into each of the 22 pages of Thoth's book and then later hiding them with the inclusion of 56 additional cards. The code to unlock them was concealed in the 22 verses of Psalm 119. The initiated priests 'spoke face to face with God' by turning them over in their mind's eye in meditation and, over the centuries, handed down the secret knowledge of that exotic experience by a judicious tradition of initiation.

1   2

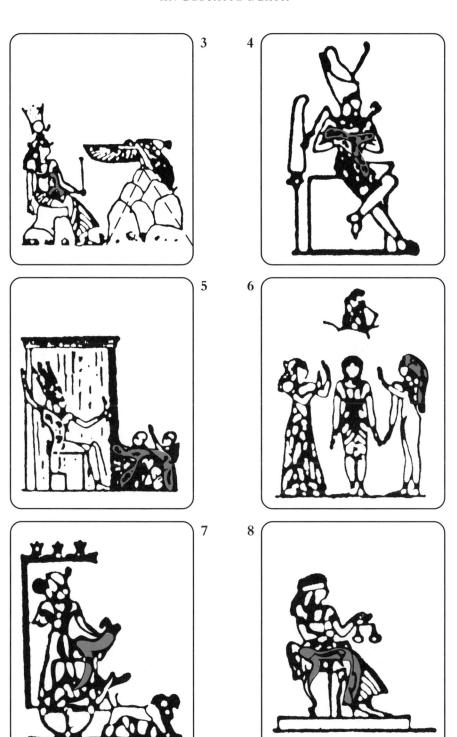

15

16

17

18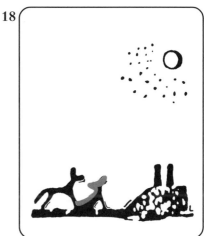

19

20

21 22

Each page of Thoth's 22-page book has the 22 Divine letters secreted into it. The coloured areas define the Letters of Light. Note the pyramid hidden in the rocks on Page 3 (The Queen). Page No.5 (The Priest) had two sacred letters secreted into it. Can you see the uncoloured one? The concept of the concealed letters is also preserved in the tomb of Miraroka at Saqqara where 22 female dancers inscribed on a stone wall are shown with their arms and legs in various positions that depict, in outline, each of the sacred symbols of Thoth.

An ancient hieroglyphic symbol depicted a pyramidal shape with a smaller, similar shape, upon its apex, denoting the Benben. It was generally drawn like this: ⟁ In Thoth's book, that symbol is secreted into the vertical stand in front of the Magician on the first page. There are other subtle areas of hidden clues leading to a greater understanding of the depth of Thoth's book. For example, the line of the crook held by the Pilgrim (No.9) forms part of his costume, and the hats on the figures on pages 11 and 14 conceal the emblem of Eternity.

The substance of the Secret in the Bible is an instance where supernatural intrusion into mundane affairs is clearly recognizable for the basis of the Secret was not invented by mankind. Mankind wrote the scriptures but their under-meaning is superhuman and transcendental. The words are dead but the letters are alive, and every letter in the original Torah is inspired, not every word. The use of the Sacred Language serves to explain the reason why the Bible was always considered a divine book; it was composed in words written in one way, but understood in another. Concerning those ancient writings, it is seen that the biblical stories are of the earthly world but written in a celestial language. The secret of the 'Secret' was one that allowed a trained person private access to an elevated and more subtle state of being for its very essence was sourced from a higher mind principle – or another plane of existence – a higher consciousness, 'the shining Paradise of God'.[14]

The Torah itself is a fabricated collection of writings that carries within its pages a profound underlying spiritual message. Its true meaning is engraved in the letters themselves and is to be understood by the personality when it is open to receive it. Its narrations are the mantle in which is clothed a sublime revelation of spiritual liberation. The letters, or spirals of energy, in which the Torah was originally written are not inventions of mankind but were used by man for recording certain myths, laws and thoughts. They are elements or reservoirs of divine power and their meditative use 'opened a door in Heaven'[15] and provides for the temporary release of the soul from the body to enter and observe the world of eternal life.

Such a mystical 'death' required drastic preliminary discipline, necessary to establish a state of consciousness in which the liberated soul was guided into its own interior principle – into a state of the highest rapture. The subject saw flashes of light and felt divinely 'anointed'. In the attainment of ecstasy, he discovered for himself his relationship to God and experienced union therewith. After the sublime experience, the subject was reunited with his physical form to resume his temporal life, but with an implicit awareness of a higher state of being. He came back to waking consciousness with a realization of his own divinity and was aware of life eternal, the world of immortal (iMMortality) beings and the wisdom of God. Such is the power of the Secret in the Bible. Socrates remarked that 'those who are acquainted with the Mysteries insure to themselves very pleasing hopes against the hour of death'. The 'end revealing' of the Mysteries of the Mystery Schools required a strong herbal or narcotic drink and a smack on the forehead with a wooden mallet to hopefully release the Soul but not kill the candidate. Ancient Australian Aborigines used 'Dream Smoke', but with the Secret, the process was entirely different. It was an internal, personal meditation, one that a knowing person could quietly do alone at home, every day, at leisure, whenever the need to talk to God arose.

The Holy Grail of Eternal Life

So here, at last, we find the Holy Grail. It is hidden in the words Pshat, Ramaz, Darash and Sud. Those four words hold the secret to the true interpretation of the Torah and led to a narrative in the book of Genesis defining what the Holy Grail really was. Controversy raged for centuries as to whether the Grail was a cup or a platter, though it is generally depicted in art as a chalice of considerable size and unusual beauty. According to a popular Christian legend, Joseph of Arimathea brought the Holy Grail to Glastonbury Abbey in England. From the evidence available, it would be erroneous to ascribe a Christian origin to Grail symbolism. Some believed the Holy Grail to be the perpetuation of the holy cup used far back in the rites of Adonis and Atys. A communion cup or chalice was used symbolically in several of the ancient Mysteries and the god Bacchus was frequently portrayed in the form of a vase, cup or urn.

The origin of the Grail myth is curiously elusive. That is because very few persons knew the Secret in the Bible and how it evolved. Sufficient foundation for it may be found in various folklore which contain many accounts of magic cauldrons, kettles, cups and drinking horns, one said to have been the red and black spiral horn of a unicorn. The earliest Grail legend described it as a veritable 'horn of plenty'. Its contents were inexhaustible and those who were served from it never hungered or thirsted. Another account stated that no matter how desperately ill a person might be, he or she could not die if they 'beheld the cup'. They were said 'to be drinking the elixir of youth from the fountain of eternal life'. The medieval Rosicrucians were undoubtedly in possession of the true secret of the Grail legend, much of its symbolism having been covertly incorporated into that Order. The most obvious of all keys to the Grail mystery is their 'rose' on the cross, a symbol that received very little consideration in relation to what it depicted.

In the ancient religion of Nature Worship, the ever-flowing Grail signified the bounty of the harvest by which the life of mankind was sustained. Like Mercury's bottomless pitcher, the Grail was seen as the inexhaustible fountain of natural resource. That opinion supported the claim that the story of the Grail was an elaboration of the myth of the Pagan 'Cup of Plenty' that was preserved by reason of the subtle manner in which it was engrafted upon the cult of Christianity. That was actually a variation of what the Grail really was.

In the Ancient Mysteries the Holy Grail, always green in colour, was symbolized as a perpetual self-feeding, cup-shaped seedpod. It was frequently employed as an emblem of germination and re-growth, 'a fruit tree yielding fruit whose seed is inside itself'.[16] It signified the regenerative forces in mankind. The actual quest for the Holy Grail could therefore be seen as the eternal search for truth and answers to the riddle of existence. In it, we see a variation of the Masonic legend in the Lost Word so long sought by the Brethren of the Craft. That was a Secret Word of Power, representing the base root and nucleus of our being. It was given earlier in this book.

Though the computerized world of the 3rd Millennium may know a thousand secrets, the ancient mystical world of the Egyptian Magi knew only one. That one was greater than the *thousand* secrets that breed selfish motives, darkness, sorrow, egotism, lust and materialism. The *one* secret conferred higher understanding, kindness, giving, light, truth and life eternal. Egyptian priests believed that the very essence of life was brought to Earth from a place of everlasting light and eternal life. In the *Book of the Dead*, it is called the 'Isle of Fire'. The learned Tibetan lamas called it the 'Island in which grows the Peach-tree of Immortality'. The author of the ancient Zohar[17] wrote of souls passing before God in the 'Room of Love' from which they departed to descend to spend their allocated time on Earth. The outcome of that divine 'reception' was that God made the soul swear to fulfill its earthly mission and attain the 'knowledge of the Mysteries of the faith' that will purify it for its return to its homeland. By means of its awakening through the Panther Secret in the Torah, it gained new strength and helped complete the mystical cycle of life. Whether you realize it or not, every person who completely read this book was, unknowingly, initiated, 'beheld the cup', and attained the 'knowledge of the Mysteries' needed to purify their soul before its return. The Gospel of Thomas[18] recorded:

> …there are five trees in Paradise which remain undisturbed summer and winter and whose leaves are never changing. Whoever becomes acquainted with them will not experience death.

That is a clear allegorical reference to the first five books of the Bible and you, my friend, through the pages of this book, have now become fully acquainted with them.

II

WORDS OF TRUTH

This page is for documentation of the sixteen 'Words of Truth' concealed in each chapter of this book. The number of dots represents the number of letters in each word and chapter numbers are written above the corresponding dots.

1	2	3	4
" · · · · ·	· · · · · ·	· ·	· · ·

5	6	7	8
· · · ·	· · ·	· · ·	· · · · · · ·

9	10	11	12
· · ·	· · · · · · ·	· · · ·	· · ·

13	14	15	16
· · · ·	· · · · · ·	· ·	· · · · · · · · · · ."

Albert Einstein (1879-1955) said: 'The most beautiful thing we can witness is the mysterious. He to who this emotion is a stranger, who can no longer pause to wonder and stand rapt in awe, is as good as dead; his eyes are closed'.

II

BIBLIOGRAPHY

A list of principal authorities consulted, referred to, or quoted in the preceding work.

Special note

Due to mergers, closure or relocation of some publishing houses, efforts to trace a number of copyright owners proved difficult. If such works are referenced in this book, copyright is hereby acknowledged and grateful appreciation is extended to those persons (dead or alive) whose thoughts and talents assisted in the development of this book. Any omissions, errors or oversights should be brought to the attention of the author for correction and appropriate acknowledgement in reprints.

About the Contemplative Life, Philo, First Century

A Concise History of Freemasonry, R. F. Gould, London, 1903

Adepts, The (4 Vols), M. P. Hall, Los Angeles, 1949

A Dictionary of Biblical Tradition, David Lyle Jeffrey, William B. Eerdman's Publishing Co., Grand Rapids, Michigan

A Dictionary of Comparative Religion, S. G. F. Brandon, London, 1970

Adventures in Immortality, George Gallop Jnr. with William Proctor, USA 1983

Aegyptiaca, (History of Egypt), Manetho, c. 305-285 BC

Ammiani Marcellini Rerum Gestarum Libri, Leipzig, 1875

Among the Dead, F. B. Maguire, Bloomsbury, London, 1933

An Archaeological Biography, Neferiti, P. Vandenburg (Trans. Hein, R), Book Club Associates, London, 1978

Ancient Egypt (Second Ed.), A. R. David, Equinox Books (Phaidon Press Limited), London, 1988

Ancient Egyptian Dictionary, R. Johnson and E. Rumbel (in Cairo Library)

Ancient Egyptian Doctrine of the Immortality of the Soul, Wiedemann, 1895

An Illustrated Encyclopedia of Mysticism and The Mystery Religions, J. Ferguson, Thames and Hudson, London, 1976

An Encyclopedia of Occultism, Lewis Spence, 1929

Apocryphal New Testament, M. R. James, Oxford, 1953

A Dictionary of Philosophy, A. Flew, Pan Books, London, 1979

A Lexion of Freemasonry, A. G. Mackay, Charles Griffin and Company, Limited, Strand, 1883

A Galley of the Chinese Immortals, L. Giles, London, 1954

Ancient Fragments, I. P. Cory, London, 1832

Ancient Times, James Henry Breasted (2nd Edition), Ginn and Company, London, 1944

Antiquités Égyptiennes, 1883

Antiquities of the Jews, Josephus, First Century

Arguments of the Emperor Julian, The, (originally called, *Against the Khrestians*), Thomas Taylor (Translator), London, 1818

Art of Easter Island, The, Thor Heyerdahl, George Allen and Unwin Ltd, 1976

Atlas of Ancient Egypt, Baines and Malek (For *Time Life Books*), Equinox, Oxford, 1984

A Successive Inquiry into Hermetic Mystery, Mary Ann Atwood, William Tait, Belfast, 1918

Baconiana, T. Tenison, 1679

Bacon's Secret Disclosed, Granville C. Cunningham, 1911

Beasts, Men and Gods, F. Ossendowski, New York, 1922

Beginnings of Architecture, The, S. Giedion, Princeton, 1993

Bel of Babylon, H. Rawlinson, London, 1891

Best Kept Secret, The, Dr. A.A. Muller, London, 1933

Bible and the Tarot, The, Corinne Heline, De Vorss and Co., U.S.A., 1969

Bible Fraud, The, Tony Bushby, The Pacific Blue Group, Hong Kong 2001 (Website address; www.thebiblefraud.com)

Bloodline of the Holy Grail, Sir Lawrence Gardner, Publ. By Element Books, 1996

Book of Ben, sometimes called the *Book of the Nine Entities*

Book of Enoch in Review, The, Professor M. J. C. Wait, Cambridge, 1897

Book of God's Judgment

Book of the Five Days over and above the Year, Egyptian papyrus

Book of Zohar, The, or the *Book of Splendor*

British Museum Dictionary of Ancient Egypt, Ian Shaw and Paul Nicholson, Publ. for the Trustees of the British Museum by the British Museum Press, 1995

Bygone Beliefs, Stanley H. Redgrove, London, William Ryder, 1920

Cairo, Egypt Tourist Authority, 1997

Catalogue of the Mayer Collection, Egyptian Antiquities, Gatty, 1895

Catholic Encyclopedia, The (*Cath. Ency.*), 15 volumes, plus index, 1907-1914

Chaldean Account of Genesis, G. Smith, undated but pre-1900

Chambers's Biographical Dictionary, W & R Chambers Ltd, London, 1968

Christ in Art, Mrs. Jameson, available in the British Library, London

Cipher of Genesis, The, Carlo Suares, Bantam Books, 1973

Collected Fruits of Occult Teaching, A. P. Sinnett, London, 1920

Columbus of Literature, The, W.F.C. Wigston, c. 1902

Commentary on the Gospel of John, St. Augustine, circa 410

Craft Masonry: The Perfect Sign and Grips, A Masonic Publication, 1872

Crata Repoa or *Initiations of the Egyptian Priests*, Berlin, 1770

Crucifixion of Truth, The, Tony Bushby, Stanford Books, 2004

Daniel and the Revelation, Uriah Smith, Pacific Press Publishing Company, London, 1881

Daughter of Amun (A Novel with Historical Notes about Pharaoh Hatshepsut), M. Caldecott, Arrow, London, 1989

Dawn of Civilization, The, Professor Maspero, Oxford, 1901 Edition

De Iside et Osiride, Leeman's Ed, c. 1880

Description of Egypt, Jomard, undated, but pre-1901

Destruction of Men, in *The Dawn of Civilization*, Professor Maspero, 1901

Dictionary of Classical Mythology, Religion, Literature and Art, Oskar Seyffert, Random House, 1995

Dictionary of Islam, London, 1895

Dictionary of Proper Names and Places in the Bible, O. Odelain and R. Seguinean, 1981

Dictionary of Rare Words, Isaac Burrows, Cambridge, 1830

Dictionary of Sects, Blunt

Dictionary of the Bible, original edition by James Hastings D.D., revised by F.C. Grant and H. H. Rowley, 1963

Discovering Ancient Egypt, Rosalie David, Michael O'Mara Books Limited, London, 1993

Diverting History of the Count of de Gabalis, The, Montfaucon de Villars, London, 1714

Dictionnaire Egyptien, Champollion, c. 1890

Dictionary of Christian Antiquities, Dom Cabrol, Rome, 1880

Dictionary of Hieroglyphs, Brugsch, c. 1892-93

Did Jesus Live 100 BC? G. R. S. Mead, Theosophical Publishing Society, 1903

Discoveries at Ephesus, J. T. Wood, London Longmans, Green and Co. 1877

Doctrine of Justification, The, James Buchanan, D. D. LL.D., Baker Book House, Grand Rapids, Michigan; from 1867 printing by T Clarke, Edinburgh, reprinted 1977

Early History of the Ancient Israelites, The, Professor Thompson, E. J. Brill, Leiden, The Netherlands, 1992

Early Jesuit Travelers in Central Asia, C. Wessels, The Hague, 1924

Ecclesiastical History, Johann Mosheim (1694-1755)

Eclipse in Egyptian Texts, The, Lepage- Renouf, Paris, c. 1860

Egypt, Thomas Young, Supplement to *Encyclopedia Britannica*, 1819

Egypt before Written History, Parthey's Edition, 1886

Egyptian Mysteries, Samuel Weiser, Inc. Maine. USA 1988

Eleusinian and Bacchic Mysteries, The, Thomas Taylor, 1875

THE SECRET IN THE BIBLE

Elliott's Delineation of Romanism, 1884

Encyclopedia Biblica, four volumes; Adam & Charles Black, London, 1899; American Reprint, The Macmillan Co., New York, 1914

Encyclopedia Britannica-Edinburgh Edition, Printed for A. Bell and C. Macfarquar, 3rd Edition in 18 Volumes, 1797

Encyclopedia Britannica, 18 Volumes, James Moore's Dublin Edition, 1790-97

Encyclopedia Britannica, 9th Edition, 24 Volumes, A. and C. Black, 1875-1889

Encyclopedia Britannica, particularly Volumes 8, 9, 10 and 11, 1907

Encyclopedia of Freemasonry, Albert G. Mackey, McClure Publishing Co. 1917

Egyptian Book of the Dead (Originally 1895, Dover Publications Inc., NY. 1967)

Egyptian Book of the Dead, Lepsius's Edition, c. 1880

Egyptian Mythology, V. Ions, London, 1968

Encyclopedia of Religion and Ethics, Ed. By James Hastings, T. & T. Clark, Edinburgh, 1914

Ennead of Heliopolis, The, Professor Gaston Maspero, 1890

Esoteric Buddhism, A. P. Sinnett, London, 1903

Excavations at Giza, Selim Hassan, with the Assistance of Mahmoud Darwish, Cairo Govt. Press. Bulaq, 1944 (Full Set at the Ashmolean Library, Oxford)

Expedition in Mesopotamia, Oppert, c. 1850

Eyes of the Sphinx, The, Erich Von Daniken, trans. by Erich Graefe, Leipzig

Fame and Confession of Rosie-Cross, Trans. Thomas Vaughan, 1625

Fifty Years in the Church of Rome, Chas. Chiniquy (Banned by the church), First printed 1885

First and Second Book of the First Lords, The

Followers of Horus, The, a Turin fragment of the *Canon of the Kings*

Francis Bacon's Personal Life, Alfred Dodd, Rider and Company, London, pre-1953

Freemasonry and the Bible, H. L. Haywood (Masonic Edition), William Collins, Sons and Co. London, 1951

Freemasonry of the Ancient Egyptians, Manly P. Hall, Philosophical Research Society, Inc. L.A., 1971 reprint from original printing in April 1, 1937

Freemasonry; Its Aims and Ideals, J.S.M. Ward, William Rider and Son Ltd., London, 1923

From Fetish to God in Ancient Egypt, Sir Wallis Budge, c. 1930

Genesis of the Grail Kings, Lawrence Gardner, Bantam, Feb.1999

Giants in the Earth, Anthony Roberts, Llanfynydd, Wales, Unicorn, 1974

Gibbon's Rome, undated

Glimpses of Masonic History, Bishop Leadbeater, 1954

Gods of Eden, The, The Dahlin Family, Avon Books, N.Y. 1993

Gods of Egypt, Dr. Rouge, The Alexandrian Prescriptions, Egypt, 1868

Gods of the Egyptians, The, Wallis Budge, Vol. 1, British Museum, London, c. 1930

God of the Witches, The, Oxford University Press, Oxford, 1952

Grand Mystery, The, a rare Masonic publication, 1724

Great Pyramid and its Builders, The, Lytle W. Robinson, The William Byrd Press, USA, reprinted 1960

Great Pyramid, The, Tom Valentine, Granada Publ. First Published by Panther Books, Ltd in Great Britain in 1977

Great Women Initiates, H. Bernard, Amorc. Inc, San Jose, USA 1984

Glimpses of Masonic History, C. W. Leadbeater, The Theosophical Publishing House, Madras (Undated)

Great Secret of Count Saint Germain, The, Dr Raymond W. Bernard, Health Research reprint, undated

Harmonic 33, Captain Bruce L. Cathie, 1968

Harmonic Conquest of Space, The, Bruce L. Cathie, Adventures Unlimited Press, 1998

Head of Osiris, The, A. S. Hughes, Egyptian Assoc, London Chapter, 1931

Hidden Symbols of the Rosicrucians, The, Harold Bayley, Baconiana, 1903

Hidden Tarot Mysteries, Professor L. S. Draper, Russell Square, London, 1922

Himalayas—Abode of Light, N. K. Roerich, Bombay, 1947

Histoire de la Magie, undated but c. 1760, trans. by Luigi Bruno, 1906

Histories, Herodotus c. 484-430 BC

History of Magic, Joseph Ennemoser, Henry G Bohn, London, 1854

History of Magic, Lynn Thorndike, Macmillan, New York, 1934

History of Freemasonry, The, R. F. Gould (Four Volumes), Thomas C. Jack, London, 1882

History of Protestantism, The, Rev, J.A. Wylie (Author of *The Papacy*), Cassell and Company Limited, London, Paris and New York (3 Volumes Undated)

History of the Holy Mecca, Syed Ahmed, London, 1870

How the Great Religions Began, J. Gaer, New York, 1954

Immortals, The, Derek and Julia Parker, Barrie & Jenkins Ltd, 1976

Initiations and Initiates in Tibet, A. David-Neel, London, 1931

Initiations of the Egyptian Priests, or, *Crata Repoa,* Berlin, 1770

Introduction to the Talmud and Midrash, Herman L. Strack, Harper Torchbooks, Harper and Row, N.Y. First Edition 1931

Inscriptions of Sinai, The, Jaroslav Cerry (Ed), Egyptian Exploration Society, London, 1955

Irenaeus of Lyons, trans. John Keble, London, 1872

Jewish Encyclopedia, N.Y. 1903

Jewish War, Josephus, Book 2

Kebra Nagast, Sir E. A. Wallis Budge, c. 1930

Kennys' Masonic Cyclopedia and Handbook of Masonic Archaeology, History and Biography, George Kenny, London, 1878

Keys of Enoch, The, J. J. Hurtak, Publ. By 'The Academy for Future Science', Calf. USA. 1977

Krishna and Orpheus, E. Schure, London, 1909

Larousse Encyclopedia of Mythology, London, 1960

Legendary History of Egypt, The, Rosellini's Version, 1856

Lehnert and Landrock, Orient Art Publishers, Cairo, Egypt

Leiden Papyrus, The

Lives of the Necromancers, William Godwin, Harper and Brothers, N.Y. 1835

Macmillan Dictionary of Women's Biography, The, J. S. Uglow, Editor, Macmillan, Bristol, U.K. 1982

Magi – The Quest for a Secret Tradition, Adrian G. Gilbert, Bloomsbury, London, 1996

Magical Mystical Sites, Elizabeth Pepper and John Wilcock, Sphere Books Ltd, London, 1976

Mahatma Letters, London, 1926

Manners and Customs, Wilkinson, pre-1900

Maori Symbolism, Ms Ettie A. Rout, Kegan Paul, Trench, Trubner & Co., Ltd. Broadway House, London, 1926

Masonry Dissected, Pritchard, 1730

Monastery of Jade Mountain, The, P. Goullart, London, 1961

Monks of Athos, The, R. M. Dawkins, 1936

Mountains of the Pharaohs, The, L. Cottrell, London, 1955

Mysteries of the Crystal Skulls, The, Chris Morton and Ceri Louise Thomas, Thorson, Imprint of Harpercollins Publ. 1997

Mythic Image, The, Joseph Campbell, M.J.F Books, New York

Mysteries of Mithra, Franz Cumont, Translated by Thomas J. McCormick, Open Court Publishing, Chicago, 1910

Myth of Eternal Return, The, Mircea Eliade, Translated by William Trask, N.Y. Pantheon, 1954

Mystery of Francis Bacon, The, William T. Smedley, John Howell, San Francisco, 1910

Mysterious Origins of Man, The, Michael Cremo, and Richard L. Thompson' Govardhan Hill Publishing, USA, 1993

Natural History, Pliny (Caius Plinius Secundus), First Century

New Dawn Magazine, New Gnosis Communications International Pty. Ltd., Melbourne, Australia, ed. David Jones

New Larousse Encyclopedia of Mythology, 1984

New Testament Apocrypha, E. Hennecke, London, 1963

Nexus New Times, Nexus Magazine Pty Ltd, Australia, ed. Duncan M. Roads

Occult Science in India, L. Jacolliot, New York, 1884

Occult Theocracy, Lady Queenborough (Published Posthumously), The Christian Bookclub of America. Cali. 1933

Old World Civilizations, The University of Queensland, Australia

On the Mysteries, particularly those of the Egyptians, Chaldeans and the Assyrians, Iamblichus, Fourth Century, trans. Professor Thomas Taylor, (1821 reprint, London; Stuart and Watkins, 1968)

On the Shores of Endless Worlds, Andrew Tomas, Sphere Books Limited, 1974

On the Religion of the Babylonians, H. Rawlinson, c. 1891

Origin of Islam, Yasser S. Farah, Damanhur Press, Alexandria, Egypt, 1969

Oxyrhynchus Papyrus, 654 and 655

Persian Scriptures, The, Lower Book

Physics of Immortality, The, Frank J. Tipler, Doubleday, WA, 1994

Proceedings of the Society of Biblical Archaeology, Brugsch, 1892-93

Pyramidographia, John Greaves, Professor of Astronomy at Oxford, 1646

Pythagoras, E. Schure, London, 1906

Rama and Moses, E. Schure, London, 1910

Records of the Past, A. H. Sayce, Professor of Assyriology, Oxford, vols. 1-11, c. 1898

Records of Rome, The, 1868, available in the British Library

Religions of India, Barth

Religion of the Ancient Babylonians, A. H. Sayce, Professor of Assyriology, Oxford, c. 1892

Remarks on Egyptian Papryri and on the Inscriptions of Rosetta, Thomas Young, 1815

Repellers of Wolves, John Telfer, Pre-publication manuscript, 2003

Researches in Sinai, Sir W. M. Flinders Petrie, John Murray, London, 1906

Researching the Origins of Egypt, J. de Morgan, c. 1890

Resuscitatio or, *Bringing into Publick Light, Several Pieces hitherto Sleeping,* Dr. William Rawley, 1657

Riddle of the Pyramids, The, K. Mendelssohn, Sphere Books, London, 1977

Ritual of Embalmment, Ancient Egyptian Papyrus

Rosicrucians and Freemasons, Thomas de Quincey, c. 1612

Rosicrucian Pamphlets of 1614, The

Rosicrucians–Their Rites and Mysteries, The, Hargrave Jennings, Routledge, London, 1887

Royal Road, The, Stephen A. Hoeller, The Theosophical Publishing House, Ill. USA, 1975

Sallier Papyrus, The

Secret Doctrine, The, H. P. Blavatsky, The Theosophical Press, Ill. USA, 1946

Secret History of Ancient Egypt, The, Professor Thomas Taylor, translator of Iamblichus' writings, 1821

Secret Oral Teachings in Tibetan Buddhist Sects, A. David-Neel, San Francisco, 1971

Secrets of the Christian Fathers, J. W. Sergerus, 1685

Secrets of the Great Pyramid, Peter Thompkins, Publ. Allen Lane

Secrets of the Occult, Burland, Cottie A. Ebury Press, London, circa 1968

Secret Search in Egypt, A, Paul Brunton, Rider and Company, 1947

Secret Societies, The, Charles William Heckethorn, University Books, New Hyde Park, N.Y. (Two Vols)

Secret Teachings of All the Ages, Manly P. Hall, The Philosophical Research Society Inc., L.A., Calif. 1901

Seven Tetracts, The

Shambala; Oasis of Life, Andrew Tomas, Sphere Books Limited, 1977

Skulls and Initiation, L. Eddington, West End Associates, London, 1901

Society in Imperial Rome; Michael Massey, Cambridge University Press, 1982

Society for the Preservation of the Architectural Resources of Egypt, The Palm Press, Cairo, No. 4, 1996

Some Difficulties of Belief, Rev. T. Teignmouth Shore, MA, Mayfair, London (Undated)

Spear of Destiny, The, Trevor Ravenscroft, Sphere Books Limited, London

Symbolism of the Gods of the Egyptians and the Light They Throw On Freemasonry, T.M. Stewart, The Baskerville Press, London, 1927

Symbolic Masonry, H.L. Haywood, G.H. Doran, N.Y. 1923

Symbolic Prophecy of the Great Pyramid, The, H. Spencer Lewis Phd., The Rosicrucian Press, San Jose,

California, First Ed, 1936

Synopsis of Sixteen Cycles

Ten Lost Books of Moses, The, Daggett Publishing Co., Chicago, Ill. USA, 1934

Tell el Amarna Tablets in the British Museum, The, Publ. by Bezold- Budge

The Aboth of R. Nathan; Sayings of the Jewish Fathers, Printed in different editions of the Talmud, Venice 1622 and Amsterdam, 1778

The Day They Wrote the Bible, John Cosin, Bishop of Durhan, d. 1672

The First Sex, E. G. Davis

The Great Controversy, Ellen G. White Laymen For Religious Liberty, Inc. Florida, first published 1888

The Templars: Knights of God, E. Burman, Aquarian Press, Wellingborough, 1986

The Temple, John M. Lundquist, Thames and Hudson, 1993

The Universal Jewish Encyclopedia, New York

Tibet—Past and Present, C. Bell, Oxford, 1968

Trails to Inmost Asia, G. N. Roerich, New Haven, 1931

Transcendental Magic, Eliphas Levi, Riders London, 1962

Travels in Egypt, Richard Pococke, publ. 1743

Travels in Egypt and Nubia, Frederick Lewis Norden, 1757

Two Republics, Alonzo T. Jones, Review and Herald Publishing Co., Battle Creek, Mich. USA, 1891

Uncovering the Secret Tradition, Universal Life Newsletter, Cleveland, Australia, 2001

Universal History (12 volumes), Diodorus Siculus, First Century

Unpublished Records of the Craft, Brother. W. J. Hughan, 1599

Vedas, The

Vines Expository Dictionary of New Testament Words, W.E. Vine, M.A. 1996

Warrior Queens, The, A. Fraser, Manderin, London, 1989

Wars of Gods and Men, The, Zecharia Sitchin, Avon Books, 1985

What Happened in History, G. Childe, London, 1954

When Time Began, Zecharia Sitchin, Avon Books, 1993

Where Did Jesus Die? J. D. Shams, Qadian (Punjab), India, 1959

White Goddess, The, R. Graves, Faber and Faber, London, 1977

With Mystics and Magicians in Tibet, A. David-Neel, London, 1931

Women and Freemasonry, D. Wright, William Riser and Son Ltd., London, 1922

Women's Mysteries, M. E. Harding (Introduced by C. G. Jung), Rider London, 1989

Women Warlords, T. Newark, Blandford, London, 1989

World Mythology, Roy Willis, Henry Holt and Company, N.Y. 1993

Year of the Goddess, The, L. Durdin-Robertson, Aquarian Press, Wellingborough, 1990

Research assistance

Sincere thanks are extended to staff members of research centres, libraries, societies, institutions and publishers who generously offered access to documents and granted copyright and reproduction rights for re-use of material produced or held, by their organizations. Special acknowledgment to:-

Alexandrian Library (Bibliotheca Alexandrina), Manuscripts and Rare Books Division, Dr. H. E. Mohesen Shebab

Al Mu'allagah Church, Old Cairo, Archives and Antiquities Department

Awareness Quest: Australian Archaeological Anomalies and Suppressed Information Distributors; Website: www.awarenessquest.com

Bible Society, The (International), Stuttgart (Bible Copyrights)

British Museum, Copyright approval, Sinai Bible

Brother Phillip and the monks of St. Leonards (Australia)

Bureau of Research and Survey, New York, USA

Church Surveys, Boston University, USA

Egyptian Archival Division, Cairo

Joshua Books, Australia; Website: www.joshuabooks.com

Pontifical Biblical Institute of Jerusalem

Professor Karl von Ritchie (Translations)

Rare Manuscripts Division, British Library, London, UK

Shed 20, and the Group of Five (Australia)

The House of Silver, 1986

The New Zealand Theosophical Society (Archival Library)

ENDNOTES

CHAPTER ONE

1   2 Cor. 12: 3-4.

2   *The Monks of Athos*; R. M. Dawkings, 1936.

3   *Catholic Encyclopaedia*, 1908,Vol. IV, Pg. 583.

4   *Institutes of Christian History*; 1755.

5   *Commentary to Matthew*; {XII; 13} Book II.

6   *Gospel of Thomas*; 1:1.

7   *Gospel of Thomas*; 39/114.

8   *Gospel of Thomas*; 13/114.

9   *The Eleusinian and Bacchic Mysteries*; Thomas
     Taylor, 1875.

10   Matt 10:13.

11   *The Book of Zohar*; the *Book of Splendor* of the
     Cabalist writings.

12   *Epip; Haer*; XXXIII; IV, pg. XLI, 560.

13   *Quabbalah*,Vol. iii; folio 1526, pg. 102, quoted
     in Myers.

14   *Huet*, Origen, Origeniana, 167.

15   4: 22-25.

16   Isa. 34:4.

17   *Jewish War*, Josephus, Book 2, Chapter 12,
     Sect. 2.

CHAPTER TWO

1   *Collins Concise Encyclopedia*, 1977.

2   *Glimpses of Masonic History*, C. W. Leadbeater,
     The Theosophical Publishing House, Madras
     (Undated).

3   Mariette, *Les Mastabas*, pp. 252, 253, 254, 275.

4   *Dictionnaire Egyptien*, Champollion, c. 1890.

5   *Life of Constantine*.

6   *Glimpses of Masonic History*, 1954; pg. 324.

7   *The Macmillan Dictionary of Woman's Biography*,
     J. S. Uglow, 1982, pg. 215.

8   *The Sunday Express*; London; July 7, 1935.

9   *The First Sex*, E. G. Davis, Pg. 82.

10   A.M.O.R.C. Inc; Pg. 59.

11   *The Crucifixion of Truth*, Tony Bushby, Stanford
     Books, 2003.

CHAPTER THREE

1   Zech. 6:7.

2   *Herodotus*, Introduction, Book IV,
     MCMLVIII.

3   *Universal History*,Vol. 1, page 50.

4   *The Destruction of Men*, 1.2; Professor Maspero,
     Pg. 110.

5   Chap. xvii. 9. 29.

6   *New Larousse Encyclopedia of Mythology*; pg. 11.

7   vol.i., pl.ii., No. vi. 11. 2,3.

8   *Book of the Dead*, Naville's Edition, pl.x. ii; 6,7.

9   *The Dawn of Civilization*, Professor Gaston
     Maspero, 1901, pgs.110-111.

10   *Epic of Gilgamesh*.

11   *Wonders by Sea and Land*.

12   *Secret Teachings of All the Ages,* Manly P. Hall, The
     Philosophical Research Society Inc., L.A., Calif. 1901.

13   *Life of Paulis*, The First Hermit; Chapter VIII.

14 *Histories.*

15 *De Civitate Dei*, xvi, 8; p. 315.

16 Genesis 6:4.

17 *Book of the Arc of Bon*, xv: 39.

18 *Le Papyrus magique*, Harris, pp. 116-117.

19 *Historische Inschriften*, vol.ii, pl.xxxv.

20 Turin fragment of the *Canon of Kings.*

21 *Histoire de la Terre*, Page 154.

22 *Heroica;* pg. 35.

23 *Chambers's Biographical Dictionary*, London, 1968 Ed., Pg. 1023.

24 *Natural History;* VII; XVI.

25 Gen. 6:4.

26 24:13.

27 Jas. 26:25.

28 *Ecclesiastical History*, Eusebius.

29 *Sethantes*, 111: 20-33.

30 Enoch 9: 5.

31 *The Book of Enoch in Review*, Professor M. J. C. Wait, Cambridge, 1897, pg. 78.

32 *Enoch* 15: 3-4.

33 *Kebra Nagast*, Pg. 188, Sir E. A. Wallis Budge.

34 *Synopsis of Sixteen Cycles*, 11:13.

35 Enoch 14:5.

36 Enoch. 15: 8-9.

37 Enoch 22:13.

38 *The Lord's First Book*, 1:20; also, *Second Book of Lords*, 11:13.

39 Enoch 16:3.

40 Jer. 2:18, Syrian Bible.

41 *Papyrus 3229* in the Louvre.

42 *The Dawn of Civilization*, Professor Gaston Maspero, 1901, pp. 162-163.

CHAPTER FOUR

1 Jud. 1:8.

2 2 Samuel 5:6.

3 12: 40.

4 *Encyclopedia Britannica*, Eleventh Ed, Vol. III, 1910, pg. 867.

5 Gen. 15:16; Ex. 6:16-20; Num. 26:5-9.

6 12:40.

7 *Catholic Encyclopedia*, Vol. II; June 1, 1911, pg. 656.

8 *Encyclopedia Britannica*, Vol. III; 11ᵗʰ Ed. 1910, pg. 864.

9 E. J. Brill, Leiden, The Netherlands, 1992.

10 *Dictionary of the Bible*, Pg. 863, Edited by James Hastings, D.D., 1914.

11 *Ibid,* now called the Sinaitic Peninsular.

12 *Encyclopedia Judea,* Book 12, Mount of Horeb.

13 3:1.

14 Ex. 9:11.

15 Ex. 33:6.

16 *Description of Egypt;* Vol. 1; Jomard, undated, but pre-1901.

17 *Memorandum and Articles of Association;* Pg.1.

18 *Nexus,* Lawrence Gardner; Feb/Mar 1998. Pg. 55 onwards.

19 Ex. 19:18.

20 *The Oxford Dictionary of the Christian Church;* 1974; pg. 168.

21 *Catholic Encyclopedia,* Vol. 14, 1912, pg. 780.

22 Heb. 3.

23 *Encyclopedia Britannica*, Vol. III; Eleventh Ed. 1910, pg. 864.

24 Jer. 29:10.

25 11 Chron. 36; 22; 23; Ezra 1:1-14; Isa 4:28.

26 *2 Macc.* 2:13. *Old Testament* Apocrypha.

27 *2 Macc.* 2:15. *Old Testament* Apocrypha.

28 2 Kings 22:8.

29 *Jewish Encyclopaedia,* New York, 1903.

30 *Encyclopaedia Judaica Jerusalem,* 1971.

31 2 Kings 23:2.

32 *The Lost Scrolls of the Essene Brotherhood,* The, E.B. Szekely, International Biogenic Society, 1989.

33 Ezra 7:25.

34 Ezra 7:12; 21.

35 Ezra 7:11.

36   e.g. Ezra 8:18.

37   Ezra 22:8.

38   4 Ezra 37.

39   4 Ezra 23-26.

40   Ezra 14:37.

41   4 Ezra 14:42.

42   *Apion,* Josephus; I,8.

43   Mark 4:12.

44   Numbers 2: 9.

45   *Numbers;* Chapters 1 and 2.

46   Neh. 8:18.

CHAPTER FIVE

1   *Stomata,* v. 7.

2   Gen. 15:1.

3   Gen. 15:1.

4   1 John; 1.

5   Luke 12:2.

6   *The Adepts* (4 Vols.), M. P. Hall, Los Angeles, 1949 Reprint.

7   *Babylonian Gemara;* Sanhedrin; 103a.

8   John 18:19.

9   Matt. 5:17.

10   Mark 15:3.

11   *Adverse Judeaus.* C. IX, last paragraph.

12   b. Sand., 106b.

13   Palestinian and Babylonian.

14   *Sanhedrin;* 67a.

CHAPTER SIX

1   *Resuscitatio* or, '*Bringing into Publick Light, Several Pieces hitherto Sleeping*', Dr. William Rawley, 1657.

2   *The Martyrdom of Francis Bacon;* Alfred Dodd, Pg. 141; undated, but c. 1940.

3   *The Mystery of Francis Bacon;* circa 1910, Pg. 128.

4   *Francis Bacon's Personal Life,* Alfred Dodd, Rider and Company, London, pre-1953.

5   *The Rise of English Culture;* Edwin Johnson, Preface.

6   *The Martyrdom of Francis Bacon;* Alfred Dodd, 1945 Pg. 32.

7   *Ibid;* Pg. 149.

8   1 Kings 7:21.

9   *The Early History and Antiquities of Freemasonry,* Fort, p. 351.

10   *The Secret Shake-speare;* Alfred Dodd, MCMXLI.

11   *Bacon and the Rosicrucians;* W.F.C. Wigston; Also see, *The Mirror of Pallas.*

12   *Francis Bacon's Cipher Signatures;* Frank Woodward.

13   *The Secret Shake-speare;* Alfred Dodd, MCMXLI; Also; *The Martyrdom of Francis Bacon;* also by Alfred Dodd.

14   *Baconiana,* T. Tenison, 1679, Pg. 28.

15   2 Kings 18:4.

16   1 Kings; 5 onwards.

17   1 Kings, 8-10.

18   Gal. 4:24.

CHAPTER SEVEN

1   *Meteorolog.,* 1, xiv.

2   *Herodotus,* ii, 4; of xcix.

3   *The Dawn of Civilization,* Professor Gaston Maspero, 1901, p. 3.

4   *Travels in Egypt and Nubia,* Frederick Lewis Norden, 1757.

5   *Travels in Egypt and Nubia;* Frederick Lewis Norden, 1757.

6   *On the Mysteries, particularly those of the Egyptians, Chaldeans and the Assyrians.*

7   *Das Pyrmidenkapitel in al- Makrizis 'Hitat',* also, *The Eyes of the Sphinx;* As translated by Erich Graefe; Leipzig; Erich Von Daniken; Pg. 254 – 273; also, *The Return of the Gods,* Erich Von Daniken, Pg. 151.

8   *Antiquités Égyptiennes,* 1883.

9   ii, 134.

10   *Pastor of Hermas,* cited in *Isis Unveiled;* Book ii; Theology, Pg. 245.

11   Pg. 1270.

12 *Description de l' Egypte*, Jomard, Vol. V.
pp. 672-674.

13 Josephus; First Century Historian.

14 *Description*, Jomard, Vol. v.

15 *Operations*, Vol 1, pp. 261, 262.

16 ii.134.

17 i, 63.

18 Herodotus, ii. 129.

19 *Histories*.

20 Routledge and Kegan Paul Limited, 1963.

21 *Old World Civilizations*, The University of
Queensland, Pg 58.

22 5:12, Syrian Bible, 1876.

23 *Travels in Egypt and Nubia*; Frederick Lewis
Norden, 1757. Pg. 104.

24 *Histories*, Herodotus.

25 *Kebra Nagast* pgs. XV; XVI.

26 *Collected Fruits of Occult Teaching*, A. P. Sinnett,
London, 1920.

27 *The Gods of the Egyptians*; Vol. 1. Pg. 471-2
and Vol. II; Pg. 361.

28 *Catalogue of the Mayer Collection*, Egyptian
Antiquities, Gatty, 1895.

29 'the alluvial plains of Mesopotamia', *Lakeland
Bible Dictionary* p. 142.

30 Gen. 11: 2-4.

31 Oppert; Vol. i, pg. 200. c. 1850.

32 Isa; 46; 1.

33 Gen. 11: 3.

34 *The Dawn of Civilization*, Professor Gaston
Maspero, 1901, pp. 593-596.

35 *Society for the Preservation of the Architectural
Resources of Egypt*, The Palm Press, Cairo,
No. 4, 1996.

36 Jer. xliii. 13.

37 *Dictionnaire Egyptien*, Champollion, c. 1890.

38 *Jer.* xliii. 13, King James Bible, 1971.

39 34; 14.

40 *Encyclopedia Biblica*, 1914; also, Jer. 52:17-20.

41 Aboth; 5; 8.

42 Jer. 52: 17-20.

43 *Encyclopedia Biblica*, 1914; also, Jer. 52:17-20.

44 *Fifth Tablet of the Creation Legend*, Pg. 70.

45 *The Indian Review*, Del Mar, 1903.

46 Gen. 11:31.

CHAPTER EIGHT

1 *The Dawn of Civilization*, Professor Gaston
Maspero, 1901, pg. 517.

2 *Histoire de la Magie*; based in part upon the
authority of Iamblichus, from, *On the
Mysteries, particularly those of the Egyptians,
Chaldeans and the Assyrians.*

3 *Ammiani Marcellini Rerum Gestarum Libri*,
Leipzig, 1875.

4 Source; The Sydney Morning Herald, 11th
October. 1994.

5 Dr. Selim Hassan.

6 *Fame and Confession of Rosie-Cross*; Trans.
Thomas Vaughan, 1625.

7 *The Diverting History of the Count of de Gabalis*,
Montfaucon de Villars, London, 1714.

CHAPTER NINE

1 *Ancient Egypt*, extracted from the *Book of the
Dead*, Professor Gaston Maspero, 1901, 2nd Ed.

2 2 Kings 22: 8.

3 *New Larousse Encyclopedia of Mythology*; pgs. 14-15.

4 *The Pyramids of Giza*; Howard Vyse; Vol. ii,
pgs. 71, 72.

5 *Gibbon's Rome*, Vol. iii, pg. 146.

6 Ibid, pg. 146.

7 *Rosicrucians and Freemasons*; Thomas de
Quincey, c. 1612.

8 *The Rosicrucian Pamphlets of 1614.*

CHAPTER TEN

1 *On the Mysteries, particularly those of the
Egyptians, Chaldeans and the Assyrians,*
Iamblichus, Fourth Century.

2   *Bacon's Secret Disclosed*, Granville C.
    Cunningham, 1911.
3   *On the Mysteries, particularly those of the*
    Egyptians, Chaldeans and the Assyrians;
    Iamblichus.
4   *Oxford Bible*, 26:5, 1896.
5   *An Encyclopedia of Occultism*, Lewis Spence,
    publ. 1920, Pg. 143.
6   *The Columbus of Literature*; W.F.C. Wigston, c. 1902.
7   *Song R*: 4:19.
8   19, 20, 21.
9   *Initiations and Initiates in Tibet,* A. David-Neel,
    London, 1931.

CHAPTER ELEVEN

1   *The Gods of the Egyptians*; Wallis Budge, Vol. 1.
2   *Shambhala: Oasis of Light*; Andrew Tomas.
    Sphere Books, London. 1977.
3   Publ. for the Trustees of the British Museum
    by the British Museum Press, 1995.
4   From interview with Dr. Zahi Hawass:
    Published by *The Irish Times*, April 18ᵗʰ 1999.
5   *The Religion of the Ancient Babylonians,* A. H.
    Sayce, Oxford, p. 216.
6   *The Dawn of Civilization*, Professor Gaston
    Maspero, 1901, pg. 636.
7   *Das Traumgesicht* Gudea's, Zimmen, vol.iii, pp
    232 -235.
8   *Manners and Customs*, Wilkinson, 2ⁿᵈ Ed.,
    Undated but c. 1880.
9   5: 17.
10 *When Time Began,* Zecharia Sitchin, Pg. 194,
    Avon, 1993.
11 *History of the Holy Mecca*, Syed Ahmed,
    London, 1870; also, *Origin of Islam;* Yasser S.
    Farah, Alexandria Press, Damanhur, 1969)

CHAPTER TWELVE

1   *Encyclopedia Judaica*, Ed. Cecil Roth,
    Jerusalem, 1974.

2   Haer; V6-17.
3   *Religions of India*, Barth; pg.169.
4   Numbers 21: 8.
5   2 Kings 18:4.
6   Ex 20:4.
7   *Isis and Osiris,* Plutarch, pg. 80.
8   2 Kings 18:4.
9   *Isis and Osiris*, Plutarch.
10 *Book of the Dead,* Ritual, Chp. 85.
11 *The Bible Fraud*, Tony Bushby, 2001, p. 167.
12 Ibid, p. 173.
13 Deut. 4:36.
14 *On the Mysteries, particularly those of the*
    Egyptians, Chaldeans and the Assyrians,
    Iamblichus, Fourth Century.
15 Ibid.
16 *Shambhala: Oasis of Light*; Andrew Tomas,
    Sphere Books, London, 1977.
17 *Encyclopedia Britannica,* 9ᵗʰ Ed.Vol. 18, pg. 134.
18 Deut. 13:1.
19 Dan. 12:7.

CHAPTER THIRTEEN

1   *De Iside et Osiride*, Leeman's Ed, pp. 37, 51, 52;
    c. 1880.
2   Ibid.
3   *The Dawn of Civilization,* Professor Gaston
    Maspero, 1901, pg. 176.
4   Gen. 32:30.
5   Matt. 27:62-63.
6   Luke 2:42.
7   Luke 3:23.
8   Matt. 4:1-2.
9   *Commentary on the Gospel of John*; Augustine,
    Vol. 1; pg. 240.
10 2 Samuel 5:4 and 1 Kings 11:42.
11 Deut. 25:3.
12 Hebrews, 6:4.
13 *Annobius*, liv, 5 (54: 5).

14 *Crata Repoa* or *Initiations of the Egyptian Priests,*
Berlin, 1770.

15 19:14.

16 14:2.

17 1 Kings 7:21.

18 Referenced in the Bible: 1 Kings 7:17.

19 Judges 12:5-6.

CHAPTER FOURTEEN

1 Luke 23:64.

2 Ex. 3:5.

3 pg. 42.

4 *New Catholic Encyclopedia,* Vol. IV; Pg. 475.

5 *Origin of Religion Belief;* Draper, Pg. 252.

6 *Christ in Art,* Mrs. Jameson; Vol. 2, Pg. 317.

7 Mark, 15; 23.

8 Luke 27:51.

9 Luke 23:53.

10 Luke 23:53.

11 *Book of Wars,* Cp. L, pgs. 5-15.

12 Luke, 24: 3.

13 Sabinius of Hereclea c. 326, *The Bible Fraud,*
Tony Bushby, p. 212.

14 John; 3: 4.

15 *Book of the Dead.*

16 Diodorus; Liv. 1.

17 *Contra Celsus;* Bk. I; lxvii and. Bk. 111; chp. xliv.

18 *The Arguments of the Emperor Julian;* T. Taylor
Trans.; London; 1818; *The Bible Fraud;* Tony
Bushby, pgs. 164-180, Australia, 2001; The
Pacific Blue Group.

CHAPTER FIFTEEN

1 *Society in Imperial Rome;* M. Massey, 1982,
Pg 103.

2 *Dictionary of Greek and Roman Antiquities:*
Sibyllini Libra.

3 *Annales Ecclesiastici* (12 Vols.), Cardinal Caesar
Baronius, Vatican librarian and Catholic
historian, 1538-1607.

4 *The Master Key,* Ian Brown, London, 1794.

5 *Encyclopedia of Freemasonry,* Albert G. Mackey,
1917, Pg. 87.

CHAPTER SIXTEEN

1 *Ecclesiastical History,* Johann Mosheim (1694-
1755), Christian historian.

2 *Life of Constantine,* attributed to Eusebius,
Fourth Century.

3 *Encyclopedia Judaica Jerusalem,* 1971.

4 41:23, *The Common Translation Corrected,*
Oxford, 1718-1724.

5 Gen. 28.

6 Hag. 13b.

7 2 Cor. 12: 3-4.

8 Gen. 32:30.

9 *Enneads;* 4. 8. 1.

10 15/114.

11 5; 21-24.

12 *The Mysteries of Osiris and Isis.*

13 Ex. 33:11.

14 *The Mysteries of Osiris and Isis.*

15 *The Mysteries of Osiris and Isis.*

16 Gen.1: 11.

17 2; 253a.

18 19/114.

INDEX

1 Chamber of Ordeal
2 Royal Arch of the Solstice
3 Hall of Initiates
4 Temple of the Grand Orbit
5 Well of Life
6 Hall of Truth in Light
7 Temple of Isis
8 Hall of Ascent
9 Hall of Truth in Darkness
10 Passage of the Veil
11 Chamber of the Second Birth

12 Hall of Judgment
13 Stone of God
14 Chamber of the Triple Veil
15 Gate of Death
16 Chamber of the Open tomb
17 The Instrument of Resurrection
18 Gate of Coming Forth by Day
19 Chamber of Upside-downness
20 Throne of Radiance
21 Passage of the Polestar
22 The False Door

THE MASTER PLANS

Drawn by the author
No. 1 © AC Bushby 2003

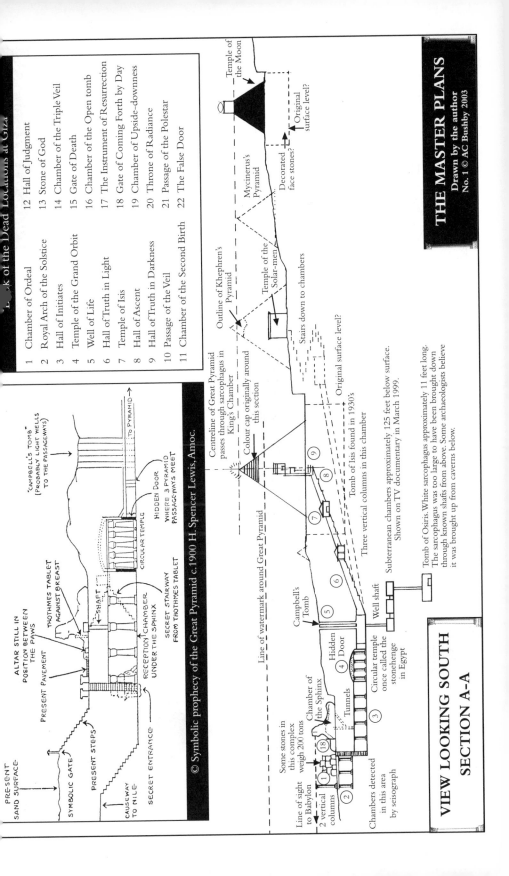

© Symbolic prophecy of the Great Pyramid c.1900 H. Spencer Lewis, Amoc.

"CAMPBELL'S TOMB"
(PROBABLY LIGHT WELLS TO THE PASSAGEWAYS)

TO PYRAMID →

ALTAR STILL IN POSITION BETWEEN THE PAWS

THOTHMES TABLET AGAINST BREAST

PRESENT PAVEMENT

SYMBOLIC GATE

PRESENT SAND SURFACE

PRESENT STEPS

CAUSEWAY TO NILE

SECRET ENTRANCE

HIDDEN DOOR

CIRCULAR TEMPLE

SHAFT

WHERE 3 PYRAMID PASSAGEWAYS MEET

RECEPTION CHAMBER UNDER THE SPHINX

SECRET STAIRWAY FROM THOTHMES TABLET

Temple of the Moon

Original surface level?

Mycinerus's Pyramid

Decorated face stones?

Outline of Khephren's Pyramid

Temple of the Solar-men

Stairs down to chambers

Original surface level?

Centreline of Great Pyramid passes through sarcophagus in King's Chamber

Colour cap originally around this section

Line of watermark around Great Pyramid

Three vertical columns in this chamber

Tomb of Isis found in 1930's

Subterranean chambers approximately 125 feet below surface. Shown on TV documentary in March 1999.

Tomb of Osiris. White sarcophagus approximately 11 feet long. The sarcophagus was too large to have been brought down through known shafts from above. Some archaeologists believe it was brought up from caverns below.

Campbell's Tomb

Hidden Door

Well shaft

Circular temple once called the stonehenge in Egypt

Chamber of the Sphinx

Tunnels

Line of sight to Babylon

2 vertical columns

Some stones in this complex weigh 200 tons

Chambers detected in this area by seisograph

VIEW LOOKING SOUTH

SECTION A-A

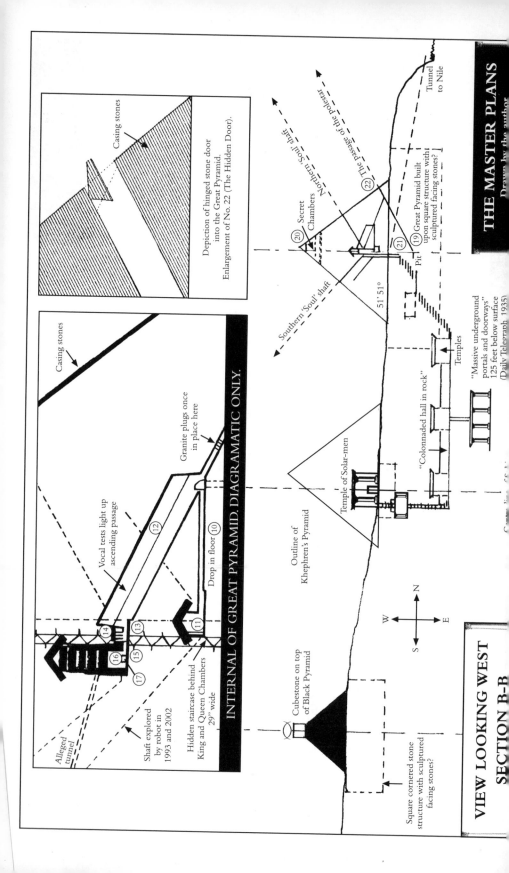

THE MASTER PLANS

Drawn by the author

Tunnel to Nile

㉒ The passage of the polestar

Secret ㉒ Chambers Northern Soul shaft

Southern Soul shaft

51° 51'

㉑ Pit

㉚ Great Pyramid built upon square structure with sculptured facing stones?

Temples

"Massive underground portals and doorways" 125 feet below surface (Daily Telegraph 1935)

"Colonnaded hall in rock"

Casing stones

Depiction of hinged stone door into the Great Pyramid. Enlargement of No. 22 (The Hidden Door).

INTERNAL OF GREAT PYRAMID. DIAGRAMATIC ONLY.

Casing stones

Granite plugs once in place here

Vocal tests light up ⑫ ascending passage

⑩ Drop in floor

⑭ ⑬ ⑪

⑯ ⑮ ⑰

Alleged tunnel

Shaft explored by robot in 1993 and 2002

Hidden staircase behind King and Queen Chambers 29' wide

Outline of Khephren's Pyramid

Temple of Solar-men

N
W — E
S

Cubestone on top of Black Pyramid

Square cornered stone structure with sculptured facing stones?

VIEW LOOKING WEST

SECTION B-B

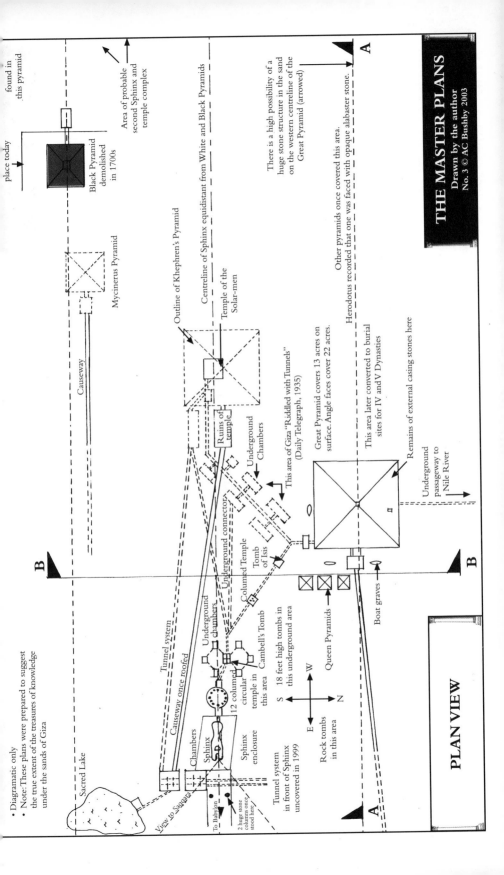

THE MASTER PLANS

Drawn by the author

No. 3 © AC Bushby 2003

PLAN VIEW

- Diagramatic only
- Note: These plans were prepared to suggest the true extent of the treasures of knowledge under the sands of Giza

found in this pyramid

place today

Area of probable second Sphinx and temple complex

There is a high possibility of a huge stone structure in the sand on the western centreline of the Great Pyramid (arrowed)

Other pyramids once covered this area.

Herodotus recorded that one was faced with opaque alabaster stone.

Black Pyramid demolished in 1700s

Mycinerus Pyramid

Causeway

Outline of Khephren's Pyramid

Centreline of Sphinx equidistant from White and Black Pyramids

Temple of the Solar-men

Ruins of temple

Underground Chambers

This area of Giza "Riddled with Tunnels" (Daily Telegraph, 1935)

Great Pyramid covers 13 acres on surface. Angle faces cover 22 acres.

This area later converted to burial sites for IV and V Dynasties

Remains of external casing stones here

Underground passageway to Nile River

Sacred Lake

Tunnel system

Causeway once roofed

Underground connector

Columned Temple

Tomb of Isis

Underground chambers

Cambell's Tomb

View to Saqqara

To Babylon

2 huge stone columns once stood here

Tunnel system in front of Sphinx uncovered in 1999

Sphinx

Chambers

Sphinx enclosure

12 columned circular temple in this area

18 feet high tombs in this underground area

Rock tombs in this area

Queen Pyramids

Boat graves

S
W — E
N

B   B

A   A

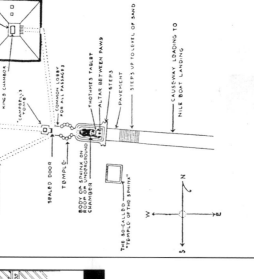

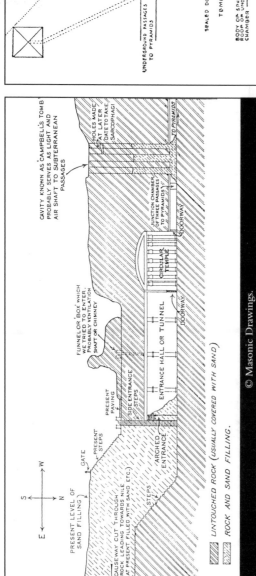

© Masonic Drawings.